IDSA Asian Strategic Review
2007

Published by Academic Foundation
in association with the
Institute for Defence Studies
and Analyses (IDSA), New Delhi

Asian Strategic Review 2007

IDSA

Edited by *S.D. Muni*

ACADEMIC FOUNDATION
NEW DELHI

First published in 2008
by

ACADEMIC FOUNDATION
4772-73 / 23 Bharat Ram Road, (23 Ansari Road),
Darya Ganj, New Delhi - 110 002 (India).
Phones : 23245001 / 02 / 03 / 04.
Fax : +91-11-23245005.
E-mail : academic@vsnl.com
www. academicfoundation.com

in association with :

Institute for Defence Studies and Analyses, New Delhi
www.idsa.in

IDSA Asian Strategic Review 2007
edited by S.D. Muni

ISBN 13: 978-81-7188-667-8
ISBN 10: 81-7188-667-1

Typeset by Italics India, New Delhi.
Printed and bound in India.

CONTENTS

V

Statistical Appendix

Contributors

Alok Bansal	*Research Fellow, South Asia, IDSA*
Ashok Behuria	*Research Fellow, South Asia, IDSA*
Abanti Bhattacharya	*Associate Fellow, East and South-East Asia, IDSA*
Vishal Chandra	*Associate Fellow, South Asia, IDSA*
Shanthie Mariet D'Souza	*Associate Fellow, USA and Europe Studies, IDSA*
Shebonti Ray Dadwal	*Research Fellow, Energy Security, IDSA*
Sreeradha Datta	*Research Fellow, South Asia, IDSA*
Gulshan Dietl	*Professor, Centre for West Asian Studies, JNU*
Namrata Goswami	*Associate Fellow, Internal Security, IDSA*
Gurpreet Khurana	*Research Fellow, Military Affairs, IDSA*
V. Krishnappa	*Research Fellow, Military Affairs, IDSA*
Ajey Lele	*Research Fellow, Modeling and Net Assessment, IDSA*
Arpita Mathur	*Associate Fellow, East and South-East Asia, IDSA*

M. Mayilvaganan .... *Associate Fellow, South Asia, IDSA*

Rajesh Kumar Mishra .... *Associate Fellow, Weapons of Mass Destruction, IDSA*

Ashutosh Misra .... *Research Fellow, Griffith Asia Institute, Brisbane*

G.V.C. Naidu .... *Senior Fellow, East and South-East Asia, IDSA*

Raviprasad Narayanan .... *Associate Fellow, East and South-East Asia, IDSA*

Rajiv Nayan .... *Research Officer, USA and Europe Studies, IDSA*

A.K. Pasha .... *Professor, Centre for West Asian Studies, JNU*

Smruti Pattanaik .... *Research Fellow, South Asia, IDSA*

S. Samuel C. Rajiv .... *Research Assistant, Military Affairs, IDSA*

Meena Singh Roy .... *Research Officer, Russia and Central Asia, IDSA*

P. Stobdan .... *Centre for Strategic and Regional Studies, Jammu University*

Preface

It gives me great pleasure to place before the wider strategic community IDSA's *Asian Strategic Review 2007*. IDSA had earlier brought out a series of annual surveys titled *Asian Strategic Review*, between 1993 and 98. Thereafter, the series was discontinued. The current volume seeks to revive that effort. This survey is an analysis of events and developments of the year 2006 and early part of 2007. It also attempts to assess their impact on India.

The main focus of the volume, divided into four sections, is on developments pertaining to Asia. However, recognising the diverse 'push' and 'pull' factors impinging on a country's strategic posture, the volume starts off by analysing issues which the Advisory Committee of Experts guiding the publication of this survey felt were of immediate relevance. Accordingly, the first section, titled "International Security Issues" has articles analysing India's responses to the global energy security challenges, the emerging military technologies and their security implications for India, the 'global war on terror', the debates surrounding the future of the nuclear non-proliferation regime, especially in the light of new proposals to strengthen or replace the existing regime, and the resurgence of Russia.

The next three parts contain indepth analyses of major events in South Asia, East Asia and the Asia–Pacific, and West and Central Asia—all regions in India's immediate/extended strategic neighbourhood. The section on South Asia has articles analysing the developments in the India-Pakistan bilateral relationship, specifically the peace process and the difficult internal situation in Pakistan. The subsequent contributions discuss the instabilities in India's immediate neighbourhood—in Bangladesh, Sri Lanka, Nepal, and Afghanistan.

The section concludes with an analysis of the 'purposes' and 'strategy' of left-wing extremism in India.

East Asia witnessed some significant developments during the past year, like the 9 October nuclear test conducted by the Democratic Peoples Republic of Korea. The section covering this region, experiencing 'economic dynamism and political flux', begins with an overview of major developments, notes the changes in the contours of the Sino-Indian and the Sino-Japanese relationship, consequent to high-level bilateral visits or changes in political leaderships and analyses the ramifications of Pyongyang's 'brinkmanship'. The section ends with a write-up on the cooperative responses to low-intensity threats in the Indian Ocean region.

West Asia occupies an important place in India's strategic neighbourhood. Some of the issues discussed in this section are the positive impetus given to the India-Saudi Arabia relationship after the visit of His Excellency the King of Saudi Arabia in early 2006, Iran's nuclear programme, developments in Israel-Palestinian relations, and an appraisal of the second Israel-Lebanon war. It also contains an article discussing the role of major powers in central Asia and the issues concerning India.

The volume concludes with a reference section containing important data for major countries in Asia on defence expenditure, armed forces personnel, major platforms and equipment inventories, nuclear forces, including the number and type of warheads and delivery systems, major ongoing conflicts and their current status, and the top 20 energy producing and consuming countries in the region.

We are grateful to Prof. S.D. Muni, distinguished South Asia expert and Visiting Fellow, IDSA for his many insightful comments on the manuscript and the meticulous manner in which he edited this volume. His vast experience and varied expertise has considerably enhanced the quality of this Review. We are also thankful to the distinguished members of the Advisory Committee, set up to guide the publication of the volume. These eminent experts included, apart from Prof. Muni, Lt. Gen. V.R. Raghavan, Rear Adm. Raja Menon, Amb. Shekhar Dasgupta, Amb. Virendra Gupta, Deputy Director, IDSA, Shri. Sujit Dutta, and Dr. G.V.C. Naidu, Senior Fellows, IDSA.

They have guided the work of this volume to its completion through their helpful suggestions, incisive comments, encouragement and participation in the deliberations of the Committee, despite their many preoccupations.

Special thanks are due to the Deputy Director, IDSA, Amb. Virendra Gupta for coordinating the work of this volume. Able research assistance was provided by Shri. S. Samuel, C. Rajiv, who apart from contributing a chapter on North Korean nuclear developments, also compiled the reference tables in the statistical appendix. Ms. Priyadarshini Singh, Energy Security Cluster, IDSA, prepared the table dealing with the energy producing/consuming countries.

It is our belief that this volume will be of value to those engaged in the study and practice of international relations and security. It should also be useful to universities, colleges and institutions engaged in research and teaching of international relations.

— N.S. Sisodia

Introduction

Asia Unbound: An Overview

S.D. MUNI

The present century is not the Asian century, not yet. But Asia's presence and weight is being felt and acknowledged widely. The strategic contours of the unfolding global reality cannot be defined or fathomed without reference to Asia. All major international economic, political, strategic, humanitarian, and environmental developments and decisions carry an unmistakable Asian imprint; be it in bold or faded shades.

Economic Rise

Economic dynamics of world politics is driven by Asia's economic rise, led by the rise of China and India. These two Asian giants have tripled and doubled their respective shares of world GDP over the past two decades. Leaders of western developed economies are projecting the rise of China and India to their electorates as a threat to energise their countries' economies and make their hard economic reform decisions credible, legitimate, and acceptable. A new term "Chindia" has been coined to project the combined weight of the Chinese and Indian economies for this purpose. There are scholars and analysts working out projections of competition between the two; if and when India will overtake China; or who will last longer in sustaining the higher growth rates; with what implications for Asia and the world; and so on. These issues may not be pertinent in the coming years as there are areas where India and China are cooperating with each other to mutual advantage; to sustain and enhance their economic dynamism and help Asia grow simultaneously. There is, however, no doubt that for the coming two to three decades, these two giant Asian economies will continue to grow at the fastest pace.

It is not only China and India that are rising in Asia. Japan too has revived its economy and there are other dynamic economies of the Republic of Korea, Vietnam, Thailand, Malaysia, Indonesia, Taiwan and Hong Kong (as economies independent of China), and Singapore. Most of the traditionally poorer South Asian countries are also doing well. In the Central and West Asian regions high oil prices for the past decade and more have added considerable economic muscle. The only fastest growing economy of Europe, Russia, is increasingly reinforcing the Asian component of its Eurasian identity. The rising Asian economies have reinforced global concerns about energy availability and costs on the one hand and environmental scare on the other.

Strategic Assertion

Economic surpluses have also induced and augmented Asia's military modernisation. Asian countries appear not at the top but quite prominently in the list of the first ten military spenders and arms importers, according to the SIPRI (Stockholm International Peace Research Institute) for the year 2006. China, with India, accounts for 40 per cent of the military spending in Southern Asia. China has managed to leave behind even Japan, for the first time, in military expenditure. India and China are also the largest importers of arms in Asia.

Asia is also the focus of global strategic concerns. Proliferation of nuclear and missile capability is primarily Asia based, though the revival of Cold War terminology between the US and Russia with regard to missile control regime and defence systems adds another complicating and wider aspect to this issue. China's demonstration of anti-satellite weapon capability has taken the arms race to space and may fuel the race for arms and military technologies among the Asian majors. While Israel remains a clandestine nuclear weapon state, India and Pakistan put their nuclear cards on the table in 1998 and are seeking global recognition of their new status. India seems closer to achieving this status with the possible finalisation of the Indo–US civil nuclear deal, but Pakistan has persisting hesitation in rooting out its clandestine proliferation networks built and nursed by the (in)famous nuclear scientist A.Q. Khan, under Pakistani state's patronage. There are deep concerns at the international level regarding the possibility of Pakistan's nuclear facilities coming under the control of a radical Islamist regime or being abused by terrorist groups such as al-Qaeda and the Taliban for delivering dirty bombs. North Korea's search for nuclear weapon status as a bargaining chip for its search for regional and economic security has almost been acquiesced in by the US under the package worked out by China within the Six-Party Talks formula. There are lingering concerns in Japan, however, about North Korean missiles and nuclear ambitions. Iran, it is claimed, is inching faster towards the acquisition of nuclear weapons. The US Ambassador to the International Atomic Energy Agency (IAEA), Gregory Schulte, has alleged in June 2007 that Iran is moving faster on the path of uranium enrichment and is hiding its other facilities like the heavy water plant at Arak from IAEA inspections. Iran continues to deny all such allegations and speculations. There are speculative reports about even Japan not being averse to reconsideration of its nuclear option as its aspirations and initiatives for a strategic and political role in Asia gather momentum. Reports are also appearing about Myanmar trying to access nuclear technology as it explores uranium deposits in its territory with the help of Russia.

The "global war on terror" (GWOT) is being fought on many fronts, but Asia remains its main theatre. Iraq and Afghanistan are on the boil, without any signs of stability and order over the long horizon. The best of the Western analysts and policymakers concede that the challenge of terrorism has been worsened by the way GWOT has been conducted. There are no indications that the US is either willing or even capable of evolving a meaningful exit strategy from Iraq or Afghanistan. On the contrary, the US has decided to stay put in Iraq, Congressional pressures on President George W. Bush notwithstanding. US and NATO (North Atlantic Treaty Organization) forces are also digging deep into Afghanistan, and the search for newer access and base facilities is going on unabated in Central and South Asia. There are indications of a strong strategic and long-term drive under cover of GWOT to consolidate a unipolar world order. Eric Rouleau, a former French diplomat-turned-journalist has described

GWOT as "new imperialism."[1] GWOT also does not adequately address many other local and regional menaces of terrorism. India and its Jammu & Kashmir region continue to be haunted by cross-border terrorism. Eelam War IV has been revived in Sri Lanka where the world's most efficient terrorist group, the Liberation Tigers of Tamil Eelam (LTTE), has even acquired air capability. The unique opportunity of mainstreaming the Maoists in Nepal and facilitating the building of a viable and inclusive democracy there is being frittered away to cultivate narrow diplomatic advantages and preferred vested interests. In West and Central Asia newer groups of Islamist extremists are joining jihad in increasing numbers against the so-called 'infidels' of their world.

Asia has witnessed a phenomenal upsurge in people's power; to fight for their rights and resist injustice and domination by their own state as well as by intruding forces. This upsurge has been helped by what can be termed as an explosion of information, aspirations, and identity. Many of Asia's popular movements, violent or otherwise, clearly reflect this explosion fuelled by poor governance and spread of globalisation. At times, the conflict and contradictions between aspirations and identity also erode the strength of the people's power and make it vulnerable to intruding interests. The developments in Iraq, Afghanistan, and Palestine are not simply results of terrorism; they are also robust manifestations of the people's will and power to resist what appears to them to be unjust and unacceptable. In April 2006 Nepal showed an unprecedented demonstration of the people's power against an internationally backed autocratic monarch. There is a clamour for democracy almost everywhere in Asia. China witnessed thousands of protests, many of them violent, in its countryside during 2006. There are no doubt reversals of this trend in some places such as Thailand, Central Asia, Myanmar, and even Bangladesh, but these reverses may prove to be short-lived. The broader direction of political processes towards liberalisation and democratic accountability is unmistakable.

---

1. Rouleau, Eric (2007). "The 'Global War on Terror' and the 'New Imperialism'", *Middle East Online*, 13 June. At *http://www.middle-east-online.com/english/Default.pl?id=21068*

Cooperative Engagement

In the midst of economic rise and political upsurge in the region, Asia's major players have displayed a remarkable degree of constructive resilience in approaching issues of conflicts and tensions between themselves. China's proactive role, with full Japanese cooperation in the Six-Party Talks to help resolve the question of North Korean nuclear build-up, brought relief to all concerned, though the situation in North East Asia will need careful monitoring. The sharpening discord between Japan and China was also handled with diplomatic finesse with the visit of the new Japanese Prime Minister Shinzo Abe to China in October 2006 and of the Chinese Premier Wen Jiabao to Japan in April 2007. The ice between the two countries first 'broke' and then 'melted' during these visits. They now claim to be strategic partners of each other. This positive development in the context of their growing economic cooperation will surely help in promoting greater stability and integration in the South East Asian and Asia-Pacific regions. Rooting out long-term rivalry stemming from traditional historical experiences and misunderstandings will, however, still need sustained efforts on the part of China and Japan.

India and China also started sincerely addressing their contentious bilateral issues since the mid-1990s. The bilateral confidence-building agreements of 1993 and 1996 committing them to avoid use of force in their mutual dealings paved the way for a meaningful dialogue on the complex border issue. Resolution of the issue may still take time and courage but the overall direction of the dialogue is constructive. The growing comfort level between the two giant neighbours has given a boost to their trade and economic relations. China is now an Observer in SAARC (South Asian Association for Regional Cooperation), which will facilitate greater economic interaction in the South Asian region. No less important has been the peace process between India and Pakistan, set in motion since January 2004. For the first time in several decades, the two adversarial neighbours seem to be seriously engaged in addressing the Kashmir question for a reasonable and viable settlement. Political uncertainties around General Pervez Musharraf's regime in Pakistan have created anxieties in the progress of the peace process but a consensus is building across various shades of political opinion in Pakistan in favour of a stable and cooperative bilateral relationship with India, even while areas of conflict and disagreements persist between them.

The US as Asian Player

The United States is an Asian power; not geographically but in every other sense of the term, particularly strategically. The implications of Asia's rise and assertion for the US presence in this continent are being intensely speculated upon. There are those who believe that its absence from the East Asia Summit (EAS) and the Shanghai Cooperation Organisation (SCO) reflect a pressure on America's strategic space in Asia. The strategic proximity between China and Russia is also to some extent balancing the US initiatives and outreach in Asia. Some of the US basing rights in Central Asia, as in Uzbekistan, have been terminated and its access to the Manas base in Kyrgyzstan is also under pressure.

While Russia is individually restraining US influence in Central Asia, China seems determined to do so in East Asia. Oil-producing countries in West Asia are pegging their crude prices on to the Euro, shifting from dollar. Even Saudi Arabia, a close traditional ally of the US has started looking East than West, as its growing trade with China and diplomatic initiatives towards India indicated in 2006.

The SAARC also admitted Iran as an observer at its 2007 New Delhi Summit much against the US pressure to the contrary. India and Pakistan are also going ahead with their gas pipeline project with Iran ignoring US objections. If moves like Russia–China–India and India–Brazil–South Africa trilateral cooperation groupings gain strength and anchor, the US room for strategic play in Asia and the world cannot remain unaffected.

These arguments need to be balanced against an equally powerful set of facts and assumptions to the contrary. ASEAN (Association of South East Nations) is the fourth-largest export destination of the US, amounting to $50 billion worth of goods. US private investment in ASEAN exceeds $80 billion. US strategic presence is welcomed and desired by various Asian countries for diverse reasons of balancing their regional adversaries, containing regional major powers, and consolidating political regimes against domestic challenges. Though the US itself was kept out of the EAS, its allies such as Australia and Japan, and friends such as Singapore and India may not allow this grouping to hurt or confront vital US interests in the region. Yet, to counter the possible clout of the EAS, the US has stepped up its efforts to strengthen and enlarge the Asia-Pacific Economic Cooperation (APEC) grouping.

The US is a critical ally of the regimes in Pakistan and Afghanistan and its influence in the fluid political processes of Nepal and Bangladesh is substantial. US intentions may be debated in India but President Bush's popularity rating in India exceeds that of the US rating, and India desperately needs the Bush administration's support to clinch the civil nuclear cooperation deal. Besides the huge US and NATO military presence in Iraq and Afghanistan, the US has nearly 150,000 troops stationed permanently in Asia, from Oman to Japan. It is also trying to build a security structure in Asia where none of the regional powers, particularly China, can dictate and dominate developments on its own. The US also seems determined to prevent China from browbeating Taiwan militarily or diplomatically into merging with the mainland.

The moves towards building a strategic grouping of the US, Japan, Australia, and India, with the main purpose of hedging China, are significant in this respect. This group had first come into existence to coordinate rescue efforts when Tsunami hit the Indian Ocean littoral states in December 2004. The US cannot and will not give up its presence in Asia in the foreseeable future, nor is there any real possibility of China and Russia together, or the collective weight of Asia's assertion, decisively denting that presence in the decades to come. However, greater assertion and effectiveness of the Asian powers in Asian affairs and greater engagement between them on constructive lines may in the long run create constraints on the US sway and manoeuvrability in Asia.

Asia is unbound in its energy, agility, resilience, and self-confidence to shape the emerging terms of reference of world politics. It will maintain its economic dynamism and political buoyancy in defining Asian priorities and nudging the world to adjust to these priorities. The challenge for Asia to turn this century into its own comes from within, from its turbulent political orders. Asia has demonstrated its capacity to create affluence and prosperity. It has to ensure credible governance to spread this prosperity among its people equitably through efficient and fair distributive mechanisms.

I

International Security Issues

1

Global Energy Security Challenges

India's Response

SHEBONTI RAY DADWAL

From an energy perspective, 2006 will be remembered for volatile oil prices. From $78.40 a barrel in July the price of international crude dropped to a little over $50 in October, rose slightly in November following an announcement by OPEC (Organisation of Petroleum Exporting Countries) of a 1.2 million barrels per day (mbd) cut, and declined to around $46 in January 2007. Analysts attributed rising prices to paucity of spare crude, paucity of refinery capacity, depleting reserves, and political tensions in producing regions and states; the declining prices were attributed to unusual weather patterns, high US inventories, and lowering of tensions in the Gulf region.

Prices began to rise in the last months of 2000, mainly because energy demand from reviving Asian economies swelled. Low oil prices during the 1990s had shrunk investment in oil exploration, consequently lowering production. Pressure from environmental lobbies partly contributed to dwindled investment in oil refineries. Most of the world's premium oil sources, being off limits for foreign investors and thus being deprived of crucial state-of-the-art technology, also curtailed production. Many Gulf States disallow foreign stake in their upstream oil sectors; in Iran and Iraq the political climate discourages investment. Devastating storms off the US coast, including Katrina and Rita, destroyed several oil production and refining facilities, adding to market woes.

OPEC's growing clout was another factor. With around two-thirds of the world's proven oil reserves located in the Persian Gulf region, the importance of OPEC, which accounts for 40 per cent of world oil production, is poised to rise to 45 per cent over the next 10 years as non-OPEC production falls. If, as reported, Sudan, Angola and Brazil join the cartel, OPEC's power will grow.[1] Continuing political turmoil in the major oil-producing regions also contributed to the price rise. According to some analysts, the damage to Iraq's oil industry, the cost of military commitment in the Gulf region, and the threat that the conflict could spread in the region, added a $20 premium to oil price.[2]

The spectacular rise in prices spawned the theory that world oil reserves had virtually reached 'peak' production levels. Excess capacity was reported to have declined from around 11 mbd in the 1980s to as low as 2 mbd, the bulk of it located in Saudi Arabia. Therefore, if a crisis were to occur in any country exporting more than 2 mbd or supply from any one region was disrupted, crude supply would tumble.

Politicisation of Energy

Some energy producers such as Russia, Iran, Algeria, and some Latin American countries, displayed an inclination to use energy to get political leverage. Moscow suspended gas supplies to Ukraine in early 2006 and oil supplies in early 2007 to Belarus, demanding better prices. Though Moscow argued that it was scrapping subsidy on prices to some of its former allies, it appeared to be the Kremlin's way of pressurising them not to go with the United States in its policy on NATO expansion and the presence of US troops in Central Asia.[3] Russia supplies 25 per cent each of Europe's oil and natural gas.[4] The European Union (EU) has been pressing Moscow to ratify its Energy Charter allowing foreign companies access to Russia's energy pipeline network. Russia has refused on the ground that some provisions in the Charter are damaging to its interests, particularly the Transit

1. *International Herald Tribune* (henceforth IHT), 13 December 2006.
2. IHT, 8 January 2007.
3. "Russia 2006: 'A Year of Muscle and Missteps'", Radio Free Europe Radio Liberty, 28 December 2006. *http://www.rferl.org/featuresarticle/2006/12/d6adc178-4b45-4f10-ac09-97dfbf370b47.html*
4. EU-Russian Energy Dialogue, Euractive.com, 28 November 2005. *http://www.euractiv.com/en/energy/eu-russia-energy-dialogue/article-150061*

Protocol on transit across third countries. Russia has also declined to liberalise its energy market.[5]

In 2005, Moscow signed an energy cooperation agreement with Algeria, giving Russian companies access to Algerian oil and gas fields. Algeria supplies around 10 per cent of Europe's gas consumption. The EU energy commissioner Andris Piebalgs saw in this agreement prospects of a cartel detrimental to European interests.[6] Another gas cartel combining Russia, Iran, and Qatar is also being mooted.

In Latin America, Venezuela and Bolivia forced foreign oil companies to renegotiate production contracts, gaining greater control of their energy sectors and demanding higher royalties. Oilfields operated by two recalcitrant international companies were seized. Even as the UN Security Council mooted imposing sanctions on Iran to deter it from going ahead with its announced launch of a uranium enrichment plant, the Islamic Republic threatened to cut off oil supplies.

After decades, the oil market had become favourable to the sellers, but prices dropped by 25 per cent from September 2006 to the end of the year. Market forces were reacting to the high prices, combined with large US inventories and the unusually mild winter in the Northern Hemisphere. A Saudi–US led initiative to prevent the producers, particularly Iran, from benefiting from increased oil revenues, also contributed to the price fall. Riyadh stated that it planned to increase production by 2 mbd over the next two years and opposed any further production cuts by OPEC. From end January 2007, however, oil prices began rising again, with a rise in demand and escalating US–Iran tensions.

Consumers' Dilemma: The Asian Theatre

Against rising prices, oil-importing countries scrambled to secure their supplies, leading to intense competition and giving rise to disputes for control over energy blocks in overlapping territories. At the same time, there were also regional initiatives for accommodation.

5. Curtin, Joseph (2006). *Energy Policy Newsletter*, Institute of European Affairs, Jill Donaghue (ed.), November. *http://www.iiea.com/images/managed/publications_attachments/Energy%20Newsletter%20November.doc.pdf*
6. IHT, 25 January 2007.

On 15 December, 2006 the energy ministers of China, the US, India, South Korea, and Japan, which together account for almost 50 per cent of the world's oil consumption, met for the first Five Country Energy Ministers' Roundtable Conference in Beijing. The discussions focused on energy security, stability, and sustainability; strategic oil stocks; diversification of energy mix and energy alternatives; investments and energy markets; challenges and priorities of international cooperation; and energy conservation. The participants also agreed to institutionalise the dialogue mechanism.[7]

Various other groupings, such as the G-8, Asia-Europe Meeting (ASEM), ASEAN, APEC (Asia–Pacific Economic Cooperation), and EAS (Organisation of East Asian States) also held high-level discussions on enhancing their collective energy security. The Cebu Declaration on East Asian Energy Security, emanating from the EAS meeting, set a wide range of goals, including a promise to "mitigate greenhouse gas emissions through effective policies and measures" and urged member countries to "consider the use of hydropower, nuclear power and biofuels like ethanol..."[8]

India's Search for Energy Security

India's economy, with an average growth rate of 6–7 per cent over the last decade and higher projected growth rates in the foreseeable future, is both dependent on fossil fuels—coal, gas for the power sector, and oil for the transport sector—and is also highly energy intensive. High oil price volatility and the growing political uncertainty in the Gulf region, from where most of India's energy is sourced, are therefore a cause for concern in India.

Diversification of sources, acquisition of foreign energy assets, and intensifying its search for domestic hydrocarbons have been India's options for ensuring its energy security. Its New Exploration Licensing Policy (NELP) has not enthused the major international oil companies. Diversification of sources and asset acquisition has, therefore, been the preferred options. Since the late 1990s Indian national oil companies

7. *http://www.indianembassy.org.cn/press/20061219_1.htm*
8. IHT, 15 January 2007.

have been bidding against Chinese firms for foreign energy assets, albeit not very successfully. In early 2006 the two countries signed a memorandum of understanding (MoU), followed by another at the end of December, to cooperate on energy issues, including in joint bidding for assets.[9] Subsequently, there have been successful joint bids in Syria, Colombia, and Sudan.

The Iran–Pakistan–India (IPI) and Turkmenistan–Afghanistan–Pakistan–India (TAPI) pipeline projects are uncertain both due to concerns over security as well as pricing patterns. Similarly, pricing differences are holding up a 2005 LNG (liquefied natural gas) deal between India and Iran.

India's Integrated Energy Policy, published in December 2006, recommends spreading its energy supply net further and looking at all fuel options, both non-renewable and renewable, including nuclear energy. Earlier on 31 May, 2005 New Delhi entered into an energy dialogue with Washington, which sought to build upon the broad range of their existing energy cooperation and develop new avenues of collaboration in all sectors of energy, including oil, gas, and power; develop cooperation on clean coal technology; promote the development and deployment of clean energy technologies and energy conservation practices and "action on issues associated with civilian uses of nuclear energy and its control."[10] On 18 July, 2005 the two countries signed a civilian nuclear energy cooperation deal, whereby the US promised to "work to achieve full civil nuclear energy cooperation with India as it realises its goals of promoting nuclear power and achieving energy security."[11]

During the visit of President Vladimir Putin of Russia to New Delhi in January 2007, the two sides agreed on all-around cooperation in energy. Prime Minister Manmohan Singh commented on the occasion that energy security was the most important emerging dimension of the Indo–Russian strategic partnership. Two working groups were set up to examine areas of cooperation in both the

9. *Economic Times*, 17 December 2006.

10. "India-US Energy Dialogue Joint Statement". Washington DC. 31 May 2005. *http://newdelhi.usembassy.gov/iprjune022005.html*

11. Ibid.

upstream and downstream sectors. Moscow has also shown keen interest in participating in the IPI project. Russia also agreed to provide India with four nuclear reactors, besides opening up its upstream oil and gas sector to Indian investment.

India is also seeking enhanced ties with other countries both to its east and west, and with both consumers and producers. Summing up India's energy strategy, the minister for external affairs, Pranab Mukherjee, said at the 7th International Oil and Gas Conference and Exhibition (Petrotech 2007) in January 2007 that "given energy's crucial place in the scheme of things, global cooperation and understanding...is essential and inescapable." Underlining the need for balancing and harmonising the interests of both producers and consumers, he said that "there is in reality a natural alliance between the producers and the consumers, both being two sides of the same coin, in a relationship of mutual dependence and cooperation."[12] Significantly, eleven petroleum ministers from countries representing OPEC and other producers as well as consumers participated in the conference.

There must be interdependence between and among energy producers and consumers to ensure energy security. Just as consumers need security of supply, producers need growing markets. Interdependence would entail making cross investments in energy infrastructure, both in the upstream and downstream sectors, as also cooperation for safe transportation of energy amidst increased incidence of piracy and terrorism. Networks of pipelines are also required to link producing regions with markets at great distances. There is also need for cooperation in efficient technology and conservation along the energy chain, and a serious look at alternative energy resources.

12 *http://www.petrotech2007.com/detailnew.asp?fol_name=news&file_name=news&curr_f=8*

2

Emerging Military Technologies

Security Implications for India

AJEY LELE

Recent wars (the Gulf Wars, Kosovo, and the Afghanistan campaign) have shown that technological advantage is a 'force multiplier'.[1] Numerous conflict issues amongst states, mostly based on historical animosities and unresolved border issues, still pose a potential for future wars. This chapter broadly discusses the relevance of modern technologies in warfare and its security implications for India. The realm of nuclear technologies is not considered here.

The success of technology in various war-waging mechanisms during the last one or two decades has dictated a revolution in military affairs (RMA). Soviet officers such as Marshal Nikolai Ogarkov argued that technological breakthroughs would give conventional weapons a level of precision as effective as that provided by tactical nuclear weapons.[2]

The military aspects of information revolution include new tools and processes of war waging such as information warfare (IW), network-centric warfare (NCW), integrated command, control, computer, communications, intelligence, surveillance, reconnaissance (C^4ISR), systems of systems, etc. In consequence, in future war-

1. A force multiplier is a factor that dramatically increases the combined effectiveness of a military force. These could include factors like morale, training, weather, and geographic features.

2. Hashim, S. Ahmed (1998). "The Revolution in Military Affairs Outside the West", *The Journal of International Affairs*, Vol. 51(2): 434. Spring.

The author wishes to acknowledge the research assistance provided by Shri. Vinod Kumar, Associate Fellow, IDSA.

waging platforms like aircraft, ships/submarines and tanks are expected to be more technology dependent than human dependent.[3]

India and RMA

As India's military capabilities have increased, it has managed to exploit opportunities, as evident in the 1971 War. The response to the coup attempt in the Maldives in 1988, the massive effort of civilian evacuation undertaken during the 1991 Gulf War, and the 2004 Tsunami relief operations also show that India has developed a capacity for rapid response. Capability of effective counter military action was in evidence in its handling of the Kargil crisis.[4] Intelligent investment in technology is one of the reasons for India's military successes.

However, India is investing more in indigenous development of technologies which is, at times, time consuming and develops a lag in global standard of technologies. Indian armed forces have a mix of conventional and emerging technologies. India could be said to have opted for hybrid RMA, based on indigenous research and development (R&D), combined with imported combat system, sensors, and precision weapons. Systems integration skills and cultural changes like quicker decision making, flatter force structures, combined-arms task forces, rapid acquisition cycles, capable defence science organisations, and creative software skills become essential in such a dispensation.[5] Probably, China comes in the same category.

In the middle decades of the twentieth century technological developments in the military sector used to find application in the civilian sector. Now the case is the reverse. Currently, technologies like microelectronics, telecommunication, information technology (IT), advanced materials, and biotechnology are in the forefront of the civil sector and have direct utility in the military sector.[6]

---

3. Joshi, Akshay (2001). *Information Age and India*. New Delhi: Knowledge World. pp.xxii–xxiii.
4. Cohen, P. Stephen (2001). *India: Emerging Power*. New Delhi: Oxford University Press. p.154.
5. Dibb, Paul (1997-98). "The RMA and Asian Security", *Survival*, Vol. 39(4): 93–116. Winter.
6. Chari, K. Sridhar (2003). *Info-Nano-Bio Technologies, their Coming Convergence, and the Implications for Security*. Bangalore: National Institute of Advanced Studies. pp.16-18.

Accessing New Technologies

Most of these technologies are being used (or developed) either independently or jointly to design and develop military hardware/ software. Technology appraisal tends to become unconnected when done from an exclusively defence perspective. It is more pragmatic to carry out technology assessment in a 'strategic context' by doing a macro-level analysis of overall growth of technology in a state, technology collaborations, future plans, defence agreements, joint military exercises undertaken, etc.

A major technological initiative for India came in the form of the Indo–US commitment in November 2001 when the two countries agreed to a strategic partnership. This commitment was furthered during January 2004 by identifying specific areas of cooperation under the banner of Next Steps in Strategic Partnership (NSSP). The areas identified were: civilian nuclear activities, civilian space programme, and high-technology trade.[7] These discussions further culminated in the Indo–US nuclear deal which was agreed in principle on 18 July 2005, and formally signed on 2 March, 2006. This deal has provisions for cooperation in high technology also. The deal states that joint research, training, and the establishment of public–private partnership would be undertaken as part of the US–India High-Technology Cooperation Group (HTCG). It further emphasises the need for building up closer ties in space exploration, satellite navigation, and launch.

Among the other more notable defence agreements that India has signed are those with France (February 2006), Germany (September 2006), and Russia (January 2007). The agreement with France covers cooperation in defence material and transfer of technology,[8] including codevelopment and coproduction of high technology defence equipment.[9] The agreement with Germany, the first defence pact between the two countries, encompasses joint training, technology transfers, and coproduction of high technology military hardware. The

7. Correll, R. Randall, "US–India Space Partnership: The Jewel in the Crown", *Astropolitics*, Vol.4(2): 160.
8. *http://www.defenseworld.net/defexpo2006/defexpo2006.asp/var/10290-DefenseAerospacePressnews-1*
9. *http://www.defensenews.com/story.php?F=1546932&C=europe*

agreement mostly covers cooperation in the field of Navy and in electronic and surveillance systems, in which Germany recently has made major breakthroughs.[10] German companies such as Rheinmetall AG are involved in a big way in development of highly advanced products and system solutions. The range of products extends from reconnaissance, fire control and command systems to guided weapon platforms and unmanned aerial vehicles (UAVs).[11] This agreement would help India to broadbase its military equipment suppliers. The agreements with Russia cover license-production and technical documents for the RD 33 series-3 aero engines and a general contract for RD 33 series-3 aero engines and associated products. The two sides also signed a protocol of intent for the joint development and production of multi-role transport aircraft and the protocol of the Sixth India–Russia Inter Governmental Commission on Military Technical Cooperation.[12] These agreements widen the agenda to encompass non-defence strategic areas such as IT and space research.

Exercising to Learn and Choose

In 2006, India participated in various military exercises with a few friendly countries, as follows:[13]

(a) Joint anti- and counter-terrorism exercises with the US forces between 16 and 31 January 2006 at Choubatia, Uttar Pradesh and during October 2006 (code-named *Shatrujeet*) in Belgaum, Karnataka. These exercises were useful in understanding how modern-day equipment could be used in urban warfare settings.

(b) India participated in the multinational exercise *Valiant Shield 2006* in Guam, hosted by the US in January 2006.

---

10. *http://www.ndtv.com/morenews/showmorestory.asp?category=National&slug=India%2C+Germany+sign+defence+pact&id=92806*

11. *http://www.rheinmetall-detec.de/index.php?lang=3&fid=620*

12. *http://www.india-defence.com/reports/2834*

13. For information the main newspaper referred was *The Hindu* and the main websites referred were:
http://www.shadow-wars.com/pg5b.html,
http://www.sepiamutiny.com/sepia/archives/cat_military.
html, http://www.hindu.com/2003/10/06/stories/2003100602700500.htm,
http://indiannavy.nic.in/pres01.htm,
http://www.hcilondon.net/bilateral-relations.html

(c) The thirteenth maritime bilateral exercise between Indian and Singapore navies (*SIMBEX*) was conducted from 26 February to 8 March, 2006. The exercise was important for validating technologies useful for purposes like anti-piracy interdiction and anti-submarine operations.

(d) The Indian Navy conducted joint naval exercises off the coast of Goa in April 2006 with the French Navy in which French nuclear-powered carrier *Charles De Gaulle* participated.

(e) One of the biggest joint exercises was carried out with the British Royal Navy (*Konkan 2006*, 17-29 May 2006) off the west coast between Goa and Mumbai.

(f) The sixth round of Indo–US joint naval exercise, *Malabar-06*, was conducted off the Goa coast during October–November 2006. The exercise involved advanced exercises including anti-submarine operations, maritime interdictions, weapon firings, and a simulated 'war at sea'.

(g) An Indian Army team participated in Exercise *Cambrian Patrol* in mid-Wales from 27 October to 5 November 2006, with army teams from the British regular and Territorial Army and Royal Air Force. Army teams from Canada, Lithuania, Latvia, Denmark, France, and the Czech Republic also took part.

These joint exercises indicate that India is interested in seeking technology and practical experience in areas of underwater operations, supersonic flights, space reconnaissance, and high technology military hardware. Particularly the naval exercises helped Indian forces to understand the nuances of anti-submarine warfare (ASW), check the effectiveness of ASW sensors, validate their communication preparedness for interoperability, and learn more about amphibious operations. The anti terrorism exercises essentially taught the Indian forces to handle asymmetric threats. The gain is not a specific technology but an overall package of techno-strategic aspects of warfighting. Also, since the civilian component in various deals (particularly the Indo–US nuclear deal and various other space deals) is more dominant, it would be difficult to pinpoint security-related technologies. These joint exercises help in understanding the compatibility problems of various items of equipment that the Indian defence forces already possess with the technologies they intend to procure. Also, these exercises help them to understand the relevance of RMA technologies in military doctrines.

India's Technology Priorities

India is looking for technologies in microelectronics, communication, space, biotechnology, nanotechnology, IT, sensors, and composite materials.[14] Though India's space assets have no specific military functions, they are capable of performing a number of military tasks.[15]

India's Cartosat launches have boosted its remote sensing services with high-resolution images. Cartosat I (launched in May 2005) has a resolution of 2.5 metres. Cartosat II (launched on 10 January 2007) has a one-metre resolution, putting it on par with Ikonos of the US. (The highest resolution is provided by the Quickbird, at 60 centimetres). These imageries would provide digital elevation maps for urban and rural development, land and water resources management, disaster and environmental impact assessment, and also in surveillance and reconnaissance operations.[16]

India is collaborating with Russia in its Global Navigation Satellite System (GLONASS) constellation. Most of India's military hardware is of Russian origin; GLONASS would naturally offer a compatible navigation solution. Since the other global navigational systems like GPS (Global Positioning System) and 'Galileo' do not offer military applications, over time India is expected to have a larger stake in GLONASS, and could be involved in production and joint use as partners.[17]

At the same time it needs to be emphasised that ISRO (Indian Space Research Organisation) focuses essentially on civilian use of space. The knowledge thus gained is not being fully incorporated in

---

14. President A.P.J. Abdul Kalam first formulated the triad of security-related future technologies as "nano-bio-info", while speaking at the Silver Jubilee celebration of the Indian Navy's Weapons and Electronic System Engineering Establishment (WESEE) on 1 July, 2004. See *The Hindu*, 2 July, 2004. Also see *http://presidentofindia.nic.in/scripts/eventslatest1.jsp?id=601*
15. Mistry, Dinshaw (1998). "India's Emerging Space Programme", *Pacific Affairs*, Vol. 71: 163.
16. Indian Express (2007). "ISRO's Four-in-One First", *Indian Express*, 9 January.
17. *Indian Express*, New Delhi, 30 January 2007.

defence preparedness. No spy satellite has been launched after TES (Technology Experiment Satellite), launched during 2001. It was reported that the Indian Navy was very keen to launch a spy satellite for communication and high-resolution space imaging,[18] but ISRO did not take sufficient interest in this project.

On the IT front a few private firms have been employed to create and provide task-specific software and hardware solutions. They are in the process of developing defence communication networks.[19] The Indian Army has deployed 'Sathi', the integrated GPS-enabled battle computer with radio that a solider can carry in his palm to access and mark military maps.[20]

India took its first successful step in ballistic missile defence in November 2006. In this test a surface-to-surface Prithvi-II missile was shot down over the Bay of Bengal by another missile fired seconds later. This missile, named as AXO (Atmospheric Intercept System), was fired from the Wheeler Islands off Chandipur in Orissa. AXO is a modified Prithvi-II. Official reports claim that the missile was supersonic, highly manoeuvrable, and was launched using its own mobile launcher. This is probably a part of India's ongoing efforts to develop a home-grown ballistic interception system.[21]

In biotechnology the military relevance is more from the point of view of addressing the threats occurring either due to natural disasters or on the country's population from biological weapons. During the bird flu crisis India successfully produced a vaccine to contain this threat. This proficiency could be useful in handling bioweapons.[22] Biotechnology is also showing promise in 'preventive security' through biometrics, which takes automated measurements of certain psychological or behavioural traits for purposes of human

18. Deccan Herald (2004). "Navy Approaches ISRO for Spy, Communication Satellite", *Deccan Herald*, 12 August.
19. Mishra, Gaurie (2005). "HP, TCS Focus on Defence Services". 20 September; *http://www.zdnetindia.com/news/national/stories/128336.html*
20. Bhogle, Srinivas (2006). "Technology Review 2005" in Satish Kumar (ed.), *India's National Security Annual Review 2006*. New Delhi: Knowledge World. p.242.
21. *http://www.sspconline.org/article_details.asp?artid=art107*
22. Authors' discussions with Dr. H.K. Pradhan, Director, High Security Animal Disease Laboratory, Bhopal.

recognition.[23] In the identification mode a biometrics system identifies a person from an enrolled population by searching database for a match. In the verification mode it uses biometrics to authenticate a person's claimed identity, based on his or her previously recorded pattern.[24] Such devices could be of great use at airports, high-security government and scientific establishments, and towards handling infiltration along the borders.

Nanotechnology, also called "platform technology",[25] is still in its infancy and demands more research for its military utility. Assembler nanotechnology and artificial intelligence (AI) together are expected to create a high level of instability in the internal system if the present 'warrior culture' continues. Just as nuclear weapons made 'major' war obsolete between nuclear-armed nations on the basis of deterrence, nanotechnology can make deterrence obsolete, as "it would not be possible to maintain stable armed peace between nano-technologically armed rivals." It is expected that untested, secret, even 'virtual arsenals' would undermine confidence in the ability to retaliate or resist aggression. Warning and decision times would shrink. This may force actual and perceived power balances to shift dramatically and abruptly.[26] Companies like Tata Steel, Tata Chemicals, Mahindra & Mahindra, Nicholas Piramal, and Intel have invested around $250 million in nanotechnology.[27]

DRDO (Defence Research and Development Organisation) has undertaken certain initiatives for making the country self-sufficient in a number of strategic materials, e.g. technology for fullerenes and carbon nanotubes, which have potential applications in stealth, smart materials, and nanoelectronics. It is reported that Agharkar Research Institute (ARI), an autonomous, grant-in-aid research institute of the

---

23. Woodward, D. John Jr. (2005). "Using Biometrics to Achieve Identity Dominance in the Global War on Terrorism", *Military Review*, September-October: 31.
24. Arden Berment Statement for Record on Border Security/Visa Act for the Subcommittee on Immigration Committee on the Judiciary, United States Senate, 12 April. 2002.
25. Jackson, Shirley Ann (2006). "International Cooperation: Multiplying Strength, Sharing Benefit". 24 March. *http://www.rpi.edu/president/speeches/ps032406-kanpur.html*
26. Chari n. 6: 90.
27. D'Monte, Leslie (2006). "India Thinks Big about Nanotechnology". 17 March. *http://inhome.rediff.com/money/2006/mar/17nano.htm*

Department of Science and Technology (DST) would be providing nanoparticles to the defence establishment.[28]

In other areas of military technology like battle tanks, light combat aircraft (LCA), etc. the process of self-reliance is not paying adequate dividends. There has been a sixteen-year delay for the Arjun tank and twelve years for just Phase I of the LCA Tejas.[29] Agni-III strategic missile (5000–8000 km range), test-fired on 9 July, 2006 after postponing the test three times, also failed to fully meet mission objectives. This is a setback to the Indian triad of nuclear counter-strike capability.[30]

India's revised budget estimates for R&D during 2004-5, 2005-6, and 2006-7 were Rs 547 crore, 511 crore, and 510 crore, respectively, indicating that no fresh R&D initiatives were undertaken. However, the budgeted estimates for 2007-8 show more than 20 per cent increase in R&D allocations.[31] This signifies that India is not only looking for off-the-shelf purchases of technologies but proposes to indigenise also.

Responding to the Challenge Ahead

India's neighbours China and Pakistan conducted a few joint exercises during 2006. The exercises that the Chinese conducted with the Central Asian countries are essentially seen in terms of cultivating goodwill. *Friendship-2006*, a China–Pakistan exercise, was an anti-terrorism exercise. China also held a joint naval exercise with the US (joint search and rescue operations) in November 2006. Pakistan also undertook a two-week anti-terrorism exercise with the US. China and Pakistan have also concluded a few defence agreements, leading to defence collaboration and purchase of arms. China is undertaking major investments in the space sector. It has already developed and

---

28. *http://www.nanowerk.com/news/newsid=1123.php*; Indian Express, 9 December 2006.
29. Aroor, Shiv and Amitav Ranjan (2006). "6,000 cr Wasted, 10-yr Delay & They Want 150,000 cr More", *Indian Express*, 12 November.
30. *http://www.bharat-rakshak.com/MISSILES/Agni.html*, "The development of India's nuclear weapon delivery systems indicates that a classic nuclear triad force—with distinct land, sea and air components—will eventually be created", in W.P.S. Sidhu, "Asian nuclear testing: India sees safety in nuclear triad and second strike potential", *Jane's Intelligence Review*, PSA-2135 (1 July 1998).
31. *http://www.indiabudget.nic.in*

tested technologies like manned space missions, which in the long run may find utility for its military programmes. On 11 January, 2007 China fired an anti-satellite weapon to 'kill' its own ageing weather satellite, thus demonstrating to the world its capabilities and willingness to take future warfare to outer space.

Today, when the need to maintain operational vigilance and military balance in the subcontinent has become a major imperative for India, it becomes essential that the state tender various modern military technologies to its armed forces. This is possible when a developing state like India adopts a multifaceted approach like purchase and transfers of technology from the techno-savvy nations, encourages research, development and production within the country, provides adequate budget facilities for indigenous development, and learns from the various bilateral or multilateral military exercises. India's progress in all these areas is encouraging but with a major scope for further development. For obvious reasons, all the technologies of military relevance would not be readily available for a transaction, hence India cannot avoid self-development in this area. Against this backdrop, India needs to develop a more mature and realistic strategic technology vision, based on its security requirements to build up its defences.

3

Global War on Terror

The Long War to Nowhere

SHANTHIE MARIET D'SOUZA

> Great harm has been done to us. We have suffered great loss. And in our grief and anger we have found our mission and our moment. Freedom and fear are at war. The advance of human freedom—the great achievement of our time, and the great hope of every time—now depends on us. Our nation—this generation—will lift a dark threat of violence from our people and our future. We will rally the world to this cause by our efforts, by our courage. We will not tire, we will not falter, and we will not fail.
>
> —"Waging and Winning the War on Terror", *http://www.whitehouse.gov/infocus/achievement/chap1-nrn.html*

More than five years after President George W. Bush's declaration of 20 September 2001 initiating the Global War on Terror (GWOT) the achievements of GWOT remain at best modest. While the threat from radical Islam—the focus of GWOT—continues to loom large, several other radical ideological movements have gained ominous muscle.

A Long 'War'

Internationally, terrorist incidents have been proliferating, notwithstanding claims of the proponents of GWOT that it is a unique formula to enervate Islamist terror groups.[1] On the other hand, the

1. President Bush explaining the objectives of GWOT stated on 11 October 2001, "The attack (9/11) took place on American soil, but it was an attack on the heart and soul of the civilized world. And the world has come together to fight a new and different war, the first, and we hope the only one, of the 21st century. A war against all those who seek to export terror, and a war against those governments that support or shelter them." See 'President holds prime time news conference'. 11 October 2001. *http://www.whitehouse.gov/news/releases/2001/10/20011011-7.html*

failure of GWOT has quietly passed monopoly over violence from state sponsors to proliferating sub-state groups. The US State Department's annual Country Reports on Terrorism (CRT), 2006, indicates that 14,338 terrorist attacks took place in 2006, 3,185 more than in 2005, a 28.5 per cent increase. These strikes claimed 20,498 lives, registering a 40.2 per cent increase over 2005.[2] The worst affected were the Near East and South Asia,[3] with Afghanistan and Iraq as epicentres. A study by the *Mother Jones* magazine finds that between the two periods September 2001 to March 2003 and March 2003 to September 2006 there has been a 607 per cent increase in the incidence of terrorism.[4]

Studies indicate that GWOT is about to become the second-most expensive conflict in American history, after World War II.

> With enactment of FY 2007 appropriations, Congress has approved a total of about $510 billion for military operations, base security, reconstruction, foreign aid, embassy costs, and veterans' health care for the three operations initiated since the 9/11 attacks: Operation Enduring Freedom (OEF) covering Afghanistan and other counter terror operations, Operation Noble Eagle (ONE) providing enhanced security at military bases, and Operation Iraqi Freedom (OIF), Iraq.[5]

Professor Joseph Stiglitz of Columbia University, who was chairman of the Council of Economic Advisers under President Clinton, co-authored a study in December 2006 that predicted that the Iraq conflict alone will eventually cost US taxpayers more than $1 trillion.[6] As a share of GDP, however, defence spending is less than in earlier times. In his testimony before the Senate on 6 February 2007, Steven M. Kosiak, Vice-President for Budget Studies, Center for

2. "Sharp rise in terrorist attacks in 2006: State Department says most attacks in Iraq, Afghanistan", 30 April 2007, *http://www.msnbc.msn.com/id/18399660/*. For the *Country Reports on Terrorism 2006*, United States Department of State, April 2007, see *http://www.state.gov/s/ct/rls/crt/2006/*
3. CRT 2006 notes, "By far the largest number of reported terrorist incidents occurred in the Near East and South Asia. These two regions also were the locations for 90 per cent of all the 290 high-casualty attacks that killed 10 or more people.", n.2: 327.
4. The study, "Iraq Effect: War has Increased Terrorism Sevenfold Worldwide", was conducted by Peter Bergen and Paul Cruickshank, research fellows at the Center on Law and Security at the New York University School of Law. See *http://www.motherjones.com/news/featurex/2007/03/iraq_effect_1.html*
5. Belasco, Amy (2007). *The Cost of Iraq, Afghanistan, and Other Global War on Terror Operations since 9/11*, Congressional Research Service (CRS) report for the Congress. 14 March. *http://www.fas.org/sgp/crs/natsec/RL33110.pdf*
6. Montgomery, Lori (2007). "The Cost of War, Unnoticed", *Washington Post*, 13 May.

Strategic and Budgetary Assessments, said:

> Notwithstanding the high cost of current military operations, spending on defense today accounts for a significantly smaller share of gross domestic product (GDP) than it did during either of these past wars. At the height of the Korean (1953) and Vietnam (1968) Wars, total spending on defense (including both war-related spending and funding for Department of Defense's "peacetime" force structure, modernization and readiness requirements) absorbed about 14.2 per cent and 9.4 per cent, respectively, of GDP. By comparison, total spending on defense (again, including both war-related and other programmes and activities) is likely to absorb some 4.5 per cent of GDP this year.[7]

GWOT and International Terrorism

While launching GWOT in Afghanistan, the US President declared in October 2001:

> The truth of the matter is, in order to fully defend America, we must defeat the evildoers where they hide. We must round them up, and we must bring them to justice. And that's exactly what we're doing in Afghanistan—the first battle in the war of the 21st century.[8]

More than five years after the commencement of Operation Enduring Freedom, violence in Afghanistan is worsening. CRT 2006 notes that Afghanistan witnessed 749 terrorist strikes in 2006, compared to 491 attacks in 2005. More than 4,000 people were killed in fighting, a quarter of them civilians, and more than 170 foreign soldiers.[9] The Taliban, after their ouster from Afghanistan have found safe haven in the bordering regions of Pakistan. Pakistan has tried to contain the Taliban's violence within its territory by signing peace deals with them,[10] but the latter taking advantage of these deals have

---

7. "The Global War on Terror (GWOT): Costs, Cost Growth and Estimating Funding Requirements", *http://www.senate.gov/~budget/republican/hearingarchive/testimonies/2007/2007-02-06Kosiak.pdf*
8. "President holds Prime Time News Conference", n.1.
9. "Fact Box—Military Deaths in Afghanistan", 7 May 2007, *http://www.alertnet.org/thenews/newsdesk/SP199432.htm*
10. Under the peace deal, signed in August 2005, the militants are to halt attacks on Pakistani forces in Pakistan's semi-autonomous North Waziristan region and stop crossing into nearby eastern Afghanistan to attack US and Afghan forces hunting al-Qaeda and Taliban militants. See "Pakistan Signs Peace Deal with pro-Taliban Militants", *International Herald Tribune*, 5 September, 2005.

been launching frequent strikes in Afghan territory. They even briefly tried to recapture Kandahar. Attacks by the insurgents have escalated from 130 a month in September 2005 to 300 in March 2006 and to 600 by November 2006.[11] The US-backed President Hamid Karzai, virtually known as 'mayor of Kabul',[12] has been unable to extend his authority to afflicted provides further eroding his legitimacy. Land under cultivation of poppy, said to be the main source of funds for the Taliban, has grown from 8,000 hectares to 165,000 hectares between 2001 and 2006.[13] Recurrent Taliban attacks, including suicide bombings, have hampered reconstruction activities under foreign aid of $3 billion a year, and eroded the people's confidence in the ability of the multinational forces to secure the country. The situation in Afghanistan is mired by lack of both development and security and the insurgents are exploiting the situation to their advantage. The rising level of violence would continue unabated in 2007.

In Iraq, another theatre in GWOT, American objectives have been stated as follows:

> Iraq is the central front in the global war on terror. Failure in Iraq will embolden terrorists and expand their reach; success in Iraq will deal them a decisive and crippling blow. [...] Iraq would become a safe haven from which terrorists could plan attacks against America, American interests abroad, and our allies.[14]

Here, too, civilian fatalities have reached alarming levels, with the propped up administration unable to cope with the insurgent violence. According to CRT 2006, 6,600 incidents of terrorist attacks took place during the year in Iraq, which accounted for 45 per cent of the worldwide incidents of terrorism. The number of people killed in these incidents, about 13,000, accounted for 65 per cent of the worldwide total of terrorism-related deaths. Kidnapping by terrorists soared by 300 per cent in Iraq over 2005.[15] Fatalities among the US

11. Scott, Cameron (2007). "Assessing ISAF: A Baseline Study of NATO's Role". March. *http://www.basicint.org/europe/NATO/afghanistan.pdf*
12. Robinson, Simon (2002). "Karzai's Kabul? Fit for a King", *Time*. 18 April.
13. McDougall, Dan (2007). "Afghans Hit Hardest by Biggest Opium Crop", *Guardian*. 13 May.
14. "National Strategy for Victory in Iraq", Executive Summary, 30 November 2005. *http://www.whitehouse.gov/infocus/iraq/iraq_national_strategy_20051130.pdf*
15. "Sharp Rise in Terrorist Attacks in 2006 ...", n.2.

forces have surpassed the body count in Vietnam.[16] 'Guerrillaisation of insurgency' in Iraq has essentially turned into sectarianism, civil war, and insurgency against the occupying force.

In Africa, 65 per cent more attacks, 420 compared to 253 in 2005, were counted in 2006, largely due to turmoil in or near Sudan, including Darfur, and Nigeria where oil facilities and workers have been targeted.[17] In Europe, CRT 2006 notes, while no major terrorist attacks took place, "foiled plots and concerns over increasing radicalisation among immigrant youth served as stimulus for increased cooperation and efforts to strengthen counter-terrorism capabilities. [...] Terrorist activity and the presence of terrorist support networks in Europe remained a source of concern."[18] Around 498 attacks were carried out in the EU in 2006 and a total of 706 arrests in 15 Member States with France, Spain and the UK being most severely affected by terrorism.[19] The foiled London airplane plot and the trolley bomb case of Germany where primarily targeted towards civilians and critical transportation infrastructure.

While half of all the terrorism arrests were related to Islamist terrorism particularly in France, Spain, Italy, separatist terrorists carried out 424 attacks in the EU, the most affected being France (60 percent of the attacks) and Spain, particularly in Basque regions and Corsica. Despite the unilateral cease fire declared in March 2006, Euskadi Ta Askatasuna (ETA) mainly used Taldes Y to carry out a high number of low intensity attacks and the attack at the Madrid airport on 30 December 2006 resulted in high casualties depicting its capabilities to strike with well-prepared, and coordinated attacks against high profile targets. In 2006, left-wing and anarchist terrorists carried out 55 attacks in the EU mainly targeting Greece, Italy, Spain and Germany.[20]

---

16. By December 2006, *Newsweek* reported, almost 3000 US soldiers were dead and 22,000 were injured in Iraq. *http://www.huffingtonpost.com/2006/12/12/25000-us-troops-dead-or-_n_36186.html*
17. "Sharp Rise in Terrorist Attacks in 2006 ...", n.2.
18. "Country Reports on Terrorism 2006", n.2: 48-49.
19. *EU Terrorism Situation and Trend Report 2007*, TE-SAT, \Europol, Netherlands, March 2007.
20. Ibid.

South East Asia, which for the Bush administration formed the 'second front' in GWOT, posed similar challenges for the US efforts.[21] An al-Qaeda affiliate, Jemaah Islamiyah (JI), which carried out several attacks including the October 2002 Bali bombings, is reported to have demonstrated significant ability to adapt and regenerate. Even with its leadership and organisation damaged the group represents a serious threat in Indonesia and southern Philippines. In May 2007, the International Crisis Group (ICG) estimated JI's cadre strength at 900, operating under a new military structure under "Afghan-trained militant Abu Dujana." The cadres include an assassination squad with focus on assassinating senior police, prosecutors, and others in authority in the JI's base of Indonesia.[22]

Neo al-Qaeda

Debilitated by GWOT, al-Qaeda has reinvented and reinvigorated itself through fission and operates through 'sub-contracting' to maintain deniability and avoid detection. Terrorist attacks across the world have indicated that:

> the new generations of fundamentalist terrorists do not share the same group history as the ones the US and its allies have been fighting most frequently since 9/11. The non-aligned nature of many of the new cells established in Europe and Australasia, for example, have a more international identity, greater independence and looser structures.[23]

The rise of these multiple micro actors, each adopting the techniques and ideology of its dominant partner, and each with an objective of 'striking at the distant enemy' through 'localised attacks', has expanded the conflict arena beyond state borders, increasingly assuming a 'trans-national' or 'stateless' form. Al-Qaeda and affiliated groups have struck in Algiers, Casablanca, Madrid, London, Istanbul, Karachi, Bali,

---

21. For a detailed analysis of US counter-terrorism policy in South East Asia see David Gracia (2004). "US Security Policy and Counter-Terrorism in Southeast Asia", *UNISCI Discussion Papers*, Unidad e Investigación Sobre Seguridad y Cooperación Internacional, May.
22. "Indonesia: Jemaah Islamiyah's Current Status", Briefing, International Crisis Group, 3 May 2007, *http://www.crisisgroup.org/library/documents/asia/indonesia/b63_indonesia_jemaah_ islamiyah_ s_current_status_new.pdf*
23. Gorka, Sebastian (2004). "Al-Qaeda's Next Generation", *Terrorism Monitor*, Vol. 2(15), 29 July.

Mombassa.[24] A plot was also discovered in August 2006 to bring down several transatlantic airliners flying between Britain and the US.

It is also reported that a new generation of leaders has emerged under Osama bin Laden to cement control over al-Qaeda's operations. Mark Mazzetti notes, for example:

> In contrast with the somewhat hierarchical structure of al-Qaeda in Afghanistan before 9/11, the group's leadership is now more diffuse, with several planning hubs working autonomously and not reliant on constant contact with bin Laden and Ayman al-Zawahiri, his deputy. Much is still not known about the backgrounds of the new leaders; some have adopted *noms de guerre*. They are said to be mostly in their mid-30s and have years of battlefield experience fighting in places like Afghanistan and Chechnya.[25]

According to US intelligence and counter-terrorism sources, the new leaders rose from within the organisation after the death or capture of the operatives who built al-Qaeda before the 9/11 attacks. Intercepted intelligence communications between al-Qaeda's operatives in Pakistan's tribal areas point towards a complex network of human couriers employed by al-Qaeda to evade electronic eavesdropping.[26]

Globalised Terrorism

There is also increasing use of technology—such as the internet and video tapes played on television channels—for propaganda, recruitment, fund raising and operations. Michael Scheuer notes:

> Easily accessible satellite television and Internet streaming video will broaden Muslim youths' perception that the West is anti-Islamic. US public diplomacy cannot negate the impressions formed by real-time video from Palestine, Iraq, and Afghanistan that shows Muslims battling 'aggressive' Western forces and validating bin Laden's claim that the West intends to destroy Islam.[27]

---

24. Riedel, Bruce (2007). "Iraq War Strengthened al-Qaida", NPR's Day to Day, 30 April, *http://www.brookings.edu/views/interviews/riedel/20070430.htm*
25. Mazzetti, Mark (2007). "A New Generation of al-Qaeda Leaders has emerged under Osama bin Laden", *International Herald Tribune*, 2 April.
26. Mazzetti, Mark, David Rohde & Margot Williams, (2007). "The Reach of War; New Generation of Qaeda Chiefs is seen on Rise", *New York Times*, 2 April.
27. Scheuer, Michael (2005). "Al-Qaeda's Next Generation: Less Visible and More Lethal", *Terrorism Focus*, Vol. 2(18), 4 October.

It is estimated that there are about 4500 overtly jihadist websites which reproduce and disseminate the al-Qaeda leadership's messages.[28] Having lost its territorial base and physical infrastructure in Afghanistan, al-Qaeda and its affiliates have maintained their operational capabilities through the 'virtual sanctuary' for 'cyber mobilisation.'

An abysmal record of success in GWOT has not, however, deterred the Bush administration from extending its shadow to Iran,[29] which the US State Department describes as "the world's leading state sponsor of terrorism."[30] CRT 2006 particularly blames the Islamic Revolutionary Guards Corps (IRGC) and Iran's Ministry of Intelligence and Security (MoIS) for supporting many extremist groups in Iraq and elsewhere.[31] In February 2007 a BBC report detailed US contingency plans for air strikes on Iran involving targets beyond nuclear sites to include most of the country's military infrastructure—"air bases, naval bases, missile facilities and command-and-control centres."[32]

GWOT has had little or no impact on other insurgencies elsewhere in the world, such as in Jammu and Kashmir and Sri Lanka. Exploiting the safety of 'ungoverned spaces' as well as areas from where states have retreated, be it the Federally Administered Tribal Areas (FATA) in Pakistan or Afghanistan or Iraq, terrorists have converted such areas into liberated zones for hiding and planning attacks elsewhere. Several reports have indicated that mujahideen trained in such areas have been used in conflicts worldwide. 'Ungoverned spaces' are also fertile ground for establishing and maintaining linkages between insurgents with local criminals, organised crime, narco trafficking and human

---

28. Riedel, Bruce (2007). "Al-Qaeda Strikes Back", *Foreign Affairs*, May-June.
29. Several reports throughout 2005 and 2006 have speculated regarding the timing of a US attack on Iran. For example, see "Journalist: U.S. Planning for Possible Attack on Iran", 17 January 2005, *http://www.cnn.com/2005/ALLPOLITICS/01/16/hersh.iran*; "Former CIA Officer: U.S. Plans Nuclear Attack on Iran", 18 July 2005, *http://www.aljazeera.com/me.asp?service_ID=9368*; Philip Sherwell, "US Prepares Military Blitz against Iran's Nuclear Sites", 14 February 2006, *http://www.telegraph.co.uk/news/main.jhtml?xml=/news/2006/02/12/wiran12.xml&sSheet=/news/2006/02/12/ixnewstop.html*
30. *Country Reports on Terrorism 2006*, n.2: 8.
31. Ibid.: 147.
32. "US 'Iran Attack Plans' Revealed", 20 February 2007. *http://news.bbc.co.uk/2/hi/middle_east/6376639.stm*

trafficking, fostering a mutually beneficial symbiotic relationship between criminals and terrorists.

Also, the domain of terrorism is increasingly becoming urban, contrary to the classical insurgency where the domain was essentially rural. While urban centres have provided easy 'mingling spaces', the urban nature of guerrilla warfare ensures visibility by the media. The New Terrorism that employed tactics which left "many watching and not necessarily many dead" has been replaced by several strikes that left "many watching as well as many dead." The 9/11 attacks, the 2002 attacks in Bali, and the 2005 attack targeting the railway network in Mumbai are some examples of this high visibility mass-casualty trend.

Untouched Areas

The GWOT in Afghanistan and Iraq, being essentially centred on neutralising the threat from radical Islam, has in a way taken the heat off movements that are not essentially the projection of a 'religion that hurts'. Maoists have emerged as major players in the political landscape of Nepal. Left-wing extremism wreaks havoc over vast stretches of Indian territory; close to 182 districts in 16 states are said to be under the influence of the Maoists. In Sri Lanka, both the government and the Liberation Tigers of Tamil Eelam (LTTE) have abandoned the dwindling peace process and have launched a full-scale war. While the government forces have claimed to have inflicted serious damage on the outfit, three aerial attacks on Sri Lankan facilities in March and April 2007 by the LTTE,[33] in spite of their limited attainment, indicate a protracted fitful war.

In spite of its projected swathe, GWOT also leaves vast conflict afflicted areas untouched. India's state of Jammu and Kashmir, a victim of Pakistan-sponsored cross-border terrorism, in spite of incidental decrease in the number of terrorist incidents, remains a tinderbox in the subcontinent. Very little has been done in GWOT to address India's concerns. Instead "there are numerous endorsements of Pakistan's exemplary role in combating terrorism and of President

33. These attacks, dated 26 March, 14 April and 29 April, respectively targeted the main Sri Lankan Air Force base in Katunayake, the main military complex in Jaffna peninsula, and oil and gas storage facilities in and around Colombo. See Sri *Lanka Timeline-Year 2007*, South Asia Terrorism Portal. *http://www.satp.org/satporgtp/countries/shrilanka/timeline/index.html*

Musharraf's 'courageous role'" in GWOT.[34] While Pakistan's engagement on its western borders and international pressure are said to be the reasons behind the current lull in Jammu and Kashmir,[35] terror from India's eastern sector is becoming a major concern. Not only have outfits like the Lashkar-e-Toiba (LeT) established linkages with al-Qaeda to orchestrate strikes in Jammu and Kashmir, but a number of terrorist attacks that took place in 2006 indicate a continuous process of mobilisation through Bangladesh with the help of Pakistan's external intelligence agency, the Inter-Services Intelligence (ISI) and its Bangladeshi counterpart, the Directorate General of Forces Intelligence (DGFI). Such nexus has resulted in periodic strikes in several of India's urban centres.[36]

Future of GWOT

According to Erich Marquardt, the US military operations against al-Qaeda in Afghanistan

> scattered an already relatively primitive organisation. Continued US vigilance in that country and elsewhere will make it difficult for al-Qaeda to orchestrate any large-scale attacks against the United States, or even its major European allies. Yet, because of al-Qaeda's attractive ideology, similar attacks such as those that occurred in London and Madrid, in addition to those that have been executed in other capitals around the world, will continue.[37]

In future, the lethality of terrorist attacks is likely to increase with focus on critical infrastructure such as economic, transport, and even nuclear installations. Interlinkages between various radical groups are projected to grow. Terrorists have acquired new survival techniques and terrorism has become a global phenomenon, necessitating greater cooperation and coordination among affected countries. Counter-

---

34. Sahni, Ajai (2007). "CRT 2006: Loss of Confidence", *South Asia Intelligence Review*, Vol. 5(43), 7 May. *http://www.satp.org/satporgtp/sair/Archives/5_43.htm#assessment1*
35. According to the Annual Report 2006-07 of the Ministry of Home Affairs, there was a marginal decline in infiltration by 4 per cent in 2006 over 2005, from 597 recorded infiltrations in 2005 to 573 the next year. See *Annual Report 2006-07*, Ministry of Home Affairs, Government of India, p.143.
36. Routray, Bibhu Prasad (2006). "HUJI: Lengthening Shadow of Terror", *South Asia Intelligence Review*, Vol. 5(3): 31, July 2. *http://www.satp.org/satporgtp/sair/Archives/5_3.htm*
37. Marquardt, Erich (2005). "Al-Qaeda's Proliferating Ideology", Power & Interest News Report, 22 August. *http://pinr.com/report.php?ac=view_report&report_id=350&language_id=1*

terrorism needs to grow from a unilateral to a multilateral effort through a regional approach. The US Global War on Terror, despite its tall claims and noble objectives, will lead to nowhere as long as US approach to addressing the menace of terror remains mired in militaristic operations with little attention to international cooperation, development and reconstruction. The shadow of terror would only lengthen.

4

A Supranational Agency for Nuclear Materials?

RAJIV NAYAN

The nuclear non-proliferation regime, dominated by the Non-Proliferation Treaty (NPT), has been under strain for a long time. The deadlocked NPT Review Conference of 2005 was a reflection of this strain. Developments in 2006 raised further doubts regarding the efficacy of the NPT regime. All the carrots and sticks used by leading members of the NPT to dissuade Iran from enriching uranium and reprocessing plutonium failed to convince that country. On 9 October, 2006 another NPT member, North Korea, announced the testing of its nuclear device, and the intent to become a nuclear weapon country.

The international community—both academics and policymakers—has been coming out with ideas and initiatives—old, new, and recast—to make the nuclear non-proliferation regime effective. More notable among such initiatives are the six-nation talks on North Korea (involving North Korea, South Korea, China, Japan, the United States, and Russia); the Middle Powers Initiative (involving eight Non-Governmental Organisations (NGOs) working with New Agenda Coalition countries such as Brazil, Egypt, Ireland, Mexico, New Zealand, South Africa and Sweden), the proposals in the Weapons of Terror report by the Weapons of Mass Destruction Commission (involving 14 non-governmental commissioners appointed by the commission), chaired by former International Atomic Energy Agency (IAEA) chief Hans Blix; multilateral approaches to the nuclear fuel cycle (a report prepared by a non-governmental expert group and published by the IAEA). The idea of a supranational agency for nuclear materials, which has as its main advocate Ruud Lubbers, former Prime Minister of Netherlands and former United Nations High Commissioner for Refugees, is one such. Proposing to stimulate a debate, Lubbers has argued for the agency in some detail to erect a twenty-first-century framework for nuclear trade and security based on a payoff structure. In examining the proposal this essay concludes that it does not go far enough.

The Lubbers Proposal

Highlights of the proposal are summarised here:

Objective: To resolve the current impasse in the NPT-driven non-proliferation regime through a blend of effective non-proliferation initiatives and lucrative offers for peaceful application of nuclear technology.

Problems: The possibility of nuclear terrorism; the inadequacy of the existing arrangement to deal with the proliferation network (A.Q. Khan could reach the Netherlands and URENCO enrichment establishment at his will; anyone could do business with his clandestine network); the US, among other countries, was aware of A.Q. Khan's clandestine activities but there was no institutional arrangement to thwart such activities.

Solutions: A supranational agency that can amalgamate national or other identities; the agency to have ownership of the land on which sensitive nuclear production and installations are located; complete control over nuclear materials that have potentiality to become critical mass; complete international control over nuclear fuel cycle; better management of the waste problem; merging and curbing proliferating identities; strict action, including forced intervention in a country violating the commitment; denial of the right to withdraw from a treaty; 'sovereign right' of a country cannot be invoked for denying access to the IAEA; a greater role for the Security Council in enforcing non-proliferation commitment; preference for deployment of the Security Council Blue Helmets to monitor nuclear research, production, and storage.

Limitations

The classical NPT bargain had two principal elements: non-nuclear weapon countries would renounce their nuclear weapon option for peaceful uses of nuclear energy and the NPT-defined nuclear weapon countries would work for nuclear disarmament. In the classical NPT bargaining structure three elements were supposed to be in equilibrium, namely, nuclear disarmament, the quest for nuclear energy, and non-proliferation. As mentioned earlier, this bargain is under tremendous pressure from all sides. Though Lubbers advocates promotion of nuclear energy among the comity of nations, his main concern seems to be to curb proliferation, based on the Cold War structure embodied in the NPT regime, suitably refurbished to resolve the current impasse.

In the proposed structure, too, nuclear weapon countries are excluded from control until nuclear disarmament is achieved. The proposal also lacks a concrete plan for verifiable, irreversible nuclear disarmament, while admitting that the functional dimension of nuclear weapons, reflected in terms of deterrence or any other military rationale, complicates nuclear disarmament. In other words, nuclear disarmament will continue to remain a rhetoric as it is in Article VI of the NPT.

Fundamentally modelled on the European Union (EU) experience, a supranational regime refers to an understanding or agreement among nation-states on rules, principles, norms, and decision making procedures in a given issue area. In EURATOM as in URENCO the founder countries merged their national nuclear capabilities and were open to supervision. The proposed agency, however, would also have complete control over nuclear materials to the extent of infringing on sovereignty. The expressed preference for a greater role for the Security Council, in the existing circumstances where the Security Council lacks a democratic structure, would virtually mean transfer of sovereign rights of all other countries in nuclear matters to the five permanent members of the Security Council.

If, as Lubbers maintains, the sovereignty principle prevented the US President from intervening despite possessing intelligence on A.Q. Khan and proliferation involving him and his country, did it stop the American intervention in Iraq on the pretext of saving the world from weapons of mass destruction (WMDs)? No doubt globalisation has led to greater networking among nation-states but it has not obliterated the notion of sovereignty. Interactions currently may be marked by an intricate pattern of cooperation and conflict but the final authority is still vested in the sovereign nation-state. The sovereign state still provides cultural identity to its citizens by integrating state and community. David Albright writes:

> The core values of sovereignty are the following: international order among states, membership and participation in the society of states, coexistence of political systems, legal equality of states, political freedom of states, and pluralism or respect for diversity of ways of life of different groups of people around the world.[1]

Ensuring territorial and economic security is a prime concern of a sovereign nation-state. Sovereignty is considered a 'chief defence mechanism' against fissiparous tendencies and has the 'capacity to insulate oneself or protect oneself from outside influences and forces.' The world witnesses combined military exercises, integrated nuclear planning, and joint command systems, and so on, but of sovereign nation-states. If an accountable sovereign nation-state allocates resources to its population efficiently, the risk of conflict and disruption may be minimised. A supranational agency with delegated representation would be too remote to fulfil these obligations.

A strong institutional arrangement is built on consensus. Consensus will not be available in the proposed supranational agency where some countries are allowed to possess nuclear weapons and fissile materials and others are deprived of these rights regardless of their security requirements. Crisis is built into such an organisation, making the institution itself problematic.

As regards the EU and many of its functioning agencies they are generally associated with 'inherently untidy and inefficient bureaucracy.' Handing over all fissile materials to an agency which replicates or resembles an inefficient body would not be prudent. Most of the leading nuclear consortiums are Europe-centred. Europe-based consortiums, which had countering the US enrichment monopoly as an objective, failed to unite all the European countries, leading to the creation of more than one consortium. URENCO soon had a rival in EURODIF, created by France, Spain, Italy, Belgium, and interestingly,

---

1. Jackson, Robert (1999). "Sovereignty in World Politics", in Robert Jackson (ed.), *Sovereignty at the Millennium*. Massachusetts: Blackwell. p.32.

Iran. Later, when the US tried to work with these European consortiums, serious differences over interests cropped up. If Europe could not set its house in order, it is difficult to visualise a universal supranational agency, involving nations and continents of far greater diversities, for control of nuclear materials. It would also be difficult to synthesise commercial and other interests.

URENCO leaked not only to A.Q. Khan and the networked countries but also to countries such as Iraq[2] and Brazil. There is no guarantee that illicit and black or grey market supply would be checked by an agency modelled on URENCO. Many believe that whatever restriction on nuclear technology or fissile material worked in URENCO, it was because of commercial reasons and had nothing to do with non-proliferation reasons. URENCO came under controversy and was even charged by the UN for procuring uranium from Namibia without authorisation.

URENCO was also not free from concerns of plutonium hazards. Besides, a URENCO-type international organisation has to resolve several issues related to financial control and funding, especially fluctuating currency exchange rates and differential inflation. A small consortium, involving just three countries, it failed to develop centralised single centrifuge technology and had to reconcile with their national development of technologies because they had already invested substantially in their national projects.

Lawrence Scheinman, a leading advocate of non-proliferation and supporter of a multilateral approach to nuclear fuel cycle observes:

> There is no single, generic multinational formula that would be satisfactory for all technologies and all partners. While all such ventures will have to meet certain basic requirements, successful implementation of multinationalism will depend on the flexibility of its application. One of the apparent virtues of the multinational concept is that it is capable of being developed in a variety of ways, as such ventures as EURODIF, URENCO and EUROCHEMIC illustrate...Arranging multinational ownership, management, or operation does not offer any significant non-proliferation benefit by

2. Albright, David (2001). "Preventing Illegal Exports: Learning from Case Studies, Part-II", Institute for Science and International Security, 9 April, at *http://www.exportcontrols.org/albright2.html*

itself, and even could have the counterproductive effect of stimulating an unnecessary early deployment of high-risk technology. Multinational arrangements must be part of an integrated regime which covers not only the facility itself, but the material produced—although different organisations could have different responsibilities under an umbrella regime.[3]

The Baruch plan of 1946, proposed by Bernard Baruch of the US to the United Nations Atomic Energy Commission, from which the Lubbers proposal apparently draws inspiration, was only clear about various stages of control, but ambiguous about control of uranium or thorium.[4] The plan had a road map about the future of nuclear science and materials. It intended to exchange basic scientific information and atomic energy for peaceful purposes. It also proposed the elimination from national armaments of nuclear weapons and other WMDs. However, it is best known for its proposal for international control of the whole field of atomic energy. It also envisaged the creation of an International Atomic Development Authority (IADA). The Baruch Plan entrusted IADA with "all phases of the development and use of atomic energy", starting with the raw material and including:

- Managerial control or ownership of all atomicenergy, activities potentially dangerous to world security.
- Power to control, inspect, and license all other atomic activities.
- The duty of fostering the beneficial uses of atomic energy.
- Research and development responsibilities of an affirmative character intended to put the Authority in the forefront of atomic knowledge and thus to enable it to comprehend, and therefore to detect, misuse of atomic energy. To be effective, the Authority must itself be the world's leader in the field of atomic knowledge and development and thus supplement its legal authority with the great power inherent in possession of leadership in knowledge."[5]

3. Scheinman, Lawrence (2004). "The Nuclear Fuel Cycle: A Challenge for Non-proliferation", *Disarmament Diplomacy*, No.76, March/April, at *http://www.acronym.org.uk/dd/dd76/76ls.htm*
4. Rydell, Randy (2006). "Looking Back, Going Back: The Nuclear Plan that Refused to Go Away", *Arms Control Today*, June, at *http://www.armscontrol.org/act/2006_06/LookingbackBaruch.asp*
5. Atomic Archive.com. "The Baruch Plan". *http://www.atomicarchive.com/Docs/Deterrence/Baruch Plan.shtml*

Because the plan proposed elimination of the veto right of members of the Security Council over action taken for violation by nation-states, the erstwhile Soviet Union opposed it. Andrei Gromyko then proposed an alternative plan to forbid the production and use of atomic weapons and the destruction of existing stocks of atomic weapons.

Several countries opposed the Baruch Plan as it would endow a country like the US having nuclear weapons with an advantage. Some others like India, which had reserves of natural uranium and thorium, opposed international control of their resources, as there was no similar control for other energy sources like oil reserves. Control of only one source of energy was considered discriminatory.

India and the Non-proliferation Regime

In stating their perspectives on the non-proliferation regime Indian leaders and officials maintain that "a further erosion of the non-proliferation regime is not in India's interests."[6] Prime Minister Manmohan Singh has stated:

> India is a responsible nuclear power. We are fully conscious of the immense responsibilities that come with the possession of advanced technologies, both civilian and strategic. While we are determined to utilise our indigenous resources and capabilities to fulfil our national interests, we are doing so in a manner that is not contrary to the larger goals of nuclear non-proliferation.[7]

On different occasions, the Indian Prime Minister affirmed that India would not support the emergence of another nuclear weapon state. When North Korea conducted its nuclear test in October 2006 he told the media:

> India has expressed deep concern over the DKR nuclear test. It is a violation of its international commitments. India had supported the six party talks which was intended to achieve the goal of denuclearisation of the Korean Peninsula. I wish to state that a further erosion of the non-proliferation regime is not in our interest.

6. For example, Government of India (2006). Prime Minister's Office, "PM's opening statement at 7th India-EU Summit", 13 October, at *http://pmindia.nic.in/visits/content.asp?id=136*
7. Government of India (2004). Prime Minister Office, "PM's address at the Golden Jubilee function of the Department of Atomic Energy", 23 October, at *http://pmindia.nic.in/speech/content.asp?id=36*

> We do not support the emergence of another nuclear weapon state. The North Korea test highlights the dangers of clandestine proliferation. In fact India's own security has suffered due to clandestine proliferation linkages relating from our neighbours.[8]

About Iran he stated "...it is a fact that Iran had a clandestine nuclear programme for several years and it is not in our interest to have another nuclear weapon state in our neighbourhood."[9]

India relates nuclear energy to energy security, which in turn is considered essential for its economic growth. The Indian leadership supports the "forward looking approaches to enhance international cooperation in the peaceful uses of nuclear energy."[10] Although India has developed capabilities in the entire range of fuel cycle operations, including capabilities to recover plutonium from irradiated nuclear fuel, it favours constructive dialogue with other advanced nuclear weapon countries. The Prime Minister has stated, "We in India are willing to shoulder our share of international obligations provided our legitimate interests are met. India has actively embraced globalisation. There is no reason why nuclear energy production should be an exception."[11] The Indian government and the policymaking community are critical of multilateral regimes which are used to deny technology that can be put to legitimate use. The Indian government views that the founding principles of Atoms for Peace are undermined with these ineffective non-proliferation regime. The Prime Minister has stated:

> The limitations of the present non-proliferation regime should not be further accentuated by artificial restrictions on genuine peaceful nuclear applications. Technology denial and closing avenues for international cooperation in such an important field is tantamount to the denial of developmental benefits to millions of people, whose lives can be transformed by the utilisation of nuclear energy and relevant technologies.[12]

---

8. The United Kingdom Government (2006). 10 Downing Street, Press Conference with Prime Minister of India, 10 October, at *http://www.number-10.gov.uk/output/Page10184.asp*
9. Government of India (2006). Prime Minister's Office, "Representatives of Muslim Organisations Meet PM, Press Release", New Delhi, 18 April, at *http://pmindia.nic.in/prelease/pcontent.asp?id=432*
10. n.5.
11. Ibid.
12. Ibid.

Assessment

In the process of arguing for a supranational agency Lubbers has highlighted some of the contentious issues the non-proliferation system is facing. In providing a solution to these issues his proposals are hazy. His proposal for institutionalisation also remains vague. As there is no concrete timeframe for nuclear disarmament, and as long as the NPT continues to define the categories of nuclear weapon and non-nuclear weapon countries, problems would persist. It is high time that the philosophy and practice of nuclear regime was restructured—away from non-proliferation to disarmament, and away from denial and confrontation to cooperation. Nuclear India needs to undertake cautious engagement with the emerging non-proliferation regime—new, old, or recast—without walking into a trap.

5

Resurgence of Russia

P. STOBDAN

Russia's changing fortunes since the Soviet collapse in terms of its economic strength, military power, and influence in global affairs, have been a subject of keen observation. A resurgent Russia, based on the strength of its economic recovery, seems to be returning to the global centre-stage with capabilities to counterpoise the United States. This has intrinsically been associated with President Putin's ascendancy to power. The index of Putin's achievements during his six years in office as compared to the situation in Russia when he came to power on the last day on 1999 has indeed been reassuring to ordinary Russians. The debate on Russia's role in world affairs has become further sharpened as Putin's presidency draws to a close shortly. Has Russia indeed put the era of disarray well behind it? This paper tries to analyse various aspects of Russian affairs, domestic and international.

Putin and Russia's Resurgence

Russia went through an ambiguous and uncertain period during the Yeltsin era. Throughout the 1990s there were considerable misgivings about its ability to stage a comeback as a power of consequence.[1] Failure to gain control over Chechnya had tarnished Moscow's capacity to tackle its own domestic issues.

Putin has reversed Russia's declining fortunes, making a U-turn from its course to isolation, decline of power and repudiation of its superpower ambition, imbuing Russians with an invigorated multifaceted nationalism and international assertiveness.

---

1. Cohen, Ariel (2002). "Uncertainty Still Defines Russia's Role in Central Eurasia", *Eurasianet*, 19 September. Proceedings of the conference, organised by the Hellenic Foundation for European and Foreign Policy (ELIAMEP), highlight the misgivings about Russia's policy. *http://www.eliamep.gr/main.asp?cat+1&scat=1&obj=true*

From the ideological standpoint Putin wagered on the Eurasian paradigm based on Gumilev's concept of Russia's destiny as a Eurasian power. Yeltsin had a Western and Atlanticist orientation.[2] Putin's Eurasian agenda, pushed primarily by ideologues such as Alexsandr Sergeevich Panarin and Alexsandr Gel'evich Dugin, sought to rescue Russia from the fifth column and financial oligarchs working for the West and the ruin of Russia.[3] Putin opted for a "non-ideological pragmatism", avoiding introduction of radical change and concession to the West.[4] His preference was to overtly support "democratic values" and covertly strive to restore Russia's global status without confrontation. He has striven for a non-ideological "World Order", making common cause with key regions and nations in Eastern Europe, Arab world, Iran, Central Asia, the Caucasus, India, and China. Dugin spoke of a never-ending struggle between Western globalism and Russian Eurasianism: in this perspective the Cold War was "only one stage of the 'great war of continents'."[5] Bearing out this perception are the US neo-conservatives' plans to "de-construct Russia" as a challenge to the USA, which has disconcerted many Russians.[6]

Displaying pragmatism Putin's Russia acquiesced in the American military entry in Central Asia in the aftermath of the events of 11 September 2001. As Russian foreign policy analyst Alvin Z. Rubinstein wrote, "Putin's Russia is not bent on restoring the empire, much less seeking domination over the Eurasian heartland. It lacks the capability, the resources, and the ideological impetus."[7] Chechnya and Dagestan

---

2. Levkin, Andrei (2001). *"Chto Takoe Evraziya, Kazhdyy (Poka?) Ponimaet Po Svoemu"* cited in *ITAR-TASS*, 21 April.
3. Panarin, A.S. (1999). *"Global'noe Politivheskoe Progozirovanie v Usloviyakh Strategicheskoy Nestabil'nosti"* (A global political forecast under conditions of strategic instability), Moscow, *Editorial URSS*. Also see Bindyukov Nikolai and Petr Lopata (1999). *"Obsobaya Tre'ya Sila: Novyy Politicheskiy Fenomen"* (A Special Third Force: A New Political phenomenon), Moscow, *OTRK*.
4. A. Dougine, "Post-liberal era", *www.arctogaia.com/public/eng-lib.htm*
5. Dugin, A. (1998). *"Posleliberal'naya Epokha"*, *Zavtra*, Vol. 21: 7, 26 May.
6. Lepic, Arthur, "The Outrageous Strategy to Destroy Russia", *http://www.voltairenet.org/article30038.html*
7. Rubinstein, Alvin Z. (2001). "A US Policy for Russia", *Foreign Policy Research Institute*, 25 April. About Russia's quick decision to join the anti-terrorist coalition, allowing US military bases in Central Asia and the subsequent announcement to abandon bases in Lourdes (Cuba) and Cam Ranh Bay (Vietnam) see Richard Balmforth, "Russia Ends Cold War Chapter by Quitting Cuban Spy Base", *Reuters*, 18 October 2001.

and not NATO posed a threat to Russia at the time, with the growing nexus between Chechens and the Taliban/al-Qaida becoming a more compelling factor. Russia was also concerned about the possible proliferation of nuclear, chemical, and biological agents as also missile technology from the old research sites over which it lacked effective control.

Domestic Changes

The 2004 Beslan school incident that left hundreds of students dead decisively altered Russia's domestic policy. Putin announced that Moscow would appoint direct presidential nominees to the seven federal districts through a reform in the Federation Council. The President retained the right to dismiss elected governors and dissolve regional legislatures. Several legislative measures approved through the Duma (parliament) seemed to have strengthened the Kremlin's control over key components of the country's affairs.

Hard initiatives in domestic policies led to the consolidation of political forces into a three-party system: Communists, pro-presidential factions, and liberals (possible merger between the "Union of Rightist Forces" and "Yabloko"). As a result, the power composition, structure, and policy direction of the government has significantly stabilised during the last six years. No significant opposition emerged to challenge Putin in his hot pursuit on Chechnya, even though his style of functioning was severely criticised in the West. There have been marked improvements in creating media pluralism and democratisation, even though the state-owned media predominate. At the same time, the State seems to be pitted against the numerous powerful media empires, who enter the field mostly with political and financial motives. The reported attacks on independent journalists and intimidation have raised many questions about the pace and sincerity of democratisation programme in Russia.

In Chechnya, ravaged by two wars in the past twelve years, a semblance of order has been restored following a ruthless military campaign and subsequent hard policing methods. The Federal Security Service (FSB) managing to rein in July 2006 the Chechen rebel commander Shamil Basayev, who was the ringleader of the Beslan siege and other terrorist plots, seems to have finally crippled the Chechen separatist network. The elimination of Politkovskaya, a powerful critic of the Kremlin's policy in Chechnya, has also helped Moscow quell the Chechen uprising.

On the downside, the rising tide of attacks against immigrants and foreigners has cast a shadow on the direction of developments in Russia. In 2006 alone, at least 45 persons have been killed and hundreds more injured in racist attacks. There is growing assertion by ultra-nationalist groups marked by mass ethnic violence in various Russian cities. The government itself is being accused of contributing to a number of discriminatory policies against immigrants. New legislation to ban foreigners from trading at markets and street kiosks, etc. has gone against the spirit of the country's constitution and is a serious backsliding on democracy. The government also passed a law that restricts activities of non-governmental organisations (NGOs) that Putin saw as being "governed by puppeteers from abroad."

Economic Scene

Putin's strong handling of the Russian economy has made it dynamic and vibrant. The Russian oligarchs, who rose to power with Western patronage in the Yeltsin era, have been liquidated. Considering the speed at which Russia's economy was falling, its resurgence as a tiger economy in a short span of sixteen years has been incredible. Russia's GDP fell by 37 per cent in the mid-1990s. After a decade of virtually uninterrupted downslide, GDP has been rising at 4 per cent since 1999 and in 2005 it increased by 6.4 per cent. Among several key drivers behind the resurgence was energy export revenue. Rejecting the Soviet-style planning system, Russia has also successfully adopted various elements of free-market economy. Economic restructuring aimed at encouraging private enterprise is gradually reaping fruits. However, privatisation plans have not been free of obstacles, especially corruption, resulting in the concentration of economic activities and resources under mafia business control. By 2005 the state re-nationalised the private oil and gas sector.

Primarily, the import substitution effects after the August 1998 devaluation and the sharp rise in Russia's oil and gas exports were responsible for the economic growth. Besides the fiscal and monetary policies, a clear economic policy and political stability contributed to this reversal. Tax reforms have increased state revenues. Since 2000 the federal budget has consistently shown surpluses. Tax revenues for 2005 were US$153 billion and had a surplus of US$51.1 billion. The budget for 2006 recorded US$197 billion in revenues, showing a surplus of US$53 billion. Similarly, devaluation of the ruble in 1998 boosted Russia's export performance, earning US$245 billion in 2005, primarily led by oil and gas, which accounted for 63 per cent of the total.[8] Structural reforms in the financial sector, ensuring transparency and good corporate governance by reducing bureaucratic interference, cutting transaction costs and the scope for corruption, and adoption of international accounting standards have also helped significantly in stabilising the economy.[9]

Although Russia's application for membership in the WTO (World Trade Organisation) is on hold due to persistent blockage by the US on account of copyright piracy in Russia and restrictions on US exports to Russia, negotiations with the European Union (EU) in a wide variety of economic and security areas have been successful. The EU is committed to supporting Russia's WTO membership in return for price concessions on Russian gas and oil.

Russia continued to maintain strong trade ties with the Commonwealth of Independent States (CIS), especially Belarus, Ukraine, and Kazakhstan. But by 2005 trade diversification efforts have led to increase in trade with China by 37 per cent, touching US$29 billion.

The large-scale capital outflow that affected the balance of payments (a negative US$53 billion in 2005) has been reversed. In 2006 Russia's reserves had increased to US$196 billion. Unemployment is currently down at around 9 per cent and there has been an impressive pay down of foreign debt. Russia's external debt

8. For details see Library of Congress, Federal Research Division, Country Profile: Russia, October 2006.

9. President Putin confirmed these strategic priorities in his annual address to the Duma in December 2001. His priorities included transparent privatisation, the liberalisation of capital flows, accession to the WTO, judicial reform, development of a science and technology policy, industrial modernisation, and priority to export capacity.

totalled US$197.4 billion in 2004. However, its oil-fed Stabilisation Fund enabled Russia to repay substantial amounts to the IMF (International Monetary Fund) and the Paris Club of international lenders during 2005-06. Real disposable income is said to be growing steadily. Russia has also attracted a cumulative FDI of more than $110 billion till 2006, mostly in the oil and gas industry but also in the manufacturing sector as well.

With its rising economic trajectory, Russia is poised to become the sixth-largest economy in the world. Although its GDP per capita remains well below that in Western Europe, with sustained annual growth at around 7 per cent Russia's economic momentum will continue to drive up, despite high inflation. Per capita GDP is expected to be $7290 in 2007—five times that in 1999.

Increased energy revenue windfall has made it possible for Russia to establish a colossal "Stabilisation Fund" as reserved resource to deal with future crises.[10] Disbursement of this fund will help bring macroeconomic stability, increased infrastructure development, and improve social and health and education facilities to Western standards. Among economic constraints is Russia's industrial sector, which remains non-competitive since it relies heavily on defence industries and heavy manufacturing. It lacks captive markets and is short on investment and human capital. Russia's agricultural potential (32 per cent of the country's land area) also faced neglect and production fell sharply in the 1990s. Even until 2005, about 40 per cent of GDP derived from 'informal' economic activity and organised crime. The share of industrial and agricultural input to GDP dropped while the share of retail trade and services increased manifold.

Ordinary Russians seem to have quickly oriented themselves to a western lifestyle. Most Russian cities have developed up-market shops. The purchasing power of many Muscovites is said to be at par with West Europeans. But though there are no cases of starving pensioners or wages not being paid for months the real benefit of Russia's economic boom is yet to be translated on a wider scale.

10. In 2006 the Stabilisation Fund amounted about US$27 billion. The preliminary 2007 budget called for US$260 billion in revenue and US$211 billion in expenditure.

Energy Fortune

Energy sale accounted for 70 per cent of Russia' industrial production growth and one-third of its GDP in the mid-1990s. The global energy equations have changed after the events of 11 September 2001, with Russia emerging as a formidable petro-state steadily challenging even Saudi Arabia to become the world's number one supplier. Oil production has increased from 6.1 mbd (million barrels per day) in 1995 to 9.1 mbd in 2005.

Dependency on Russian energy has become imperative for many importing countries. Russia fulfils a fifth of Europe's oil and a third of its gas demand. Similarly, the US has been seeking energy alliance with Russia to reduce its dependency on Saudi Arabian oil. The demand for Russian energy supply has been ever increasing in the East, especially from its trans-Siberian pipelines and the Sakhalin Island oil deposits. The opening of a trans-Siberian oil pipeline scheduled for 2008 would significantly reorient the flow of Russia's oil to Asia. The gas company Gazprom is getting larger and is in the process of signing deals with major consumer countries, including China, India, Japan, Korea, EU states, and the US. According to plans, Gazprom should supply 20 per cent of America's liquefied natural gas (LNG) requirements in the coming years.

A law adopted in 2003 aimed to restructure the energy sector, including extensive privatisation and elimination of the Unified Energy System. In the years ahead, the energy sector is likely to see major reforms that will entail foreign investment.[11] At the same time, Russia has been working to form an OPEC-style gas cartel combining Iran and other Middle Eastern suppliers. Tough price negotiations with Europe are the main incentive for this initiative.[12]

Moscow's tendency to use energy supply as a weapon has created a series of rows. When Ukraine was drifting into the American orbit Russia raised tariffs for Ukraine from $90 to $130 per 1000 cubic

---

11. Gazprom controls an estimated 30 per cent of the world's natural gas reserves. Earlier Yukos was Russia's largest oil company. It lost most of its assets during Putin's campaign against its chief, Mikhail Khodorkovskiy. The largest state company Lukoil produces 18 per cent of oil production currently.
12. Russia, Iran, and Qatar have denied that a gas cartel is under construction.

metres. With Georgia, this policy has dramatically deteriorated diplomatic ties. A new trans-Baltic pipeline will deprive Ukraine and Poland, another state at odds with Russia, of fees for overland transit of Russian oil to Europe. In the Caucasus and Central Asia, Russia has sought to make a white elephant of the Baku-Ceyhan oil pipeline, which the Americans are plugging for, by capturing a major contract with supplier countries such Turkmenistan and Kazakhstan.[13] The Russian government is also selectively edging out world majors from dominant control of oil projects. Shell Company, for example, faced environmental controls over its operation in Sakhalin Island off the Pacific coast. At the same time, Russia's policy trend is to integrate into the global economy by diversifying from reliance on energy and metals exports.

Defence

After a sharp drop in the 1990s, production in the defence sector increased significantly beginning in 1999. Increased foreign sales, particularly to China and India, and some increases in domestic military spending have spurred growth. In 2005 military exports were estimated at US$6 billion. The defence budget has nearly quadrupled since 1999 to reach $31 billion and is likely to go up further in the face of the Pentagon's growing $620 billion military expenditure.[14]

Among the large-scale modernisation plans for strategic and conventional military power is the new weapon programme GPV-2015.[15] Introduction of new strategic nuclear assets and submarines also seems to be high in priority.[16] As late as in May 2007, Russia has gone in for the tests of a strategic RS-24 MIRV (multiple independently targeted re-entry vehicles) intercontinental missile, a new version of the Iskander (SS-26), and an advanced theatre-level

13. *http://www.rferl.org/features/2000/05/f.ru.000524145941.asp.*
14. "Is the Arms Race Back", *RIA Novosti*, 22 February 2007. *http://www.defencetalk.com/news/publish/index.php.*
15. Cooper, Julian (2006). "Developments in the Russian Arms Industry", in *SIPRI Yearbook, 2006: Armaments, Disarmament, and International Security*. Oxford: Oxford University Press, pp.431-48.
16. Matthews, Owen (2006). "Russian Nukes Redux", *Newsweek International*, 13 February.

surface-to-surface missile.[17] However, the nuclear factor is unlikely to be important for Russia's resurgence on the world scene.

Foreign Policy

Russia's post-Cold War security perception was underpinned largely by the so-called "threat from the South", a euphemism for the Islamist threat. Moscow's initial support for the US-led war against terror was based on the expectation that it would include Moscow's problems in Chechnya as well but this was not on Washington's agenda. China too questioned the US double standards concerning Islamic rebels in Xinjiang. Similarly, the Central Asian objection to US dealings with Islamist opposition groups was fully exploited by Russia to push for a rollback of US military presence from the region.[18]

Russia's economic resurgence has led to a more assertive stance towards former Soviet republics, particularly securing interest in its "near abroad" where 15 to 20 million ethnic Russians continue to live. Moscow has sought to pursue a policy not only to improve its power projection in Central Asia *vis-à-vis* Islamist radicals but also to restore its lost influence in the region. President Putin started with measures to reinvigorate the Russian-led military alliance, the Collective Security Treaty Organization (CSTO), enlarged its military presence in Kyrgyzstan and Tajikistan, and worked out a new deal with Tashkent in 2005 for rapid deployment of Russian troops to Uzbekistan in an emergency. Moscow also restored the Soviet-type subsidised sale of weapons to Central Asian states.

In 2006, Russia along with China gave a security dimension to the Shanghai Cooperation Organization (SCO), comprising China, Russia, Kazakhstan, Kyrgyzstan, Tajikistan, and Uzbekistan. Members of the SCO have been undertaking various military exercises. Russian Defence Minister Sergei Ivanov has advocated a common command and control structure for the SCO. The SCO is getting more teeth,

17. The RS-24 is a MIRVed version of the operational Topol-M (SS-25) that can carry up to ten independently targeted warheads. The R-500 is a new cruise missile adapted for the Iskander launcher previously used only with tactical ballistic missiles. See *http://www.defencetalk.com/news/publish/index.php*, 31 May 2007.

18. After the May 2005 Andijan incident, Uzbekistan served notice and the SCO called for a fixed timetable for withdrawal of all US forces from the region.

inducing even the US to apply for an observer status to the organisation. Mongolia, India, Pakistan, and Iran have already become observers in 2004-05.

Moscow's opposition to US moves against the nuclear programmes of Iran and North Korea are indicative of its assertiveness. It has given military support to Syria, including missiles, and remains committed to construct the Bushehr nuclear reactor in Iran. Convergence of interests between Russia and China has grown in many areas, from teaming up against the US plans in Iran and North Korea to key areas of military and energy cooperation. President Putin's visit to the Persian Gulf and strengthening relations with Saudi Arabia is another instance of the new Russian assertiveness. Such posturing also had direct stabilising influence over Russia's own restive Muslim Chechnya and Tatarstan. Mintimer Shaimiev, the head of the Tatarstan republic, was part of Putin's entourage to the Middle East. Russia invited the new Hamas leaders of the Palestinian government to Moscow for 'talks', symbolising a new posturing in its policy.

Moscow has used energy, weapon sales, and nuclear technology supply as tools of its diplomacy in West Asia. Russia's offer to Tehran of enriched uranium helped sidetrack temporarily Washington's tough stance against Iran. Even though the Iranians turned down the offer, Russia's image in the eyes of the Muslim world went up with this diplomatic move. Russia is not inclined to support a nuclear Iran but its diplomatic stance on the issue is critical to Russia's overall game plan on the global scene. Moreover, Moscow has chosen to focus its diplomacy over the Middle East to exploit the weakening US position in Iraq. There is also the idea of Russia's willingness to assist the Middle East countries, including Saudi Arabia, Egypt, and Turkey in the field of nuclear power development.

Russian foreign policy has shown maturity in terms of building a partnership with the EU driven by economic interests, especially attracting investment and enlarging trade. In South East Asia, Russia's interests have grown during Putin's era, especially in expanding its arms sales with ASEAN (Association of South East Asian Nations) actors. Russia's role in the Asia-Pacific region is poised to grow since

19. Leszek, Buszynski (2006). "Russia and Southeast Asia: A New Relationship", *Contemporary Southeast Asia,* Vol. 28(2): 276–96, (August).

acquiring membership of the East Asian Summit in 2005.[19] Russia has sustained its traditional interests with India by focusing on the hard market economics.

Strategic Balance

In his declaratory policy address "State of the Federation" on 10 May 2006 Putin set the roadmap for Russia in the next five to ten years. He spelt out Russia's long-term goal to rebuild its resources and capabilities to emerge as a credible counterpoise to the US. The contours of Russia's resurgence were clear when in September 2006 President Putin sat down with the key European leaders to work out the future of European energy security. It marked the significance of Russia's strategic role in European affairs.

President Putin in his second term has subtly sought to gain strategic autonomy as against his earlier 'partnership strategy' with the West. On the global scene, a host of strategic developments have converged in Russia's favour, including the fact of the United States getting bogged down in Afghanistan and Iraq. Western unease over Russia's future direction has grown substantially in the past year. Washington and Moscow have been exchanging a volley of criticism over a variety of issues, ranging from suppressing of individual rights to bullying of its neighbours. When President George Bush publicly criticised Russia's rolling back of freedoms, President Putin accused him of trying to bully Russia.[20] In early 2006, when President Putin criticised the US at the annual security conference in Munich saying that "one single centre of power—one single centre of force—one single centre of decision-making. This is the world of one master, one sovereign", the US Secretary of State for Defence, Robert Gates, who was present, suggested that old spy habits die hard, a clear reference to Putin's long KGB background. Gates had earlier categorised Russia as one element in a new axis of evil.

At the showcase G8 summit in St. Petersburg in July 2006, when President Putin was reminded by the media on Russia's democratic

20. During his visit to Luxembourg in May 2007, President Putin said that "one of their aims is to make Russia more pliable on issues that have nothing to do with democracy or human rights".

record, he responded by noting Washington's unpopular war in Iraq and a corruption scandal involving the party of British Prime Minister Tony Blair.[21] Moscow also vehemently opposed US-sponsored 'colour revolutions' in Ukraine and Georgia and attempts at overthrowing regimes in Central Asia. When Moscow shut off gas supplies to Ukraine, which resulted in disruption of gas deliveries to several European countries, US Vice President Dick Cheney accused Russia of using its vast energy resources as "tools of intimidation and blackmail." Criticism also grew over the suppression of individual rights, including the killing of high-profile journalist Anna Politkovskaya. Russia's ties with the UK particularly soured after Russia's secret services accused British diplomats of spying in January 2006. Since the incident of Alexander V. Litvinenko, a former KGB officer, who died of polonium poisoning in London in November 2006 the UK and Russia have been locked in severe acrimony.[22]

Russia is highly aggrieved at NATO's eastward expansion and US plans to set up a missile defence shield in Central Europe (Poland and the Czech Republic) and has threatened to freeze the Conventional Forces in Europe (CFE) Treaty in retaliation.[23] Earlier President Putin, in a State of the Nation address, said it would be appropriate to announce a moratorium on Russian adherence to this treaty until it was ratified by all NATO countries. The US intends to have ten interceptors based in Poland and a radar tracker in the Republic to counter threats emanating from 'rogue states' like Iran.[24]

---

21. "The St. Petersburg G8 summit seals Russia's resurgence as a key world player", *http://www.rferl.org/newsline/2006/07/140706.asp.*

22. "Deepening Chill Divides Moscow and the West", *New York Times*, 2 June 2007.

23. In NATO talks in Oslo, Foreign Minister Sergei Lavrov warned that Russia could pull out if the allies did not endorse it. He said, "It means that we will halt the compliance of our obligations under the treaty." The CFE treaty was signed in 1990 in Paris by NATO and the former Warsaw Pact countries to limit deployments in Europe. The treaty was adapted in Istanbul in 1999 to limit deployments on a country-by-country basis. NATO has not ratified the treaty because Moscow has failed to honour commitments made in Istanbul to withdraw Russian forces from Georgia and Moldova. "Missile shield tensions build in Europe as Russia freezes treaty", *http://www.defencetalk.com/news/publish/index.php.*

24. The US Secretary of State said, "the idea that somehow 10 interceptors and a few radars in Eastern Europe are going to threaten the Soviet strategic return is purely ludicrous and everybody knows it." *http://www.defencetalk.com/news/publish/index.php.*

Conclusion

Even though Russia may be optimistic about its future, others see Russia to be less strong than it perceives itself to be. Russia's 'spoiler mentality' may not threaten American core interest but it may easily thwart US access to energy resources in areas where Russia has got a hold. Russia's long-term direction would also depend on the future of its nexus with China. If the current trend of cooperation with China continues, Russia would only end up strengthening China's economic muscle, which in turn will pose an increasing threat to Russia itself in the longer run. Similarly, Russia is also critical to the European Union. Finally, how it deals with the Muslim world would decide the future course of the rise of Islamist fundamentalism in the world.

On its road to regaining domestic and international stature there are several challenges in Russia's way. The most serious concerns social indicators and demographic trends. At the rate the Russian population is declining, it will decline from 145 million currently to 100 million by 2050. The population of Siberia is dropping by 300 every day. Alcoholism, high rates of cardiovascular diseases, and toxic induced deaths are curtailing the life expectancy of males to 58 years. Similarly, tuberculosis, hepatitis, and HIV/AIDS are causing havoc.

Russia is still far from achieving a reasonable social security system. Improving its education system and public services, which are in a dilapidated state, would take a long time. The establishment of a democratic and plural political system is also at a nascent stage. Autocratic tendencies still run strong, and the level of trust in the judicial system is weak.

It seems unlikely that the resurgence of Russia will revive the world of bipolarisation, even though Russia has the potential to emerge as a power centre to countervail the United States in global affairs. Russia's prominence is bound to rise further as it becomes the key player in Western energy security. The rest of the world, including the EU, is keeping pace with the changing reality and approaching Russia's resurgence as a positive phenomenon and intends to gain from its endowments. The US, however, seems unprepared to reconcile to a resurgent Russia and will need to take initiatives for a deeper engagement with it to avoid a repetition of the Cold War scenario.

II

South Asia: Concerns and Hopes

6

India–Pakistan Peace Process

Gathering Momentum

ASHUTOSH MISRA

Progress in the India–Pakistan peace process over the last year or so is examined here against four broad themes, namely, security, technical, economic and trade, and people-to-people issues.

The peace process was suspended after the attack on India's Parliament House in December 2001. It was resumed in April 2003, when Prime Minister Atal Behari Vajpayee offered talks, which was duly reciprocated by his Pakistani counterpart Zafarullah Khan Jamali. Bilateral relations had plummeted by then and both sides agreed on the need to improve the atmospherics first through restoration of rail, road, air, and diplomatic links, enhancement of people-to-people contacts, and several confidence-building measures (CBMs), including new bus and train services, promoting trade and commerce across the LoC (Line of Control), and opening up of meeting points for people along the LoC. Significantly, troops disengaged following the cease fire along the LoC, International Border (IB), and the Actual Ground Position Line (AGPL) from 25 November, 2003. Prime Minister Vajpayee's meeting with General Pervez Musharraf in Islamabad in January 2004 and later the meetings of Prime Minister Manmohan Singh with General Musharraf in Islamabad in April 2005, in New York in September 2005 and a year later in Havana, Cuba in September 2006 underlined the importance both sides attached to sustained engagement. Progress in the talks during 2004 and 2005 was reviewed by the two Foreign Secretaries, Shyam Saran and Riaz Mohammad Khan, in New Delhi on 17-18 January, 2006.[1]

---

1. Joint statement, India-Pakistan Foreign Secretary level talks in New Delhi, Ministry of External Affairs, Government of India, New Delhi (henceforth MEA), 18 January 2006, at *http://meaindia.nic.in*

Security Issues

Security-specific talks were focussed on Jammu and Kashmir, conventional and nuclear CBMs, and terrorism. The two sides discussed J&K and reaffirmed their commitment to the joint press statement of 6 January 2004 issued in Islamabad on the side lines of the 12th Summit of South Asian Association for Regional Cooperation (SAARC) and seeking "peaceful settlement of all bilateral issues, including Jammu and Kashmir, to the satisfaction of both sides."[2] The talks on Jammu and Kashmir were held on 27–28 June 2004 in New Delhi, led by the Indian Foreign Secretary Shashank and his Pakistani counterpart Riaz Khokhar. No breakthrough was achieved, yet the talks were described by both sides as 'useful', 'good first step', and 'positive and concrete.'[3] At the end of the two days talks, both sides reaffirmed their commitment to the joint press statement of 6 January 2004 issued in Islamabad and sought "peaceful settlement of all bilateral issues, including Jammu and Kashmir, to the satisfaction of both sides."[4]

Jammu and Kashmir

In their January 2006 meeting, the two Foreign Secretaries discussed Jammu and Kashmir and CBMs related to that issue, especially the bus service between Srinagar and Muzaffarabad and between Poonch and Rawalakot. The discussion indicated dilution of old stances and a people-oriented approach, with pragmatism replacing polemics and one-upmanship.

General Musharraf's Kashmir Proposals

On 25 October 2004, at an Iftaar party, General Musharraf articulated his version of the Kashmir solution, primarily for domestic churning through the media. He called for "identifying" various "regions" of Kashmir on both sides of the LoC, "demilitarizing them", and granting them the status of "independence" or placing them under a "joint Indo-Pak control" or a "UN mandate."[5] He suggested:

---

2. Baruah, Amit (2004). "India, Pakistan to find a 'final' Solution to J&K", *The Hindu*, 29 June.
3. Pandit, Rajat (2004). "India, Pak Skirt Kashmir, Build Confidence", *The Times of India*, 28 June.
4. Baruah, *op. cit.*
5. Verma, K.J.M. (2004). "Mark an Area, Disarm it, Decide on Freedom or Joint Control", *Indian Express*, 26 October.

> Take Kashmir in its entirety. It has seven regions. Two of the regions are in Pakistan and five are in India. In my view, identify a region, whether it is the whole or part, I do not know. Identify the region, demilitarize the region for ever and change its status...status can be independence, condominium where there can be a joint control or there can be UN mandate...to be defined by legal people.[6]

Subsequent reports suggested that the seven regions could be the plains, including Jammu, foothills up to 7000 ft, Pir Panjal, the valley of Kashmir, the great Himalayan Zone, the Upper Indus Valley, and the Karakoram.[7] Ladakh, Kargil/Dras, Poonch, Jammu, and the Valley are parts of India. Pakistan controls Pakistan-Occupied Kashmir or 'Azad Kashmir' as Pakistan refers to it, and the Northern Areas (minus Baltistan).[8]

The proposal sought to isolate the 'Muslim majority' areas on religious basis, which New Delhi has been averse to in principle. Prime Minister Manmohan Singh, initially in New York and then in Srinagar in November 2004 remarked:

> I have made it quite clear that any redrawing of international border is something which is not going to be acceptable to us...Any proposal which smacks of a further division of our country on the basis of religion is not going to be acceptable to us...Within these two limits we are ready to look into any proposal...(Musharraf's proposals) are still not clear to us...I do not know what his plan is.[9]

The Pakistan People's Party Parliamentarian (PPPP), Pakistan Muslim League-Nawaz (PML-N), and Muttahida Majlis-e-Amal (MMA) rejected the proposals, accusing General Musharraf of conceding too much to India. Najam Sethi, editor of the *Friday Times* seemed more inclined to see the reasoning behind Musharraf's move. He noted:

> Jihad can no longer be used as a weapon of coercion in the discourse on Kashmir...Pakistan stands to gain more from any 'peace dividend' than India. The respite from long-term warring would dilute Pakistan's obsession with 'national security' and create the political

6. Ibid.
7. Ibid.
8. Ahmed, Khaled (2004). "Musharraf's 'Seven-regions' Options in Kashmir", at *http:www.thefridaytimes.com/page8.shtml* (30 November).
9. "India will not Accept Redrawing of Borders: PM", at *http://news.indiainfo.com/2004/11/17/1711pm1.html*

space to develop stable, democratic and civilian institutions. Equally, the economic resources resultant from an end to the arms race could be productively employed in development and poverty alleviation.[10]

Zahid Hussein saw in the proposals Pakistan's compulsions to abandon its old policies and think afresh following the failure of jihad as a tool. Jihad also had a boomerang effect on Pakistan in attacks on political leaders, including on Gen. Musharraf, in the wake of the 'war on terrorism', and the stricter international watch after 11 September 2001. It was in Pakistan's national interest to break the Kashmir logjam, he said.[11]

In September 2005 General Musharraf called for Indian troops withdrawal from Kupwara, Baramula, and Srinagar to boost the peace process.[12] Earlier in November 2004 Prime Minister Manmohan Singh, during his visit to the Valley, had ordered troops withdrawal from South Kashmir. The decision was criticised by opposition parties in New Delhi due to continuing terrorist attacks in Jammu and Kashmir and elsewhere in India. It has been conveyed to Pakistan that the ground situation (read continuous terrorist violence) in Jammu and Kashmir does not permit troop withdrawal from the state.

India's consistent official position has been that the 'boundaries cannot be redrawn' and the need is to move from border-centric approaches to borderless solutions.[13] Sceptics in India maintain that one should not get carried away by the semantics and look at addressing terrorism-related issues and improving the ground situation first. India has periodically raised the terrorism issue in talks, whereas Pakistan talked about 'human rights violations' and troops reduction in the state.[14]

In December 2006 in an interview to an Indian television channel, General Musharraf floated a four-point proposal; first, the borders

---

10. Sethi, Najam, "Win-no Loss Approach on Kashmir", at *http://www.thefridaytimes.com/page1.shtml.*
11. Hussein, Zahid (2004). "Kashmir: The Long Road to Peace", *Newsline*, November, p.26.
12. Hussain, Fahd (2005). "Kashmir Troops Cut to Boost Peace, Musharraf tells Bush", at *http://www.jang.com.pk/thenews/sep2005-daily/15-09-2005/main/main4.htm*
13. Ibid.
14. Swami, Praveen (2006). "Musharraf's Offer Nearer to New Delhi's Bottom Line", at *http://www.hindu.com/2006/12/06/stories/2006120604650100.htm*

would not be changed but people would be allowed free movement in the region; second, the region would have self-governance or autonomy but not independence; third, troops would be withdrawn in a staggered manner; and fourth, a joint supervision mechanism would be set up, with India, Pakistan, and Kashmir represented on it. Pakistan would have to be prepared to give up the independence or UN resolution option if this proposal could be worked out, he noted.[15] The initial response of India's policymakers to the proposals was positive, prompting them to discuss the proposals in greater depth and detail with Pakistan. General Musharraf's proposals also sent a strong message to separatist parties and groups in Jammu and Kashmir as also the Jihadis in Pakistan, that independence was no more a viable option. The All Party Hurriyat Conference (APHC), led by Mirwaiz Umar Farooq, also urged New Delhi to discuss these ideas, while asking the separatist groups and parties to support the debate on these lines.[16] For India, troop withdrawal and joint supervision remain sticking points.

Terrorism and Drug Trafficking

The second round of technical-level talks were held between the Central Bureau of Investigation (CBI) and its Pakistani counterpart Federal Investigation Agency on 21-22 March, 2006 in New Delhi.[17] These talks were being held after a span of seventeen years and dealt with key security challenges such as human trafficking, counterfeit currency, and illegal immigration. Both sides were willing to hold periodic meetings and explore possible avenues of professional training and share their experiences pertaining to criminal investigations.

The third round of talks at the level of Interior/Home Secretaries was held on 30–31 May 2006, which hailed the progress in talks between the Anti Narcotic Force (ANF) of Pakistan and Narcotics Control Bureau (NCB) of India.[18]

15. Naqvi, Jawed (2006). "Musharraf's Four-stage Kashmir Peace Plan: We Can Make Borders Irrelevant: India", at *http://www.dawn.com/2006/12/06/top1.htm*

16. Naqvi, Jawed (2007). "Mirwaiz Asks India to Consider Musharraf's Proposals", at *http://www.dawn.com/2007/02/02/top3.htm*

17. Joint statement, Second round of technical level talks between Central Bureau of Investigation (India)-Federal Investigation Agency (Pakistan), MEA, 7 March 2006, at *http://meaindia.nic.in*.

18. Joint statement, Third round of Pakistan-India Interior/Home Secretary talks on terrorism and drugs trafficking, MEA, 31 May 2006, at *http://meaindia.nic.in*.

In September 2005 the peace process facilitated the release of 435 Indian prisoners (371 fishermen) and 148 Pakistani prisoners (51 fishermen). This followed an agreement between the Home Secretaries of the two sides on 30 August, 2005. It was also agreed that the issue of prisoners would be dealt with as a humanitarian issue, keeping each other notified about any arrest made, providing consular access within three months to the arrested persons, and materialising their release as soon as the term of imprisonment was complete.

Joint Anti-terrorism Mechanism (Havana Declaration)

The peace process was suspended after the July 2006 blasts in Mumbai, owing to domestic political pressure in India. The first formal meeting thereafter came in September in Havana, where Prime Minister Manmohan Singh and General Musharraf met on the sidelines of the Non-Aligned Summit and the two leaders expressed their desire to revive the talks. Out of this meeting emerged the 'Havana Declaration', which called for setting up a joint institutional mechanism to identify and implement counter-terrorism initiatives and investigations.[19]

In principle, Pakistan always declined to accept terrorism as an issue between the two countries, but since 1997 it agreed to incorporate terrorism into the agenda of the composite dialogue process. After the July 2006 Mumbai blasts the peace process was put on hold and was formally resumed with the summit level Havana meeting in September 2006, with the establishment of Joint Anti-Terrorism Mechanism. The first formal meeting of the joint mechanism was held on 6-7 March, 2007 in Islamabad, where India provided Pakistan with evidence collected into the terrorist attacks in Ayodhya (5 July, 2005), in Sarojini Nagar, Paharganj and Govindpuri in New Delhi (29 October 2005), in Malegaon in Mumbai (11 July 2006), at the Indian Institute of Science (IISc) in Bangalore (28 December 2005) and on the Delhi-Lahore Samjhauta Express (19 February 2007), to take necessary action.[20] Regarding the Samjhauta blast, the Pakistani daily *Dawn* wrote that Pakistan was disappointed

19. Joint statement, India-Pakistan in Havana, Cuba, Ministry of External Affairs, Government of India, 16 September 2006, at *http://meaindia.nic.in*.

20. Subramanian, Nirupama (2007). "Help Track Down Samjhauta Suspect", *The Hindu*, 7 March.

at India not presenting any substantial evidence, apart from a sketch of the suspect made on the basis of inputs from witnesses.[21] In response, Pakistan also gave a comprehensive dossier with very "specific information about systematic involvement of Indian security agencies" in Balochistan, which gives a hint of the shape and tenor of future joint mechanism meetings.

Conventional and Nuclear CBMs

On 17-18 January, 2006 the two Foreign Secretaries discussed in New Delhi progress made, following the expert-level meetings, on nuclear and conventional CBMs. The two sides reiterated their commitment to finalise an agreement on "Reducing risk of nuclear accidents or unauthorised use of nuclear weapons", on which a draft was presented by India.[22] The two sides also expressed their commitment to the Lahore Memorandum of Understanding (MoU) of February 1999. The Lahore MoU was signed by former Prime Minister Atal Behari Vajpayee during his historic bus trip to Lahore, with his counterpart Nawaz Sharif. The MoU categorically reiterates the commitment of the two sides to implementing the 1972 Simla Agreement in letter and spirit, implying resolving pending issues through bilateral negotiations only. Therefore, the recognition of the Lahore MoU by the Pakistani military regime should be seen as an encouraging development for India.

The fourth round of expert-level dialogue on nuclear CBMs was held in Islamabad on 25-26 April, 2006.[23] The signing of the pre-notification of flights, testing of ballistic missiles, and operationalising the hotline between the two Foreign Secretaries are useful subsidiary measures of the agreement. The two sides also reaffirmed their 'unilateral moratorium' on conducting further nuclear tests until "extraordinary events jeopardise their supreme interests." Both sides called for regular working-level meetings to be held among all the nuclear powers to discuss issues of common concern, which reflected

21. Akhlaque, Qudssia (2007). "Terror Dossier given to India", *Dawn*, at *http://www.dawn.com/2007/03/07/top2.htm*
22. Joint statement, India Pakistan Foreign Secretary level talks in New Delhi, MEA, 18 January 2006, at *http://meaindia.nic.in*
23. Joint statement, Fourth round of Pakistan-India expert level dialogue on nuclear CBMs held in Islamabad 25-26 April 2006, MEA, 26 April 2006, at *http://meaindia.nic.in*

growing mutual understanding to take the nuclear debate from the regional to the global level.

Analysts in Pakistan have been stressing the need for Pakistan to legitimise its nuclear weapons by making common cause with India and help insulate itself from US pressures. Ayaz Amir wrote:

> The Pakistani establishment has yet to realise it but the old paradigms have shifted. The new enemy, the new threat to Pakistani security, comes from the US and its irresponsible policies in this part of the world, not India. Indian Foreign Minister (former) Natwar Singh's proposal for a shared nuclear doctrine between China, India and Pakistan is radical in its import. For it implies an ability to look for regional solutions to regional problems, free from outside interference. It also gives Pakistan protection against American designs to castrate its nuke capability.[24]

Besides, the Indian and Pakistani claims for nuclear power status and China's immediate objection to the claims, indicate the shifts which the nuclear debate in South Asia seems to have undergone over the last five years.

The third round of expert-level dialogue on conventional CBMs was held on 27 April, 2006 in Islamabad.[25] Both sides agreed to finalise border ground rules for implementation along the IB, quarterly flag meeting at local commanders' level, posts and defence works along the LoC, and speedy return of inadvertent line crosser(s). There seems to be a clear resolve on both sides to reduce trust deficit manifested through the past four conflicts, constant shelling across the LoC until 2003, and India's reluctance to abandon its current positions in Siachen.

Technical Issues

Siachen

The Siachen Glacier in the Karakoram Range is 76 kilometres long and varies in width between 2 and 8 kilometres. In this highest war zone in the world, 97 per cent of Indian casualties have resulted due to the altitude, weather, and terrain; the remaining 3 per cent being

---

24. "Republic Terrorised by Fools", *Dawn*, 4 June 2004.
25. Joint statement, Third round of Pakistan-India expert level dialogue on conventional CBMs, Islamabad, MEA, 27 April 2006, at *http://meaindia.nic.in*

caused by hostile firing.[26] Guns have remained silent in the area ever since the cease fire in 2004 along the LoC and the IB was extended to AGPL, the line dividing the troops of the two sides in Siachen.

India and Pakistan were very close to an agreement on Siachen in 1989 but domestic political considerations in India did not allow it to materialise. Since then adverse developments in Indo–Pak relations, primarily due to rise in militancy in Jammu and Kashmir, have lowered trust levels. Proposals on the prospective solution have ranged from demilitarisation, joint monitoring, to turning it into a peace park. India insists on authentication of the current troop positions as a precondition for troop withdrawal; Pakistan sees this as a formal acknowledgement of India's occupation of Siachen, even after it has withdrawn. Back-channel diplomacy has inclined India to contemplate withdrawal, provided Pakistan gives assurances of some sort that it would not occupy vacated positions. Of late, Pakistan has shown willingness to address India's concern without undermining its own official position.

Defence Secretary-level talks were held on 22-23 May, 2006 in New Delhi, without much progress. The issue was again up for discussion during the Foreign Secretary-level meetings on 14-15 November, 2006 in New Delhi,[27] where authentication of troop positions on the glacier remained the contentious point. Recently, however, Pakistan has offered to 'acknowledge' the current position of the Indian troops as opposed to 'authenticating' it, which would mean a tacit acceptance of India's claim over Siachen.[28]

Wullar Barrage Storage Project/Tulbul Navigation Project

For India, it is the Tulbul Navigation Project; Pakistan calls it the Wullar Barrage. At issue is a barrage that is to be constructed by the government of the state of Jammu and Kashmir on the Jhelum River just below Wullar Lake located about 25 kilometres north of Srinagar

26. Ahmed, Samina and Varun Sahni (1998). "Freezing the Fighting: Military Disengagement on the Siachen Glacier", *Cooperative Monitoring Center Occasional Papers*, Sandia National Laboratories, Albuquerque, March, p.10.
27. Joint press release, Defence Secretary-level talks between India and Pakistan on the Siachen issue, MEA, 24 May 2006, at *http://meaindia.nic.in/prhome.htm*
28. Gilani, Iftikhar (2007). "India Considring Siachen Proposal", at *http://www.dailytimes.com.pk/default.asp?page=2007%5C01%5C18%5Cstory_18-1-2007_pg7_1*

at about 5180 feet above sea level.[29] The name Wullar comes from the Sanskrit word 'woll', meaning 'obstacle.'[30] Pakistan says that a dam at this site would inundate Srinagar and the Valley, whereas India says it would be used to maintain navigability in the Jhelum during lean months. India abandoned the construction work pending agreement. Ten rounds of talks have been held but with little progress and the term 'Storage Project' has been added to the nomenclature at Pakistan's insistence. On 22-23 June, 2006 a Secretary-level delegation from Pakistan's Ministry of Water and Power yet again looked into the matter under the provisions of the 1960 Indus Waters Treaty but was unable to resolve the differences whether it is a storage project or a navigation project and also whether it violates the terms of the 1960 treaty.

Sir Creek

Sir Creek, a fluctuating tidal channel, is a sixty-milelong estuary in the marshes of the Rann of Kutch between the Indian state of Gujarat and the Pakistani province of Sind. The once disputed Rann of Kutch area was settled through the Indo-Pakistani Western Boundary Case Tribunal's Award on 19 February 1968 but the Tribunal excluded the creek from its purview. The dispute hinges on the demarcation of the boundary from "the mouth of Sir Creek to the top of Sir Creek" and from "the top of the Sir Creek eastwards to a point (on land) designated as the Western Terminus." Determination of the creek boundary would enable India and Pakistan to determine their maritime zones and exclusive economic zones (EEZs) and allow them to explore prospects of oil, gas, and other economic assets in the area.

Settling the matter has become urgent because under the United Nations Convention on the Law of the Sea (UNCLOS) if the contestants fail to determine their respective maritime zones by 2009 the area would be declared international waters. Technical-level talks on Sir Creek were held on 22-23 December, 2006 in Rawalpindi and a decision was taken to hold joint survey of the creek and adjoining areas and also simultaneously undertake discussions to determine

29. Noorani, A.G. (1995). "CBMs for the Siachen Glacier, Sir Creek and Wullar Barrage", in Michael Krepon and Amit Sevak (eds.), *Crisis Prevention, Confidence Building and Reconciliation in South Asia* (New York: St. Martin's Press), p.95.

30. Aziz, Mir Abdul (1986). "Wullar and the Proposed Barrage", *The Muslim*, 24 October.

maritime zones.[31] The joint survey is intended to verify outermost points of coastlines using the equidistance method.

Economic and Commercial Issues

The Commerce Secretaries of the two countries met in Islamabad on 27 March, 2006 as a part of the Joint Study Group (JSG).[32] The JSG emphasised establishing facilitation measures to enhance bilateral trade and supplement deliberations on substantive trade issues being discussed in the peace process. These facilitation measures could be very helpful in promoting trade at bilateral, multilateral, and regional levels for SAARC (South Asian Association for Regional Cooperation) countries. Within the JSG there are various subgroups on 'custom cooperation and trade facilitation measures' and 'non-tariff barriers' and working groups on 'standards and conformance and sanitary and phyto-sanitation', which meet periodically.

The third round of economic and commercial cooperation was held on 28-29 March, 2006 at Islamabad and discussed initiatives and progress made since the first round of talks in New Delhi on 9-10 August, 2005. A broad range of issues were discussed, including opening of scheduled branches of banks in each country, tea trade, shipping procedures, problems of transportation of goods through train, enlargement of export items from India to Pakistan, and feasibility of trade in IT-enabled medical services. Both sides appreciated the ratification of SAFTA (South Asian Free Trade Area agreement) by all SAARC member-states, considering it as an encouraging sign for strengthening of regional trade within the SAFTA framework.

People-to-People CBMs

LoC Meeting Points

In 2005 agreement was reached between the two countries to open five meeting points across the LoC for divided families, trade,

---

31. Joint press statement after technical level talks between India and Pakistan on Sir Creek, MEA, 23 December 2006, New Delhi, at *http://meaindia.nic.in*

32. Joint statement, Third round of Pakistan-India talks on economic and commercial cooperation, Ialamabad, MEA, 29 March 2006, at *http://meaindia.nic.in*

pilgrimages, and cultural interaction. These points include Rawalakot–Poonch (7 November), Chakothi–Uri (9 November), Nauseri–Tithwal (10 November), Tattapani–Mendhar (15 November), and Hajipir–Uri (16 November).

Technical-level talks to enhance interaction and cooperation across the LoC were held in New Delhi on 2-3 May 2006, which reviewed the operationalisation of the Srinagar–Muzaffarabad bus service since it began in April 2005 and discussed the problems with the application process for travel.[33] The long-standing Indian proposal to start truck service to enhance trade on this route also received serious consideration apart from the list of goods to be traded.

Transport Links

As per the agreed schedule, bus services between Srinagar and Muzaffarabad started on 7 April 2005, Poonch–Rawalakot on 19 June 2005, and Amritsar–Nankana Sahib (Lahore) on 20 January, 2006. The two sides also agreed that starting trade on the Srinagar–Muzaffarabad and Suchetgarh–-Sialkot route would boost economic development in the region. Pakistan has been slow on starting the Kargil–Skardu and Mendhar–Mirpur bus services, which would expose to visitors the presence of terrorist outfits and training camps in those areas. The Delhi–Lahore train service, suspended in December 2001 following the terrorist attack on the Indian Parliament House, was resumed on 11 July, 2003. The Kokhrapar–Munabao service, defunct and suspended when Pakistani fighters bombed it during the 1965 War, was resumed on 18 February, 2006. The two sides also agreed to add pilgrimage places in the existing list and increase the number of pilgrims from what the 1974 protocol provided.

On the Srinagar–Muzaffarabad bus service initially the talks were stalled because Pakistan insisted on United Nations documents as travel documents while India proposed passports for the purpose. At the second round of talks on 7-8 December, 2004 in New Delhi, Pakistan made the additional demand that the bus service be kept exclusively for Kashmiris, as opposed to India's proposal of keeping it

---

33. Joint statement, India-Pakistan technical level talks on enhancing interaction and cooperation across the LoC, MEA, 3 May 2006, at *http://meaindia.nic.in*

open for all Indians.[34] Eventually in February 2005, then foreign ministers Natwar Singh and Kursheed Mahmud Kasuri resolved these differences in Islamabad. The bus service was inaugurated on 7 April 2005, though some political parties, including the Pakistan Muslim League-Nawaz (PML-N) and Jamaat-e-Islami (JI) said that such measures would dilute the 'core' issue of Kashmir.[35] In a significant development, on 2 June, 2005 the APHC leaders led by its Chairman Mirwaiz Umar Farooq boarded the bus and crossed the LoC to meet leaders in Pakistan-Occupied Kashmir and Islamabad. The visit drew flak from the United Jihad Council (UJC) leader Syed Salahuddin and hardliners in Srinagar. An unfazed Mirwaiz also criticised the hardliners on both sides saying,

> For fear of being labelled as treacherous should we sit at home and repeat the song of UN resolutions. One lakh people have already lost their lives. Should we wait for the sacrifice of another lakh people before we begin to look at the other possible ways to resolve the issue?... There are people in Kashmir who considered talking to New Delhi as treachery. Now we are being told that even visiting Pakistan amounted to treachery. It is high time the word treachery is redefined ...when we return to Kashmir, we need to redefine certain things... certain words and phrases.[36]

Earthquake Relief

The region of Jammu and Kashmir was hit by severe tremors on 8 October 2005, causing enormous loss of lives and property, mostly in POK and Pakistan, killing over 80,000 people. The Indian Prime Minister spoke to General Musharraf on the phone assuring him all necessary help in disaster relief. India announced a relief assistance of US $25 million, in addition to relief materials in Geneva at the international conference organised by the UN Coordinator for Emergency Relief. India's Minister of State for External Affairs, Anand Sharma, represented India in Islamabad at the international conference

---

34. Singh, Onkar (2004). "Muzaffarabad Bus Service Deadlocked", at *http://www.in.rediff.com/news/2004/dec/08bus.htm*
35. "Opposition Divided over LoC Bus Service: Major Difference Between ARD, MMA", at *http://www.dawn.com/2005/02/18/top2.htm*
36. Reddy, B. Murlidhar (2005). "Time to Look for New Options: Mirwaiz", *The Hindu*, at *http://www.hindu.com/2005/06/13/stories/2005061312161200.htm*

on 19 November 2005, where he announced India's resolve to undertake reconstruction projects in health and education sectors. India provided more than 1300 tonnes of relief goods across the LoC, apart from hundreds of tonnes coming from private sources, worth a total of US $15.5 million. Five LoC points were opened and made fully functional for sending relief goods to Pakistan. Aircraft of foreign countries carrying relief materials to Pakistan were given permission to overfly Indian territory. Pakistan helicopters too were given permission to fly in the 'no-fly zone' close to the LoC for relief measures. India's offer of flying its own helicopters in the region for relief operations was, however, disallowed by Pakistan. New telephone lines were installed to enable people in Jammu and Kashmir to speak to their relatives in POK and Pakistan.[37] The difficulty which the terrain posed for relief operations prompted the two sides to think of a joint disaster management mechanism in the future to deal with natural calamities.

Promotion of Friendly Exchanges

A Secretary level delegation from the Indian Ministry of Tourism & Culture and Pakistani Ministry of Culture, met in New Delhi on 1-2 June, 2006 and reviewed the progress in friendly exchanges between the two countries.[38] These covered arts and culture, education, Ayurvedic and Unani medicine, archaeology, tourism, youth affairs, sports, and media. Exchanges such as cricket matches, visits by academics, professionals, peace activists, and media persons in recent years have also helped in significantly enlarging the scope and impact of peace constituencies that exist in both countries. There are also several institutional proposals for establishing bilateral linkages for the purpose of exchanging ideas, undertaking joint research, and organising collaborative events such as seminars, symposiums, and conferences.

The peace process has always been susceptible to domestic political compulsions. Issues such as Jammu and Kashmir, Siachen, and

37. *Annual Report 2005-2006*, MEA, p. 16.

38. Joint statement, Third round of Secretary level talks between India and Pakistan on 'promotion of friendly exchanges in various fields', MEA, 26 April 2006, at *http://meaindia.nic.in*

terrorism in particular are directly affected by them. However, in recent years there has been mutual agreement to continue the peace process notwithstanding the domestic compulsions and terrorist activities.

7

Pakistan 2006: Between Internal Constraints and External Pressures

ASHOK K. BEHURIA

In its evaluation of the performance of different states, the *Foreign Policy* magazine in early 2006 placed Pakistan at the ninth place from the bottom on its list of failed states. The indices used by the magazine were comprehensive and took into account social, political, and economic aspects.

Pakistan's internal security situation worsened in 2006. An independent Pakistani think-tank estimated that there were 657 militant attacks, including 41 of a sectarian nature during the year, leaving 907 people dead and 1543 others injured. The study put the number of people arrested for reasons of internal security at 1552, including 1094 Taliban (both local and foreign), 47 al Qaeda operatives, 198 other militants, and 213 nationalist insurgents.[1] Another estimate put militancy/terrorist-related casualties at 1471 in 2006, compared to 638 in 2005. There were seven suicide attacks, resulting in 160 deaths.[2] At the political level, the military-backed democracy showed signs of atrophy. The popular disaffection fuelling militancy in the province of Balochistan and north-western tribal areas peaked during the year and, at times, appeared quite ominous for the state of Pakistan. Opposition political parties tried all the while to corner the government ahead of the elections scheduled for 2007. Sometimes they induced a certain unease in the administration, even though they were not united.

---

1. Statistics from the Pak Institute for Peace Studies, Cited in *Dawn*, 7 January, 2007.
2. The 1,471 casualties included 608 civilians, 538 militants, and 325 security personnel. In 2005, the corresponding figures were 430, 137, and 81. Data from the South Asian Terrorism Portal (SATP), New Delhi, India. (*www.satp.org*, accessed on 12 March, 2007).

The three most nagging problems confronting the government during the year were the ethnic unrest in Balochistan, the ongoing confrontation with local Taliban in the tribal areas, and the unending violence on the sectarian front—in that order. There were other issues like the demand by the Muttaihida Majlis-e-Amal (MMA) and other opposition parties on General Pervez Musharraf to shed his uniform, and preparations by the ruling Pakistan Muslim League (Quaid-e-Azam) (PML(Q)) and other opposition parties for the elections scheduled for 2007. The military regime also had to withstand tremendous external pressure from the US, which has sustained the regime through continuous material and moral support since September 2001.

The Baloch Nationalist Unrest

The Baloch insurgency gathered momentum in 2006.[3] As the government shied from the path of dialogue, the militants intensified their activities with greater show of solidarity across tribal divisions. Not a day passed till early September without an incident of militants taking on the security forces in different parts of the province, but mostly around the capital city of Quetta and areas adjacent to Dera Bugti and Kohlu. Indications were that the Baloch movement was expanding its popular base and moving out of the control of the tribal Sardars (traditional community leaders). The Baloch diaspora in the Gulf and the West were seen to be coming together to support the resistance movement.

The government responded to the attacks and ambushes by Baloch militants through helicopter gun ships. In early January, security forces took over the house of Nawab Bugti, the kingpin of the Baloch militancy, in Sui, and killed him in his hideout using heavy artillery and helicopter gun ships on 26 August, 2006. All the political parties in Pakistan condemned the army action.

Bugti's death brought Balochis together. The grand Balochi jirga (traditional community gathering) of 21 September in Kalat, attended by some 85 tribal chiefs and 300 elders, presided over by the Khan of

3. The Balochistan Liberation Army, the Balochistan Liberation Front, and the Bugti Militia were blamed by the government for carrying out 403 terror attacks in Balochistan during 2006 that killed 277 people and injured 676 others.

Kalat, Mir Suleman Daud Ahmedzai, demonstrated this unity. After a brief slump in their activities, the Baloch rebels asserted themselves again since November 2006 with regular disruption of gas pipelines, blowing up of railway tracks, and ambushing of security forces. By the beginning of 2007, the scale and intensity of Balochi resistance had visibly gone up.

Playing with Tribal Fire

In clear contrast to his policy *vis-à-vis* the Baloch, General Musharraf adopted a more palliative approach towards the militants in the Federally Administered Tribal Areas (FATA), where the Pashtun dominate. While the government repeatedly claimed that Pakistan has amassed 80,000 of its troops in the inhospitable terrain, analysts in the US and the Ahmed Karzai government in Afghanistan have complained that the government was not doing enough in the tribal borderlands.[4] Throughout the year the security forces were competing with the militants to have nominal control over townships in North and South Waziristan. A total of 144 attacks took place in the tribal areas during the year, killing 379 people and injuring 307 others. The militants killed 39 local people alleging that they were passing on information to the US intelligence agencies.

There is disinclination among the Pashtun component within the army to take on fellow Pashtuns. The paramilitary Frontier Corps (FC), which is primarily in charge of ground operations in FATA, is overwhelmingly Pashtun in composition. Many desertions have been reported from it and even one Major General from the Orakzai tribe preferred premature retirement rather than be a party to army operations against Pashtun. Pashtun colonels who expressed reservations about the army operations have also been posted out of the terrain.[5] Pashtun constitute about 20–25 per cent of the Pakistan armed forces and about 15–22 per cent of the officer level.[6] Repetition

4. For example, see the transcript of Peter Tomsen's interview with Martin Smith at *http://www.pbs.org/wgbh/pages/frontline/taliban/interviews/tomsen.html*. Tomsen was President George Bush's Special Envoy on Afghan resistance from 1989-1992.
5. See Abbas, Hassan (2006). "Musharraf Contends with the Pashtun Element in the Pakistani Army", *Terrorism Focus*, Vol. 3(42), 31 October.
6. Ibid.

of General Musharraf's coercive Balochistan policy here could divide the army and also unleash a serious political backlash by the Islamist parties. The bulk of the leadership of the Islamist groups are Pashtun and their parties also have a significant presence in the Pashtun-dominated areas of Pakistan, spread across NWFP (North West Frontier Province), FATA, and northern Balochistan.

There is a view in Pakistan that its security operations in the tribal areas provide the anvil for the American hammer. Most of the heavy-casualty attacks on either madrassas or private houses in the tribal areas, allegedly sheltering high-value targets, have been coordinated with the US forces or carried out by the American single-handedly. The government condemned one such attack on 13 January, 2006 on Bahaur as an irresponsible US action and an assault on the sovereignty of Pakistan.[7] The political opposition launched a protest march from Peshawar to Bajaur but the government stopped it at Yaka Gund. On 1 March twelve army helicopters attacked a suspected compound in Dandy Saidgay in North Waziristan, on the day the American President started his South Asia visit. The attack left 40 persons dead and many injured, provoking many protest demonstrations in North and South Waziristan, and a suicide attack on the US embassy the next day.

Signing deals with tribal militants has been another of the government's ways of handling the problem of tribal militancy. In February 2005 the government signed the Shakai (or Wana) peace deal in South Waziristan, allegedly paying them about Rs. 50 million to pay up their debt to al-Qaeda and return to the path of peace.[8] Thereafter, the security forces faced increasing resistance from the militants in North Waziristan. From early 2006 some local militants claimed themselves as Pakistani Taliban. Not wanting to antagonise the security forces, they declared a unilateral cease fire in June 2006.[9] In return for the withdrawal of troops from the region they offered not

7. The attack was mentioned by Prime Minister, Sahukat Aziz during his trip to the US later that month.

8. Khan, Ismail (2005). "Payment to Wana Militants: Probe into Missing Millions Initiated", *Dawn*, 3 May.

9. The militants announced cease fire on 25 June, 2006, to pave the way for 'a permanent solution'. *Dawn*, 13 July, 2006.

to shelter foreign militants.[10] This truce was reportedly approved by Mullah Omar, leader of the Afghan Taliban. Mullah Dadullah and Jalaluddin Haqqani of the Afghan Taliban played a major role in convincing the local Taliban about it, the media observed.[11] On 5 September the government signed the "Waziristan Accord" with the militants. One of the terms of the accord[12] was that the government would release about 2000–2500 persons allegedly having links with the Taliban.[13] While these persons were released, the Taliban went on killing suspected informers. The US media and security establishment excoriated the deal as a brazen surrender of the Pakistani state to the militants.

From North Waziristan the focus shifted to Bajaur on 30 October, 2006 when about 80 al-Qaeda militants were killed in air attacks in the Chengai hamlet in Damadola. It was reported that the attack was conducted primarily by fixed-wing US drones though the Pakistan government claimed credit for it.[14] The militants avenged this with a suicide attack on an Army training base at Dargai in NWFP, killing 42 army cadets, and other suicide attacks on security forces. After another strike in Hamazola village near Razmak in North Waziristan, on 16 January, 2007, the North Waziristan deal died a natural death. The principal target of the attack, Baitullah Mehsud, vowed soon afterwards that he would teach a lesson to the Pakistani forces. In March 2007 the pro-Taliban tribal militants fell out with Uzbek militants in Waziristan and fought a bloody battle against them, killing more than 100 foreign militants. Government forces helped the local militants in the battle and the government projected the event as a successful outcome of the peace deals by the Musharraf administration.

---

10. For details of the demands see Khan, Ismail (2006). "Waziristan Militants Offer Cease fire", *Dawn*, 26 June.
11. Yusufzai, Rahimullah (2006). "We Advised Pak Taliban not to Fight Army: Dadullah", *The News*, 17 September.
12. For details of the accord see Pazir, Gul (2006). "Waziristan Accord Signed", *Dawn*, 6 September.
13. Wilkinson, Isambard (2006). "US Outraged as Pakistan Frees Taliban Fighters", *Daily Telegraph*, London, 15 September.
14. About Contradictory Reports see Khan, Anwarullah (2006). "82 Die as Missiles Rain on Bajaur: Pakistan Owns up to Strike; Locals Blame US Drones", *Dawn*, 31 October,; and editorial, "The Bajaur Massacre", *Dawn*, 1 November.

The Sectarian Virus

There were 41 sectarian incidents in the country during the year, which claimed 200 lives. Sunni–Shia violence erupted in Hangu and Tank in NWFP during Muharram. Intra-Sunni conflict engulfed the Khyber Agency, where the followers of Deobandi Mufti Shakir and Barelvi Pir Saif—both supporters of the Afghan jihad—attacked each other throughout the year. In Karachi, a suicide bomber on 11 April, 2006 attacked a Barelvi congregation celebrating Prophet Muhammad's birthday, wiping out the entire top leadership of the militant Barelvi organisation Sunni Tehrik.[15]

While the government has sought to fight sectarianism, it has strangely relaxed its position *vis-à-vis* certain die-hard sectarian groups like Jasih-e-Muhammad (JeM), Lashkar-e-Tayyaba (LeT), and Harkat-ul-Mujahideen (HuM), who have hooked onto Pakistan's policy of subversion in Kashmir. The Musharraf administration officially banned the JeM and LeT in 2002 but neutral observers in Pakistan would suggest that Islamabad is not sincere about containing their activities as an instrument of its foreign policy vis-à-vis India.[16] Some suggest that the involvement of some of these organisations in the assassination attempt on General Musharraf strengthened his resolve to deal with them sternly but people below him in intelligence and security agencies are tolerant of them.[17]

Other Challenges

The political opposition to General Musharraf remained divided. The two main opposition parties, PML (Nawaz) and Pakistan People's Party (PPP), made tentative moves to come together to counter him but the efforts have not borne results. The PPP is unwilling to be part of any alliance which accommodates the right-wing MMA; the PML (N) is suspicious of the PPP striking a deal with General Musharraf. The MMA has picked on the issue of his holding two posts and has demanded that he should shed his uniform before the elections; it can

15. Deobandi Sunnis regard such celebrations as un-Islamic.
16. Daily Times (Lahore), 14 May 2006, in its editorial criticized the government's policy *vis-à-vis* Jamaat-ud-Dawa (earlier Lashkar-e-Tayyaba).
17. See, for instance, Hussain, Zahid (2004). "Dangerous Liaisons", *Newsline*, January.

make use of its nuisance potential on the streets over the issue but well within the limits of General Musharraf's tolerance. The ruling PML (Q) is quietly preparing for the elections scheduled for 2007.

General Musharraf is distinctly uneasy about any genuine, open and uncontrolled political process in Pakistan and brooks no criticism of his style of functioning. The political vacuum created by the absence of a genuine political process in the country is getting filled up by assertive conservative elements and disaffected nationalist elements.

During the year the Sindhi nationalists came together in their demands for better allocation of resources, declaration of Sindhi as a national language, and reservation in jobs for communities within the provinces. The Sindhi Quami Conference, organised by Awami Tehrik on 5 March, demanded re-federalisation of Pakistan based on the principles of provincial autonomy contained in the Pakistan Resolution of 23 March 1940, and retrospective compensation for unjust acts of exploitation and crimes committed by the ruling class. The Pakhtun Milli Awami Party (PMAP) also came out with demands for recognition of the Pashto language as a medium of instruction in schools. Undercurrents of nationalist sentiments gain new life under military dispensations, which are unresponsive to such demands. Political parties seeking their share in a constricted political space often use such opportunities to mobilise people around nationalist sentiments.

Similarly, by disallowing liberal political groups to operate in the tribal areas, General Musharraf has given a handle to the religious forces in the entire Pastun belt (from NWFP till north Balochistan). The people detest his bid to bring education, healthcare, and development in tribal areas through USAID (United States Agency for International Development), the Agha Khan Foundation, and governmental agencies. Involvement of local representatives would have soothed the nerves and removed operational roadblocks.

External Pressures

The United States has used its economic assistance to Pakistan as an effective lever in dealing with the Musharraf administration, giving currency to allegations by the jihadis and pro-Taliban militants that he is surrendering Pakistan's autonomy to the US and other Western powers. Citing Alexander Haig, former US Secretary of State, former Prime Minister Benazir Bhutto described General Musharraf as an "endangered species", and said that it was primarily the annual non-budgetary allocation of $900 million coming from outside which kept the economy afloat.[18] Following Pakistan's commitment to fight terror after the events of 11 September 2001, many international sanctions against it were lifted and there was an unprecedented inflow of foreign assistance. Pakistan's debts were either rescheduled on generous terms or reduced substantially. The 2006 annual country report by the State Department claims that US assistance "played a key role in moving Pakistan's economy from the brink of collapse to setting record high levels of foreign reserves and exports."[19] The US also rolled in a $3 billion five-year assistance package in 2005 to address Pakistan's long-term needs in the health and education sectors.

The volume of diplomatic traffic between Islamabad and Washington during the year under review suggested that there was constant pressure for performance on General Musharraf from the US, especially because of the re-emergence of the Taliban and the apprehension of a major spring offensive in 2007. Media reports suggested that during his visit to Pakistan on 27 February Dick Cheney, the US Vice President, threatened Pakistan with cutting off aid if it did not step up efforts to combat al-Qaeda and Taliban forces in Pakistan.[20] So far, General Musharraf has successfully persuaded his interlocutors in the US that doing more on this front will be counterproductive for his government and the US.[21]

---

18. Bhutto, Benazir (2006). Quoted in *Dawn*, 4 April.
19. Background note: Pakistan, Bureau of South and Central Asian Affairs, October 2006, at *http://www.state.gov/r/pa/ei/bgn/3453.htm* (accessed on 12 March, 2007).
20. Reports in the US media stated that Cheney made it clear that Congress was threatening to cut aid to Pakistan "unless it sees more concrete results from the nation in combating militants' cross-border infiltration of Afghanistan". *Los Angeles Times*, 27 February, 2007.
21. Pakistan claims to have stationed 80,000 troops and lost 800 of them in action, and opened 1000 check gates along the border with Afghanistan. It has also started fencing heavily trafficked areas, and has installed a biometric identification system at the main border crossing of Chaman.

Conclusions

Though in his public utterances General Musharraf expressed his determination to extend the writ of the state to all corners of Pakistan, the writ of the state does not run fully in Balochistan and FATA. The sectarian front remains as troublesome as ever, and on the political front the religious forces are becoming more restive. The external pressures have also mounted on General Musharraf to deliver on his commitment to contain terrorism.

A country with an illiberal socio-political milieu, yet a vigorously participative political culture, Pakistan has alternated between democracy and military rule through its sixty years of independent existence. The periods of military rule have been sustained as much by lack of internal capacity for generating political alternatives as by generous external support, through acts of omission and commission, based on politics of expediency and convenience. Political effervescence at the internal level has often failed to mature into a constructive force due to external factors impeding the process of political transformation in many ways. Pressures from within for return to democracy have been defused by a spurious system of representative rule, tutored and tailored by the military dictators, often with the blessings of their foreign mentors, who have considered democracy in Pakistan less important than their own global concerns. In the process they have contributed to the fragility of the Pakistani polity and weakened the cohesive and integrative capacity of the state. The discussion of the political developments in Pakistan in 2006 substantiates this point.

8

Bangladesh: Amidst Constitutional Crisis

SREERADHA DATTA

Ever since Khaleda Zia demitted office after completion of her five-year term as prime minister in October 2006, Bangladesh has been plunged into a series of political crises. Khaleda undermined the office of prime minister through her appointment of a caretaker government of partisans. The President, Iajuddin Ahmed, in his turn usurped the powers of the caretaker government. Just days before elections to the ninth Jatiya Sangsad (Parliament) emergency was introduced in the country on 11 January, 2007. This was followed by the President surrendering his dual responsibility, which paved the way for the formation of the second caretaker government headed by Fakhruddin Ahmed. Meanwhile, parliament was dissolved without an election schedule. Under intense public pressure, the chief election commissioner (CEC) went on leave. The second caretaker government has been preoccupied with reforming the political system rather than fulfilling its primary responsibility of holding a free and fair election within ninety days of taking over. The constitutional requirement that internal emergency has to be ratified within 120 days of declaration, that is by 12 May, will not be met because parliament stands dissolved and elections are not in sight.

A decade and a half after multiparty elections were introduced, how did Bangladesh reach this point? The answer lies in the gradual erosion of some principal institutions of democracy, primary among them the office of President, Chief Advisor to the caretaker government, Election Commission, parliament, political parties, and the military.

The author wishes to thank Prof. P.R. Kumaraswamy for comments on an earlier draft.

President-Caretaker Government

The imposition of emergency was preceded by controversies surrounding the appointment of Chief Adviser to the caretaker government. According to the thirteenth amendment to the Constitution approved by the sixth parliament on 26 March 1996, a neutral caretaker government would be formed to organise free and fair elections to the *Jatiya Sangsad*. Periodic accusations of partisanship and official interference resulted in Bangladesh opting for this unique institution as a transitional arrangement after an elected government completes its five-year term. Under the provisions, the most recently retired chief justice of the Supreme Court would become head of the caretaker government. Bangladesh has so far held two Jatiya Sangsad elections under caretaker governments.

On 14 May, 2004 the four-party coalition government headed by Khaleda Zia of the BNP (Bangladesh Nationalist Party) passed the fourteenth amendment to the Constitution, increasing the retirement age of Supreme Court judges from 65 to 67 years. This in practice meant that Justice K.M. Hasan would become head of the caretaker government when the current government demitted office. The present Justice would continue his term and Justice K.M. Hasan would be the last outgoing Chief Justice to head the caretaker government. Justice Hasan had been a member of the BNP. The opposition accused the government of partisanship and facilitating the nomination of its former member to this neutral post.

Widespread public disapproval and criticism of the opposition resulted in Justice Hasan declining to head the caretaker government. The Constitution prescribes an orderly procedure to find alternative arrangements. If other retired judges of the Supreme Court are not available, Article 58(C) suggests the nomination of a non-political 'public figure' who enjoys widespread respect and acceptance. Instead of following these prescribed norms, on 30 October, 2006 President Iajuddin Ahmed concurrently assumed the office of Adviser to the caretaker government.

For many Bangladeshis this move undermined the constitutional role of and respect for the office of President and evoked widespread public protest and opposition. Out of the 10-member council of advisers appointed by the President 9 resigned on 11 January, 2007 citing the 'dictatorial' attitude of the President and lack of proper consultations. The President's brief attempt to deploy the military to tide over street protests came under more severe criticism and disapproval.

Later that day, the President resigned as head of the caretaker government and declared a state of emergency. A couple of days later, a former World Bank official, Fakhruddin Ahmed, was appointed Chief Adviser with a new council of advisers. Under the internal emergency, the caretaker government has been functioning like an interim government, which the constitution does not provide for: a caretaker government has to conduct free and fair elections within three months after assuming office.

Under Article 107 the President could seek the opinion of the Supreme Court on issues of public importance. However, after cancelling the elections scheduled for 22 January such a reference has not been made until March 2007.

The second caretaker administration immediately initiated specific reforms, including issuing of voter identity cards and correcting the voter list. A drive to purge 'corrupt' institutions and individuals was also initiated. High-profile targets of this campaign have been Tarique Rahman, son of Khaleda Zia, and some of his cronies. There have also been a few arrests of Awami League leaders but, by and large, General Ershad's Jatiya Party, and noticeably those belonging to the Jama'at, have been largely untouched. To facilitate their actions task forces vested with unbridled powers have been formed. As if this constitutional crisis were not enough, the Election Commission posed a different set of problems.

Election Commission

Pre-empting the functioning of the neutral caretaker government, as early as in 2005 the BNP-led coalition had filled the local administration with its members and supporters. To enhance its electoral chances, scores of election officers at district and Upazila levels were recruited from amongst the BNP and its coalition supporters.[1] According to various media reports the ruling coalition

1. 290 of the recent 328 recruited as *upazila* election officers had links with the coalition parties. "Corruption, Nepotism, Dog Civil Service Recruitments: Insiders Blame Political Intervention", *New Age*, Dhaka, 27 November, 2005.

filled over 700 posts with those affiliated with their parties. These appointments might be crucial for ensuring the victory of the BNP-led coalition, even under a neutral administration.

Meanwhile the CEC, M.A. Aziz, was embroiled in serious controversies with the opposition and the judiciary. On 1 January, 2006 he unilaterally decided to draw up a fresh voter list, contrary to the High Court directive to update the existing list.[2] Two of his colleagues were opposed to the move, which was seen by many as an exercise to inflate the voter list by including bogus members sympathetic to the ruling coalition.

In recent years, the Election Commission has come under severe criticism over a number of issues, which include:

- Failure to implement the delimitation laws to demarcate the parliamentary constituencies following the latest population census held in 2001.[3]
- Publishing the 'draft' of the fresh electoral roll despite a legal battle initiated by the opposition parties which was pending with the Appellate Division of the Supreme Court.[4]
- According to the Awami League and many neutral commentators the report prepared by the National Democratic Institute had identified over 120,000 fake voters' names in the electoral roll, which also missed out between six and seven million genuine voters. There were also suggestions that the fresh voter list consisted of as many as 14 million fake names.[5]
- Since August 2005 CEC Aziz had serious differences with the other election commissioners M. Munsef Ali and A.K. Mohammad Ali over the preparation of a fresh voter list. In a

2. The Daily Star (2006). "No EC Meet on Voter Listing Since Aug: Time for Fresh Enrolment ends on Feb. 20", *The Daily Star*, Dhaka, 18 February.
3. Liton, Shakhawat (2006). "2006 EC Meet Ignores Law on Demarcation of Constituencies: Last Delimitation took place 11 years ago", *The Daily Star*, 11 February.
4. Editorial (2006). "EC makes Fresh Mess", *The Daily Star*, 5 May.
5. The initial list prepared by the CEC contained 91.3 million voters. This was struck down by the Supreme Court, which directed the EC to update the existing list. The corrected list, after the court's direction, stood at 93 million. This was different from the estimation of the Bangladesh Bureau of Statistics 2001, which stated that if all the people above 18 were listed and no death had occurred, the current voters' list should be 80.2 million.

bid to bolster his position in the Commission, Aziz inducted two BNP loyalists, Mahfuz and S.M. Zakaria, as new election commissioners.

- Despite the political tension in the country, especially after President Ahmed assumed office as head of the caretaker government, on 22 November the CEC went ahead and announced that the elections to the ninth *Jatiya Sangsad* would be held on 22 January, 2007.

Amidst the crisis over the caretaker government, the opposition led by the Awami League launched a personal and concerted campaign against the CEC. Finally, on 27 November, 2006 Aziz went on a long leave. A couple of days later President Ahmed (still holding the caretaker government) reconstituted the Election Commission.

Weakened *Jatiya Sangsad*

In the 2001 *Jatiya Sangsad* elections, the Awami League refused to gracefully accept the electoral verdict which had brought the BNP-led coalition to power. Since then the opposition has been regularly resorting to extra-parliamentary methods. Members of the Awami League attended the *Jatiya Sangsad* only when they were faced with the threat of disqualification. The government, too, made it difficult for the opposition to function responsibly. The following are some examples:

- Opposition members were prevented from speaking on important national issues in parliament, sometimes by switching off the microphones.
- The formation of parliamentary standing committees, expected to be constituted following the inaugural session of the Jatiya Sangsad when a new government takes over, was delayed by almost two years.
- The government refused to discuss the arrest of Members of Parliament during various protests and agitations. They were protesting against misuses during military operation against terrorism or over corruption in the government, deteriorating law and order situation, shortage of wheat and paddy seeds, and increase of prices of fuel, gas, electricity, and water.

There were also serious differences over the conduct of elections for the ninth Jatiya Sangsad, originally due in January 2007. Given the obvious manipulation of the political system by the ruling alliance, the Awami League-led opposition parties were demanding:

- reconstitution of the Election Commission,
- preparation of a faultless voter list, and
- ensuring of an environment congenial to the conduct of a free and fair election.

The Awami League has been demanding reforms in electoral laws and made its participation in the 2007 elections conditional upon the fulfilment of its demands.[6] As has been the trend in Bangladesh, various extra-constitutional means were adopted by the opposition as they were unable to hold dialogue within the Jatiya Sangsad. This resulted in Prime Minister Khaleda Zia suggesting the formation of a committee to discuss the reform proposals outside parliament. Coalition compulsions resulted in the BNP naming members of the religious parties to this committee.[7]

This was unacceptable to the opposition. For long, the Awami League has blamed the religious allies of the BNP for the increasing number of terror attacks and undermining the political process. Objecting to the inclusion of Jama'at to the committee, the Awami League stepped up its agitation programmes, including a series of non-stop hartals.[8] In the ensuing violence in Dhaka and elsewhere in Bangladesh, in the clashes with police some prominent Awami League leaders, such as Saber Hossain Choudhury and Asaduzzaman Nur, were severely injured.

Political Parties

The major political parties have also been facing serious internal challenges. The BNP's problems could be directly traced to the rapid

6. It proposed a five-point agenda to amend the caretaker government, a 15-point programme to make the EC independent, and made 11 suggestions for the reform of electoral laws and regulations.
7. Ali, A.M.M. Shawkat (2006). "Worth a Look: Unending Debate on Electoral Reforms", *The Daily Star*, 27 April.
8. Islam, Khadimul (2006). "Scope for Talks Fades as AL plans to Scale up Street Agitation", *The Daily Star*, 12 May.

increase in extremist violence in the country ever since Khaleda returned to power in October 2001. Ironically, it was on a promise of rolling back deteriorating law and order that the BNP-led coalition won a huge mandate in the 2001 elections, but military operations, such as 'Clean Heart' and 'Spider Web' and the formation of Rapid Action Battalion were only partially successful.

The larger problem of religious extremism went unchecked. For long the ruling coalition was in a denial mode, thus aggravating the problem. The government dismissed Islamic militancy as "a conspiracy and an orchestrated campaign by some vested quarters" and "the creation of some newspapers". Islamic extremist violence, which began sporadically in 1999, peaked in 2004-05. Between 1999 and December 2005 there were over 33 major bomb blasts, most of them attributed to militant groups or individuals.[9] Official investigations were either not completed or yielded no result or led to no arrests. Attacks targeted at political leaders included the one on the Awami League leader Sheikh Hasina Wajid in August 2004 at a party rally, which killed twenty persons, including senior Awami League leader Ivy Rahman, and the assassination in January 2005 of S.A.M.S. Kibria, senior Awami League leader and former finance minister. Particularly sensational were the nationwide simultaneous bomb blasts on 17 August 2005, numbering over 300. Arguably, the unstable political conditions have benefited the "increasingly influential Islamist fringe, led by legitimate governing parties like the Jama'at but extending to the violently militant Jagrata Muslim Janata Bangladesh (JMJB) and the Jamaat-ul-Mujahideen Bangladesh (JMB)."[10]

It was the concerted international pressure, especially from its western donors, that jolted the government into action. Their expression of concern over the "deterioration of the governance situation in Bangladesh, especially the situation of law and order, political violence including recent bombings, and the climate of impunity" prompted the government to ban the JMB and JMJB. The immediate arrest of Bangla Bhai and Shaikh Abdur Rahman, leaders

---

9. The Daily Star (2005). "Udichi Again: 33 Major Blasts since 1999", The Daily Star, 9 December.

10. "Bangladesh Today", ICG Asia Report, No. 121, 23 October, 2006.

of JMJB and JMB respectively, led Khaleda Zia on 2 March, 2006 to declare Bangladesh as "a terrorism-free nation."

The influence of religion has been palpable and conservative elements found the contrived system convenient to push their narrow agenda aggressively. Investigations had revealed that the coalition members, specifically Jamaa't cadres, were contributing funds to the JMB.[11] Such reports and the failure of the government to decisively disengage from its coalition partners painted the BNP as willing partner if not a collaborator in extremist violence. The terror attacks had also precipitated a deep crisis and divisions within the BNP. A number of disgruntled BNP leaders publicly accused the ruling coalition of having links with religious extremists.

The government made only very limited and cursory attempts to investigate and unearth the underground terror links. Its lack of serious action invoked severe criticism that "underground terrorist groups have been cultivated and sheltered by those in power."[12] Mounting domestic and international pressure resulted in cosmetic changes and some quick high-profile arrests but "Bangladeshi intelligence officials believe that the arrests are unlikely to undermine the militant groups entirely."[13] Many Bangladeshis believe that a series of highly publicised mass surrenders of suspects were "more political theatre than a genuine end to a reign of terror."[14]

The opposition also has its share of woes. In its obsession to unseat the Khaleda government, the Awami League had forged an unwieldy alliance with various opposition parties. The result was that the fourteen-party coalition under Sheikh Hasina was expanded to nineteen parties, including two factions of Islami Oikya Jote led by Mizbahur Rahman Choudhury and Allama Azizul Haque, along with the Islamic Front of Bangladesh. In the process, Hasina made some odd and controversial choices. The Khaleda government's refusal to drop corruption charges against him induced former President and

11. Kumar, Anand (2003). "Islamists and Bangladesh", *Time*, 21 March.
12. "Bangladesh Today", n.10, p.3.
13. "Captures Fail to Halt Bangladesh Militants", Jane's Terrorism and Security Monitor, 12 April, 2006.
14. "Bangladesh Today", n.10.

Jatiya Party leader General Ershad to forge an alliance with the Awami League-led opposition coalition. Likewise, despite its secular orientation, Hasina forged a partnership with Khilafat Majlish Bangladesh, signing an agreement that if voted to power her government was committed to the introduction of Sharia.

Systemic Collapse

If initially there was no manifestation of popular displeasure against some of the unprecedented moves by the interim government—voices are being raised now—it was merely a reflection of the people's disappointment with their mainstream leadership. But the caretaker government is a team of appointed technocrats. The constitution restricts their scope to holding free and fair elections within three months but more than five months after Khaleda Zia demitted office Bangladesh does not have an election schedule. By undertaking revision of the voters' list it has postponed elections indefinitely. This political crisis has undermined various political institutions in the country.

The current situation would necessitate the two main political parties modifying or even abandoning some of their erstwhile positions. For example, Khaleda Zia's son Tarique looks likely to be marginalised within the BNP. The Awami League had to pull out of its last-minute alliance with Khilafat Majlish Bangladesh. The caretaker government has initiated actions against both the BNP and the Awami League to expose their corruption. Popular endorsement of this initiative has restrained rival politicians from taking to the streets.

The appointment of a neutral administration under Fakhruddin Ahmed also appears to have weakened the support enjoyed by the right-wing religious elements. Without the backing of the establishment, tacit or otherwise, the religious elements will have their wings clipped. Also, the caretaker government's actions appear to be directed against the two principal parties. So long as they are not targets of the crackdown, the religious parties can safely lie low.

From the time it returned to the barracks in 1991, the military has not shown signs of returning to the political arena. External pressures, especially from the UN, the US, and the EU, cautioned the military against returning to active politics. The present change has vested the military with a more focused and specific role in the country's politics. The emergency was introduced and enforced with its backing. But if the caretaker government collapses, proves ineffective, or becomes unpopular, the military may not remain a silent spectator.

External Players

Bangladesh has been vulnerable to external pressures and demands since it depends heavily upon western donors. A large number of non-governmental organisations (NGOs) in the country also survive upon western financial assistance. Many western countries, especially the US, have viewed Bangladesh as a model Islamic democratic nation and as a key partner in their fight against global terror. But the growing religious extremism and internal violence have dimmed the image of Bangladesh. When the British High Commissioner in Dhaka, Anwar Choudhury, expressed his fear of Bangladesh being at a serious risk of falling into the hands of Islamist fundamentalists if its political impasse continued, he was reflecting similar sentiments in other western capitals.[15] The BNP-led government faced a difficult task in assuring its developmental partners that it was in control of the situation even while being benevolent and accommodative of its Islamic coalition partners.

Since the unfolding of the crisis over the caretaker government in October 2006, a number of donor agencies and influential foreign countries announced that elections which did not ensure participation of all political parties would not be acceptable to the international community. When the caretaker government went ahead to announce dates for the ninth Jatiya Sangsad elections, the reaction of the international community was sharp and unequivocal. Early January, the UN, the EU, and the Commonwealth suspended their election observation missions in Bangladesh. Both EU Deputy Chief Observer Graham Elson and the UN spokesperson stated that under the present circumstances and due to the lack of reforms, any elections in Bangladesh would not be credible and would not meet the

15. Foster, Peter (2006). "Bangladesh at Risk of Falling to Extremists", *Daily Telegraph*, 4 December.

international standards. They seem to have been more receptive to a non-partisan administration under Fakhruddin Ahmed.

Implications for India

Under the Khaleda dispensation Indo–Bangladeshi relations were marred by the perception that India had a preference for the Awami League and Sheikh Hasina. The visit by India's Minister for External Affairs to Dhaka in February 2007 to formally invite Bangladesh to the SAARC meet in New Delhi in April 2007 was seen as an ice-breaking exercise. During the visit it was agreed that:

> ...India will grant unconditional duty-free access to import of 2 million pieces of readymade garments from Bangladesh. The issue of restrictions being placed on import of cosmetics from Bangladesh has also been resolved. The Bangladesh side has been kind enough to offer early operationalisation of Sealdah-Joydevpur passenger train service and to build a bridge over Raghnacherra river. Both sides have agreed to jointly combat terrorism, which today poses the most grave challenge to our society and threatens the rapid economic development of our nations.[16]

For implementation, however, these agreements would have to await a government to be elected.

Apprehensions in India regarding Bangladesh are twofold. One is the larger fear of democracy being subverted there. There is also growing concern about the role of the military in delaying the elections.[17]

The large-scale influx from Bangladesh taking place through the porous borders will exacerbate if the political situation in that country worsens, possibly provoking a backlash against the minorities in India. The open borders would also be used by insurgents fighting the Indian government, who have bases in Bangladesh. Past election campaigns in Bangladesh have also generally tended to generate anti-India rhetoric and feelings.

---

16. Statement of the Indian Minister for External Affairs, Pranab Mukherjee, on departure from Dhaka, 19 March 2007, at *http://meaindia.nic.in*
17. Karim, I.A. Tariq and Christine Fair (2007). "Bangladesh at the Crossroads", United States Institute of Peace, January; see also Bruce Vaughn, "Islamist Extremism in Bangladesh", CRS Report for Congress, 31 January, 2007: 4.

Conclusion

The year 2006 exposed, once again, the fragility of Bangladesh democracy. It took the country nearly two months of intense street protests to bring about a duly constituted and recognised caretaker government. Widespread public protests also resulted in the President relinquishing his post as chief of the caretaker government. Likewise, only under popular protest and threat of personal boycott did the controversial CEC leave office.

At the same time, even four months after the resignation of the Khaleda government there are no signs of an early election. The newly constituted Election Commission has started the arduous task of revision of the voter list, without any tentative date of completion. Under the constitution, the emergency would have to be ratified by parliament within 120 days or it lapses. This in practical terms means that the new Jatiya Sangsad would have to be constituted before 10 May 2007. With no definite election dates, a question mark hangs over the duration and legality of the emergency regulations.

By all accounts, the political situation under a caretaker government is at odds with the Constitution. The military is implementing the emergency. At the same time, except the political parties, the wider public including the media appear to have endorsed this non-political climate.

9

Sri Lanka: Towards Eelam War IV?

ALOK BANSAL and M. MAYILVAGANAN

Sri Lanka's ethnic conflict, commencing in 1983, has resulted in the death of over 100,000 and displacement of millions. Almost one-third of the Tamil population has been internally displaced and almost one-fourth have emigrated. The antagonistic perceptions of the two main ethnic groups—the majority Sinhala and minority Tamil—based on religion, culture, language, and history, the differences going back to the colonial period—have contributed to a wide schism between them. Unfair distribution of benefits, denial of equal access to opportunities, and unwillingness to devolve powers to areas dominated by Tamils have increasingly alienated the Tamils. Resurgence of Sinhala nationalist consciousness has worsened the inter-ethnic relationship, leading to recurring conflict since the 1950s.

The 'Sinhala only' legislation of 1956 triggered off violent demonstrations by the Tamils; in response, there were fierce anti-Tamil riots in the Sinhala south. Efforts to address the ethnic problem commenced with the Bandaranaike-Chelvanayakam pact in 1957, which addressed the issues of devolution of power and giving official-language status to Tamil. The latest was the Cease Fire Agreement (CFA) in 2002 between the Ranil Wickremesinghe government and the Liberation Tigers of Tamil Eelam (LTTE).[1] There is, however, an unbridgeable chasm between the LTTE demands and what the government is willing to concede. The LTTE has consistently demanded a separate Tamil homeland whereas the Sinhalese are not even willing to devolve minimal powers to the Tamils. After the 2002 CFA the LTTE has shown willingness to accept autonomy in a

1. Rupesinghe, Kumar (ed.) (1998). *Negotiating Peace in Sri Lanka: Efforts, Failures and Lessons*, London: International Alert.

notionally united Sri Lanka. Its proposal for an Interim Self Governing Authority (ISGA) was summarily rejected by the political establishment. The lack of consensus within the All Party Conference appointed by President Mahinda Rajapaksa in January 2006 and stiff resistance by the Sinhala nationalists on its draft political package has crashed the peace process. The latest Sinhala proposals for an All Party Conference regresses the situation to the early 1980s.

Norwegian Peace Process

The withdrawal of the Indian Peace Keeping Force (IPKF) in 1990 was followed by a number of Eelam Wars, ending in stalemate. President Chandrika Kumaratunga, with the tacit approval of India, invited Norway in 1998 to mediate. After an initial deadlock, in September 2001 Norway succeeded in convening a meeting in Geneva to explore a solution to the conflict. In 2002 a Norwegian-brokered cease fire came into effect between the government of Prime Minister Ranil Wickremesinghe, who had won the parliamentary elections on an electoral platform of working for peace, and the LTTE.

The CFA was a "well crafted, valid instrument of peace, devised for the purpose of bringing an end to hostilities and to create a positive environment conducive for meaningful negotiations."[2] The agreement was followed by a steady move towards normalisation, rehabilitation, and development, to undo decades of devastation. However, the process got derailed after the European Union (EU) branded the LTTE as a banned terrorist organisation on 30 May 2006, despite warnings that it would affect the peace process. The Sri Lankan Monitoring Mission (SLMM) thereafter found it difficult to monitor the cease fire. The government's objection to the Norwegians' role as both peace mediators and commander of the truce observers also created hurdles in their effort. The SLMM's effectiveness was undermined by its lack of mandate to oversee human rights violation besides CFA violations.

Why the Peace Process Stumbled

The Norwegian peace process crumbled in 2006 and the security forces and the LTTE took on each other with renewed vigour,

2. "Ceasefire Agreement is Foundation of Peace and must be Implemented: Balasingham", at *http://www.tamilnet.com/art.html?catid=13&artid=17260* (accessed on 31 August, 2007).

especially in the Eastern Province. Reasons for the failure of the peace process are discussed in the subsequent paragraphs.

Non-committal Approach of the Adversary Parties

Attitudes have hardened on both sides of the divide after the CFA was negotiated. The two sides came to the negotiating table in Geneva in February 2006 with rigid stances, with the government seeking an amendment to the CFA, while the LTTE stuck to its position that the A9 highway to Jaffna had to be opened. Consequently, the February talks failed. After Mahinda Rajapaksa became President in November 2005 the radical Sinhala groups have adopted a hardline position on the peace process as well as on the Norwegian role as facilitator. As a result of its thin majority in parliament and opposition from its ally Janatha Vimukthi Peramuna (JVP), the Rajapaksa government has not been able to pursue its promised peace with zeal and vigour. It may be recalled that Rajapaksa won the elections courtesy the LTTE, which did not allow large-scale voting in Tamil areas, thereby denying the UNP (United Nationalist Party) an assured chunk of votes. The LTTE perceives the CFA to be 'defunct', in view of the government offensive since early 2006.[3] The EU ban and the government's closure of transport and communication channel in the North East have also contributed to the LTTE hardening its stance.

Government's Hardline Approach

The government seems to have convinced itself of the efficacy of force in settling the issue. The military approach first succeeded in the operation at Muttur over the problem of Mavilaru water canal in July 2006.[4] Thereafter, the security forces seized control of Sampur town in early September 2006; this was the first ever territorial change in the country after the CFA. Next, exploiting their supremacy in the air,

3. Foster, Peter (2006). "Tamil Leader Declares Peace Process 'Defunct'", *The Telegraph* (UK), 28 November; "Colombo has Rendered Truce Defunct: LTTE", *The Hindu*, 30 November.

4. The standoff over the Maavilaru waterway in Trincomalee district started with the closure of sluice gate by Tamils living in LTTE-controlled areas of Mutur East-Eechchilampattu on 22 July, 2006 with the LTTE protesting against the reported insensitivity of the Sri Lankan government in addressing the drinking water problem of Tamils at Eachchilampattu. This blocked the flow of water to some 30,000 acres of ripe paddy fields and 60,000 people in nearby Sinhala settlements. The issue got aggravated when the Sri Lankan government began using military force to settle the issue.

the security forces captured the Vaharai region with minimum bloodshed, the biggest territorial loss for the LTTE. It was also the first time that the Sri Lankan Air Force jets bombed areas in Kilinochchi. Apparently, the government's reading is that the LTTE has been crippled by the former LTTE commander in the East, Karuna, switching allegiance to the security forces, and the increased international pressure on the LTTE draining its funding and thus eroding its combat potential.

Role of Other Tamil Armed Groups

The schismatic Karuna faction is collaborating with other Tamil groups like PLOTE (Siddarthan) and EPRLF (Perumal) who are opposed to the LTTE. This factor is constraining the LTTE's operational independence in the East. These groups targeted the LTTE even when the LTTE and the government were maintaining the cease-fire, which led the LTTE to accuse the government of using them as its cat's paw.

Humanitarian Crisis and Human Rights Violation

The escalation of hostility since April 2006 has shattered the hopes of the Tamils while disillusioning the international community. The closure of main A9 highway between Jaffna and Colombo, the lifeline of Jaffna peninsula, as a result of the conflict has caused severe shortages of essential commodities in the region, especially medical supplies, despite attempts to maintain supplies through the sea. The LTTE has refused to guarantee the security of shipping or aircraft supplying essential goods to Jaffna with an aim to force the government to reopen the A9 highway. Large-scale civilian casualties have been reported in air strikes by the security forces. Similarly, the LTTE's artillery attack on Palaly airbase in Jaffna led to the suspension of flights from Colombo and caused collateral damage to men and material.[5] The government restricted the operations of NGOs (non-governmental organisations), which were rendering crucial humanitarian aid. The killing of workers of the French NGO Action Contre la Faim (ACF) and attacks on local staff employed by various

5. Balachandran, P.K. (2006). "Artillery Duels and Air Action Continue in Sri Lanka", *Hindustan Times*, 12 August.

NGOs have resulted in the withdrawal of many NGO workers from the North-East in the interest of their security.[6]

Both sides have shown scant respect to the human rights of non-belligerents. The LTTE routinely uses civilians as shield and exploits their deaths as a propaganda tool. The security forces, too, attack civilian targets. In the worst incident of its kind, security forces shelled a camp for Internally Displaced People (IDPs) in Kathiraweli in Vaharai of Batticaloa district on 8 November 2006, killing 47 persons and injuring another 136.[7] The Karuna group has been recruiting children for combat role. LTTE suicide bombers and pro-government vigilante groups have been targeting individuals in and outside the zone of conflict. Terrorist attacks in Anuradhapura killed sixty-four civilians and in Habarana in the North Central Province killed at least 100 naval personnel. The unceasing displacement, abduction, and disappearance of a large number of Tamil civilians in Colombo and Jaffna have also become a sensitive issue domestically and internationally.

Elusive Sinhala Consensus

Consensus eludes the Sinhala elite on the question of devolution of power mainly because of their political myopia. In 2000 when President Chandrika Kumaratunga was on the verge of finalising a bipartisan consensus, the UNP backed out at the last moment to deny her credit for the achievement. In 2003 when Ranil Wickremesinghe's UNP government was attempting to move the peace process forward, President Kumaratunga hobbled progress by taking over two crucial ministries.[8] A glimmer of hope was seen in October 2006 when President Rajapaksa signed a political pact with the UNP to strive for consensus on national issues, including the ethnic question,[9] only to derail this achievement with his manoeuvre to defect 19 UNP

6. For details see *http://hrw.org/english/docs/2006/08/11/slanka13959.htm*; see also *http://www.hrw.org/backgrounder/asia/srilanka0906/srilanka0906webwcover.pdf*.
7. See *http://www.reliefweb.int/rw/rwb.nsf/db900SID/LSGZ-6VMDR8?OpenDocument*; see also *http://www.nvpf.org/np/english/resources/progdept/Nov06.pdf*
8. Sambandan, V.S. (2003). "Chandrika Takes Over Defence, Two Other Portfolios", *The Hindu*, 5 November.
9. See *http://www.priu.gov.lk/news_update/Current_Affairs/ca200610/20061023slfp_unp_sign_mou. htm*

legislators to his side. This presidential gambit has riled not only the UNP but the SLFP as well, with the pro-Chandrika faction and Sinhala hardliners putting pressure on the President. On the positive side, however, Rajapaksa's sleight of hand may allow him to disregard pressure from the JVP hardliners, allowing him elbow room to accommodate Tamil demands. At the same time, the JVP appears to be on the ascendant. The JVP and other radical groups had filed a petition in an Appeal Court to annul the CFA.[10] They have recently got a verdict against the merger of the North and East from the Supreme Court.[11] Sri Lanka's election system of proportional representation seems to encourage hardline stances. Politicians get elected to parliament on the support of their own ethnic groups. Since they do not have to seek support of voters of other communities, they thrive on hardline stances. A first-past-the-post system, based on territorial constituencies, would have forced them to moderate their stances in order to get votes from other communities or groups.

Perceptions of the Adversary Parties

There is a growing perception that the LTTE basically looks at all peace processes as tactical pauses for the attainment of its ultimate strategic objective—a separate state of Eelam. In the past, the LTTE accepted negotiations when it needed time for reinforcement. After its failure to capture Jaffna in 2000, the LTTE realised that it could not attain its objectives militarily. This, coupled with the changing world perception after the events of 11 September 2001, forced the LTTE to accept a cease fire and climb down from its stated objective of Eelam to autonomy (self-governing authority) within a unified Sri Lanka. Thereafter, its policy has been neither to allow a breakthrough—by making impossible demands—nor to force a breakdown of the cease fire. However, the LTTE stance seems to have changed in 2006. After the Geneva talks in February, it complained that the government side was represented by a relatively low-level delegation. In June it refused to meet the government delegation for talks on truce monitoring at Oslo because the delegation did not have a political representation and

10. See *http://www.lankasun.com/modules/news/article.php?storyid=6263*

11. See *http://www.jvpsrilanka.com/statements_page/Judgment%20on%20North%20East%20merger.htm*

also protesting against the presence of SLMM monitors from EU countries.[12] When finally the peace talks resumed in Geneva in October 2006, the LTTE demanded reopening of the A9 highway as a precondition for talks. Earlier the LTTE had pulled out of talks citing various reasons, which varied from lack of resources for the war-torn Tamil regions, to demands of safe passage for its commanders in the East.

The LTTE's military gambits have generally failed in 2006, except for its success in foiling the military offensive in Muhamalai on 11 October 2006, where it captured four battle tanks. The LTTE's attack on Army Chief Lt. Gen. Sarath Fonseka on 25 April, the suicide attack at Habarana on 16 October, which resulted in killing of 116 Naval sailors and wounding 130 others, the attempt by the Sea Tigers to raid the naval base at Galle three days on 19 October, and President Rajapaksa's brother and Defence Secretary Gothabaya on 1 December 2006 are generally viewed as acts of desperation.[13] The LTTE is therefore projecting a conciliatory face and highlighting human rights violation by the government and wants the international community to pressurise it to respect the cease fire and bring it to the negotiating table. It is likely to exploit the interregnum provided by these conciliatory moves to fortify its battered position in the Eastern Province and vanish the Karuna faction and his fledgling political party, the Tamil Eela Makkal Viduthalai Pulikal. Aware that India alone can check the Sri Lankan government's onslaught it is trying to mend fences with the Indian government: hence its statement of 'regret' on Rajiv Gandhi's assassination to test the waters. After the crackdown on pro-LTTE outfits in the West and the EU ban, the LTTE perceives a political role by India as its best option for the time being.

The Sri Lankan Army, on the other hand, appears confident of military victory, having acquired better equipment and better training and also having gained tactical advantage thanks to the defection of Karuna. Since April 2006 the security forces have been using superior artillery and recently acquired air assets to seek military victory. The

12. See *www.idsa.in/publications/strategic-analysis/2006/jul-sep06/Sukanya090107.pdf*

13. See *http://news.bbc.co.uk/2/hi/south_asia/4941744.stm*; see also *http://www.priu.gov.lk/news_update/Current_Affairs/ca200612/20061201defence_secretary_unharmed_bomb_attack.htm*

increase in government's defence spending by 28 per cent in the budget presented in November 2006 indicates a possible resort to military coercion to attain an ultimate political solution to the vexed issue.[14]

India's Stakes

India backs a unified Sri Lanka, where legitimate Tamil aspirations are incorporated within the constitutional framework. The LTTE is a terrorist organisation, which if successful, would not remain confined to Sri Lankan borders. On the other hand, but for the LTTE the government and Sinhala youth would not have even agreed to discuss legitimate Tamil demands. Also, the phenomenon of the LTTE has compelled the Sri Lankan governments to maintain good relations with India, which was not always the case earlier. Although both the ethnic groups in Sri Lanka trace their origins to India, the Tamil population in India identifies itself with Sri Lankan Tamils. The worsening humanitarian crisis in Jaffna is having repercussions in Tamil Nadu. The spontaneous and strong reaction to the Sri Lankan offensive by the political parties in Tamil Nadu indicates that the Tamil issue in Sri Lanka has resurfaced as an important determinant of internal politics in India. The large-scale influx of refugees from Sri Lanka, estimated to be 16,221 in 2006 by the UN Office for Coordination of Humanitarian Affairs, is also a cause for concern. The Government of India has reacted so far with caution despite disapproving of the Sri Lankan government's military approach and conveying its concern at Sri Lanka's attempts to seek military assistance from Pakistan and China.

The Way Ahead

Reasonable devolution of power acceptable to minorities like Tamils and Muslims, and supported by all sections of the Sinhala community, is the only possible solution to Sri Lanka's ethnic conflict. This can come about only through inclusive political processes rather than military means. Building of consensus among the majority, Sinhalese

14. "Arms on Menu as Sri Lanka Defence Spending Rises 28 pct", at *http://asia.news.yahoo.com/061117/3/2t2y0.html*

will be the first step. The political package based on the model of federalism and accepted by the Sinhalas can form the basis for further discussion between the government and Tamils. The government must strive to amend the constitution to incorporate the devolution of powers to the Tamils. It must also take steps to keep the North and East together. There is also a need to ensure that the government, and especially the armed forces, are made more representatives by incorporating Tamils in these institutions. In the effort to find a solution to the conflict the government also needs to encourage the voice of moderates amongst Tamils. The international community must offer to underwrite the constitutional provisions that guarantee devolution of power to the Tamils.

India's support, overt or covert, is essential to resolve the issue. As an emerging global power India cannot sit back and watch its neighbourhood being engulfed in anarchy. India must first impress upon the Sri Lankan government to halt its military operations and provide succour to the Tamil population in the North East. The impending humanitarian crisis must be averted at all cost. Similarly, India has to help the Sri Lankan government in safeguarding its security from the threat potentials of the LTTE—Air Tigers, Sea Tigers, and Black Tigers. Especially after the LTTE's attack on Kattunayake Air Force base, the Indian government should provide non-lethal weapons to the Sri Lankan armed forces and work towards coordinated patrolling of the Palk Strait. Thereafter it must back the Norwegian peace accord and ensure that the two sides stick to their commitments under the accord.

The international community also must attempt to bring the two parties closer to strive for a solution. The threat of curbing international aid for the development programme in Sri Lanka and strict measures like curbing the LTTE's illegal activities are certain to impact the parties in due course from deviating from the peace process. The donors have a valid stake in ensuring that peace returns to Sri Lanka and North East Sri Lanka returns to the path of economic development.

10

The Challenge of Building a New Nepal

SMRUTI S. PATTANAIK

Nepal witnessed dramatic political changes in 2006 after more than a decade of Maoist insurgency. The King's decision to directly assume power, his efforts to marginalise the political parties, and his decision to militarily annihilate the Maoists without addressing their grievances, brought about a massive popular upsurge against him, led by the political parties and the Maoists, forcing the monarchy to restore the suspended Parliament. The Maoists are now part of the interim government. This democratic transformation of a left wing radical guerrilla movement is unprecedented. Belying concerns and scepticism expressed by the international community, the alliance between the political parties and the Maoists has sustained the constraints of political and ideological differences. There remain, however, various roadblocks in implementing some of the core aspects of political understanding.

Setting the Pace of Political Reconciliation

The direct assumption of power by the monarchy on 1 February, 2005 became the catalyst in bringing together the seven major political parties and the Maoists. In a significant move, they reached a twelve-point political agreement in New Delhi on 22 November, 2005 that laid the foundation for their cooperation. Reinstating Parliament and forming an all-party government that would oversee the elections to the Constituent Assembly were the most significant point of the agreement. The popular uprising in April 2006 against the King's intransigence was the next milestone in weakening his position. King Gyanendra initially used the army to quell the demonstrations and later tried to undermine the movement by accusing it of being inspired by the Maoists. On 21 April the King asked the political parties to suggest a name for an interim prime minister, a proposal which they rejected. On 24 April, under intense pressure, the King finally succumbed to the demands of the people and reinstated Parliament. To facilitate the peace process the Maoists declared a unilateral cease fire on 25 April. On 26 May, 2006 the Maoists and the Seven Party Alliance (SPA) signed a 25-point cease fire code of conduct. On 16 June the Maoists and the SPA reached an eight-point agreement. The agreement spoke of the need to:

> bring about a forward-looking restructuring of the state so as to resolve the class-based, racial, regional and gender-based problems through Constituent Assembly elections. Transform the cease fire between the Nepal government and CPN-Maoist into permanent peace by focusing on democracy, peace, prosperity, forward-looking change and the country's independence, sovereignty and pride and express commitment to resolve the problem through talks.[1]

The eight parties formally invited the United Nations on 9 August 2006 to help disarm the Maoists and the Nepalese Army and manage their surrendered arms.

Negotiating the Future

The Interim Constitution

The agreement signed on 22 November and the arms agreement signed on 8 December 2006 further concretised the vision of the Nepalese people for a democratic future of their nation. On 16 December 2006 the SPA and Maoists signed the interim constitution, paving the way for a new Nepal. The interim constitution facilitated the emergence of an Eight Party Alliance (SPA+Maoists) leading to the Maoists joining the interim government. The interim constitution in Part 23 under transitional provisions explicitly states that "no power regarding the governance of the country shall be vested in the king" and the fate of the monarchy would be decided by simple majority at the first meeting of the elected Constituent Assembly. It also urges the political parties to follow an inclusive system to

1. *http://www.kantipuronline.com/kolnews.php?nid=76803* (accessed on 18 September, 2006).

represent women, dalits, and members from neglected and suppressed regions.

After considerable political wrangling the draft interim constitution was put into operation on 15 January, 2007. The interim constitution concentrates all power in the hand of the Prime Minister. In a subsequent amendment, a provision for the removal of the Prime Minister by two-thirds majority of Parliament was added. The interim constitution also has a provision of referendum on issues of national importance.

The government has also taken other steps to make democracy participatory. The first amendment to the constitution proposes to provide proportional representation to Madhesis, Dalits, women, and people from disadvantaged classes and regions. Article 138 was amended to make Nepal a federal state. The structuring of the federation would be decided by the Constituent Assembly.[2] The Election Constituency Delimitation Commission (ECDC), which submitted its report to the government on 12 April 2007, has added 35 constituencies to the existing 205—28 in the Terai region and 7 in the hill region—basing itself on the report of the 1991 census.[3] Additionally, the government has taken steps to make the Army representative. It has raised two armed battalions to accommodate the Madhesias in the Naya Sabuj battalion and the Kirat community in the Rupamardhini battalion.[4]

The Interim Parliament

The interim legislature comprises 330 members, as follows: 209 members from the SPA,[5] 73 from the Maoists; 10 members each nominated by the Nepali Congress (NC), United Marxist-Leninist (UML), and Maoists; 6 members nominated by NC (democratic); 3

---

2. *http://insn.org/?p=4231*
3. According to the 2001 census of Nepal, 51.57 per cent of the population lives in the Terai and 48.53 per cent lives in the hill and mountainous region. *http://www.allheadlinenews.com/articles/7007036381* (accessed on 18 April, 2007).
4. *http://www.southasianmedia.net/cnn.cfm?id=357480&category=Security&Country=NEPAL* (accessed on 27 January, 2007).
5. In the interim legislature the parties will retain the number of seats they had in the reinstated House of Representatives. Nepali Congress 75, CPN (UML) 73, NC (democratic) 42 and other smaller parties have 19 members.

members each nominated by the People's Front, Nepal Workers and Peasant Party, Nepal Sadbhavana Party (Anandi), and United Left Front. In their nominations to Parliament it appears that the Maoists have tried to have some sort of social balance whereas the Nepali Congress attempted to accommodate its members defeated in the elections and the kin of the leadership.

Election to the Constituent Assembly would be based on a mixed electoral system, with 205 members elected on the basis of the first-past-the-post system and 204 by the proportional representation system on the basis of votes won by the political parties. Sixteen members would be nominated by the interim Council of Ministers from among distinguished persons, bringing the strength of the Constituent Assembly to 425. Following the eruption of violence in the Terai (discussed later), the government has taken steps to increase the number of seats in the proposed Constituent Assembly to ensure better representation of Terai.

Interim Government

An interim government was sworn in on 1 April, 2007. Distribution of the portfolios delayed the formation of the council of ministers. To avoid contesting claims from Maoists and the UML, the post of Deputy Prime Minister was abolished. The interim government has agreed upon a common minimum programme for itself. Its main mandate is to oversee the conduct of a free and fair election to the Constituent Assembly and implement various agreements that were signed by the political parties and the Maoists, including the return of properties held by the Maoists in the course of the violent struggle.

Peace Process and Disarming of the Maoists

The detailed agreement signed on 28 November, 2006 to monitor the management of arms and armies of both the Maoists and the Nepal Army is important not only for stabilising the peace but also for establishing trust. This agreement confines the Maoists to specified cantonments and a section of the Nepal Army to the barracks. The maoist parties have agreed to dissolve their parallel government established during the insurgency. The UN has been informed of the command structure of the Maoist army, their personnel, and ammunition inventory in the cantonments. The Army is going to store its arms and ammunition at one location at Chhauni in Kathmandu whereas the Maoists are required to deposit their arms at seven camps and 21 satellite camps across the country.[6] The monitoring team is headed by the representative of the UN who is currently carrying out arms management in Nepal. The team is assisted by 111 retired Gorkha soldiers who have been trained to carry out the task of arms management. Both sides have also agreed to assist each other in marking landmines and booby traps used during the time of conflict and remove and destroy them within sixty days. Also, any weapons not registered with the UN would be seized by the government.

The agreement provides for rehabilitation of the Maoist army. It was agreed that their integration into the state security forces would be determined by a special committee. The agreement also specifies that Maoist combatants who were born after 25 May, 1988 would be automatically discharged. The agreement provides assistance packages for the voluntarily discharged personnel, though details of the assistance package are not specified.

Challenges Ahead

The challenges to political and institutional restructuring in Nepal are manifold. Serious differences of opinion in the Eight Party Alliance have delayed many agreed deadlines. Sorting out internal differences among the alliance partners has also delayed the Constituent Assembly poll. The government is yet to appoint election officials and security personnel for some 17,500 polling booths. Parliament, however, has passed two important bills related to the elections. One concerns the right, functions, and responsibilities of the Election Commission and the second pertains to the revision of voters list and delineation of the electoral constituencies.

There has been persisting tension regarding the Maoists' activities and their violation of the arms agreement. Earlier Prime Minister Koirala had suggested complete disarmament of the Maoist cadres for them to become part of the government whereas the Maoists were

6. These camps are Kailali, Surkhet, Rolpa, Palpa, Kavre, Sindhuli, Ilam.

hinting that they were only ready for 'some' kind of arms management. The UN reports that 31,152 Maoist cadres have surrendered with 3,475 weapons.[7] There is no way to authenticate whether the Maoists have faithfully abided by the agreement to surrender arms. The fear will always remain whether some of the arms could be used to terrorise people and also to affect the electoral process. There have also been allegations that the Maoist cadres are carrying arms and displaying them in public meetings. The assurance by Prachanda, Maoist supremo, to investigate the matter has not assuaged dissatisfaction. Still suspicious of the Nepal Army, which is yet to be restructured and democratised, the Maoists want to keep the option of going back to war if their basic aspirations remain unfulfilled.

Also, though the common minimum programme pledges the Maoists to return all seized properties to their owners and help return of the displaced persons respectfully, there are media reports that the Maoist cadres are engaged in extortion. Recently, there was a country-wide traders' strike that was supported by seventy business groups protesting the abduction of 25 entrepreneurs by Maoists.[8] Though the Maoists have pledged themselves to dissolve people's government and people's judiciary there are allegations that in areas dominated by Maoists these institutions continue to operate.

Rehabilitation of Maoist armed cadres will be a major challenge, given the problem of unemployment in Nepal. Already there are reports that members of the Youth Communist League (YCL) are engaged in extortion and terrorising people. The YCL, which was formed in 1990, was revived in January 2007 and is believed to be led by People's Liberation Army commanders who did not surrender to the UN. The probability of the Maoist cadres bringing their strong ideological underpinnings into any institution they are absorbed in would also make integration difficult.

Restructuring of the state and building a sound political edifice for new Nepal is also a challenge. One of the major political planks of the

---

7. UN report dated 26 April, 2007 at *http://www.reliefweb.int/rw/RWB.NSF/db900SID/EGUA-72SPXA?OpenDocument* (accessed on 1 May, 2007).
8. *www.ft.com/cms/s/36f4a4ea-d6fa-11db-8de3-000b5df10621.html* (accessed on 20 March, 2007).

Maoists and the subsequent people's uprising has been the struggle for an inclusive democracy. Their political success and proposed socio-economic programme have raised expectations among the people. This has encouraged different ethnic groups to demand representation in the interim constitution. For instance, the Newar organisation 'Newa Deya Dabbu' is critical of the interim constitution. The challenge before the country would be to meet the expectations of all the marginalised groups. Since Nepal is likely to be governed for the next two years on the basis of the interim constitution till the Constituent Assembly finalises a new constitution, many groups see the current period as their last chance to get a fair deal from the system.

The Terai issue is one such problem of marginalisation and under-representation. *The Janatantric Terai Mukti Morcha* (JTMM), that initially spearheaded the movement, challenged the political authority and is fighting for the Madhesias' rights. JTMM split and is led by two former Maoist leaders from Terai—Goit and Jwala Singh. Their demands have ranged from separatism to autonomy with right to self-determination.[9] The Terai-based Madhesi Janadhikar Forum (MJF) is also raising similar demands. Initially, violence was directed against the Paharis (hill people). Pahari–Terai tussles were prominent during the *Panchayat* regime as the government was trying to promote a nationalism that is associated with the Pahari culture. The Madhesis have always complained that they have not been given adequate representation in Parliament, the armed forces, and government services. These sentiments gained strength during the April 2006 people's uprising and are now being fuelled by both the factions of JTMM and MJF. Other militant groups that have mushroomed in the Terai are the Terai Tiger, Terai Cobra, Nepal Defence Army, and *Chure Bhawar Ekta Samaj*. The government has taken certain steps to address the grievances of the Terai people, but the latter do not seem to think they are far-going enough. In July 2006 the government distributed citizenship certificates to the people in the region. The new Nepal Citizenship Act undertakes to provide citizenship certificate to those

9. JTMM's demands include independent state of Terai, letting indigenous people of Terai to operate Army, Police, and administration in the Terai region, revenue collected from Terai to be utilised for Terai development, and cessation of infiltration of Nepalis (paharis) to the region.

born before 15 April, 1990 after they produce landownership/house ownership certificate or provide registration number in the voters' list.

The political parties and Maoists differ regarding the future of the monarchy. Koirala, after taking over as Prime Minster stated that constitutional monarchy is a part of parliamentary democracy but the Maoists are non-compromising in demanding the abolition of the monarchy, insisting that Nepal should be declared a republic before the elections. This could be because of two factors. First, the Maoists are not sure whether they will muster enough majority in the Constituent Assembly to push their agenda forward. Second, they are not sure of the political parties, especially the Nepali Congress, and some international actors. According to the latest International Crisis Group report, Gyanendra still has the support of a section of the Army and the 3000 strong palace guard.[10]

With the elections to the Constituent Assembly scheduled for 22 November 2007, the Maoists are jittery on the issue of monarchy. A clause has been inserted in the interim constitution to abolish monarchy with two-thirds majority vote if he is found to pose grave obstacles to the holding of the Constituent Assembly elections. The Maoists have been accusing the monarchy of fomenting trouble in the Terai, though it is a fact that the grievances of the Terai people are genuine. Blanket branding of people and parties as 'reactionary force' may have negative implications for the future of Nepal.

On 24 April 2007, the first anniversary of his surrender of power, King Gyanendra visited the Pashupatinath temple escorted by the Army and received a 21-gun salute from the Army. In his message to the people he also defended his role in suppressing the people's movement. There have been differences of opinion between the Maoists and the political parties on issues such as the structure of the interim government, on approaches to the Terai issue, and the schedule for the Constituent Assembly elections. A squabbling interim government would provide political space to the monarchy to gain political legitimacy and thus pose itself as an institutional necessity.

The new constitution will have to deal with many delicate issues

10. ICG Report No. 132, *Nepal Maoists: Purists or Pragmatists?*, 18 May, 2007: 22.

like distributive justice and proportional representation of ethno-linguistic groups. Negotiations on many issues will depend on the electoral strength of the Maoists, who have been vocal on such issues. The sympathies for the Maoists and their political programme may not, however, necessarily transform into ballot. After arousing expectations of a representative government in people's minds if the government fails to deliver on the ground, Nepal would head for a greater crisis of governance. The monarchy is waiting in the wings for such an opportune moment to gain political legitimacy. A positive factor of the Maoist insurgency is that it has sensitised the political parties to the people's needs and one can expect a greater responsiveness from them. From an elitist state structure, it appears that Nepal is geared towards becoming a representative one.

The interim constitution does not have a blueprint for economic capacity building. There is a need to invest in infrastructure and economic capacity building of Nepal to cope with rising expectations. Employment generation needs to be prioritised. As the attention is more on political restructuring, Nepal would find it difficult to accommodate the economic aspirations that follow such a revolutionary change.

India and the Crisis in Nepal

India is largely perceived as a supporter of democracy in Nepal. Historically, India played an important role in the short-lived democratic experiment in the 1950s. It was critical of the dismissal of B.P. Koirala's ministry and assumption of power by King Mahendra. India's sympathy has always remained with the political parties and their democratic experiment as many of the Nepalese political leaders have had close links with the Indian leaders. India has supported constitutional monarchy. Therefore, the King saw India as an impediment to his unbridled political ambition. Through the decade of the 1990s India supported the twin-pillar theory of political stability: multi-party democracy and constitutional monarchy. India was critical of direct assumption of power by the King on 1 February 2005 and declined to participate in the SAARC (South Asian Association for Regional Cooperation) summit scheduled in Dhaka that month to demonstrate its displeasure at the developments in

Nepal. However, India emphasised the twin-pillar theory and made efforts to convince the King to take steps in this regard. Prime Minister Manmohan Singh met King Gyanendra on the sidelines of the Asia–Africa Summit in Jakarta on 23 April 2005. This meeting broke the ice between the two neighbours. Subsequently, India's Minister of External Affairs visited Nepal on 21–23 July 2005, which was a high-level visit after the imposition of direct rule by the King. Though India facilitated the Maoist–SPA agreement of 22 November, 2005 it continued to work for the twin-pillar theory. Foreign Secretary Shyam Saran during his visit to Kathmandu on 14 December, 2005 emphasised that restoration of peace and stability and economic recovery of Nepal is in the interest of India. He emphasised the need for the 'constitutional forces' to work together. Even though there was perceptible anti-monarchy feeling in Nepal as demonstrated during the April 2006 popular uprising, India persisted in its advocacy of the twin-pillar theory of political stability. India was quick to issue a statement on 21 April welcoming the King's invitation to the political parties to nominate an interim Prime Minister even though the political parties and the Maoists rejected it. New Delhi's approach to the April 2006 *Jana Andolan*-II gave an impression that when Nepal is prepared for radical reforms, India is not prepared to give up its old thinking that only a constitutional monarchy is seen as a panacea for a stable Nepal. India's sympathies with the royals were intact in spite of the fact that King Gyanendra was openly playing the China card to the discomfort of India.[11] It was the King's obduracy that prompted India to rethink its Nepal policy.

In the past, India was critical of the Maoists and looked upon them with a degree of apprehension, given their similar ideological moorings with the Indian Maoists. From the beginning the Maoists contested India's argument for constitutional monarchy as they perceived monarchy as a symbol of feudalism and class exploitation. The current Indian policy seems to indicate that it has factored the people's aspiration as expressed in the April 2006 popular uprising

---

11. King Gyanendra met President Hu Jintao of China in Jakarta on the sidelines of the Asia-Africa Summit in 2005. China supported the King's effort in tackling the Maoists. Earlier, during the visit of the Nepal Chief of Army Staff to Beijing in June 2004 the two countries signed a security cooperation agreement and the Chinese promised to deliver military hardware and logistic support.

and has recognised the Maoists as legitimate political actors in Nepal.

Officially, India is supportive of the political initiatives in Nepal. It has provided various economic grants for the reconstruction of Nepal[12] but is reluctant to be directly involved in its political restructuring. India's support is crucial for Nepal. In fact, India was critical of the monarchy taking over direct power on 1 February 2005 and along with the US and the UK withdrew crucial political support to the monarchy. India suspended its defence supplies to pressurise the King to restore Parliament. But all three countries were initially reluctant to deal with the Maoists; the US still continues to have strong reservations regarding the group.

India's political support is crucial to Nepal. While addressing academics, security analysts, and policymakers in the Observer Research Foundation (ORF) in December 2006, Prachanda said, "We want to work with India because from whichever angle we see, whether historical, cultural, linguistic or geo-political, without getting involved with India in a serious interaction, the formation of new Nepal is difficult and we realise that."[13] Maoist settlement in politics would also have critical implication for the Indian Maoists. Stability in Nepal would also assuage India's own security concerns.

Conclusion

The Maoists seem unlikely to revert to their much articulated 'people's war' stage, having realised by now that decisive military victory is impossible. The timing of the twelve-point agreement also indicates that the Maoists are amenable to some serious political adjustment after they achieve substantial military strength. Their military clout also enabled them to negotiate from a position of strength. Nevertheless, there is apprehension that if the peace process fails the Maoists may go back to violence as they retain their top cadres and most of arms.

---

12. India has offered a soft credit of Rs. 7.5 billion for the execution of infrastructure development projects and has increased its aid to Nepal's budget from Rs. 1.4 billion to Rs. 2.4 billion. Additionally, it has provided Rs. 1.3 billion to build modern check posts and Rs. 1.08 billion for establishment of a trauma centre. *http://www.fesnepal.org/reports/2006/annual_report/Political_report%202006.htm*
13. Prachanda's address in ORF, "Prospects of Building a New Nepal", 1(3) (December 2006): 3.

The year 2006 demonstrated people's political aspirations and saw the end of fourteen months of direct rule by King Gyanendra. In a most significant positive development, the political parties and Maoists came together to lead a people's movement against the king. Though doubts were raised about the durability of the alliance, given their different ideologies, both of them by staying together have instilled hope in the people's mind for a new Nepal with attenuation of marginalisation and inequality.

11

Afghanistan: Growing Uncertainties

VISHAL CHANDRA

"Afghanistan in 2006 was not supposed to be like this."

—Paul Rogers, "Afghanistan under siege", 23 November 2006[1]

After more than five years of externally sponsored political process and security, Afghanistan remains years away from stability and peace. It is believed that more than 4000 people, a quarter of them civilians, and more than 160 foreign soldiers were killed in Afghanistan in 2006, as compared to about 1600 people killed in 2005. The Taliban having resurrected themselves and poppy cultivation thriving, the war on terror in Afghanistan has ebbed. A further complicating factor is Pakistan's growing assertion against Kabul.

The Taliban Crescendo

"Unlike other wars, Afghan wars become serious only when they are over."

—Sir Olaf Caroe, the last British Governor of NWFP

The Taliban demonstrated clear indications of resurgence and clout. Retired US General Barry R. McCaffrey reported in June 2006 that "the Taliban operated in small units three years ago; last year, they grew to company-sized units of 100-plus men; and for this year's summer fighting season they are manoeuvring in 400-strong battalion-sized units." The Taliban now have 'excellent weapons' and 'new field equipment' and "new IED (improvised explosive device) technology and commercial communications. They appear to have received

1. *http://www.opendemocracy.net/conflict/afghanistan_4123.jsp*

excellent tactical, camouflage and marksmanship training" and "they are very aggressive and smart in their tactics."[2]

The *Newsline* magazine of Pakistan (June 2006) reported that the Taliban were controlling twenty districts in Kandahar, Uruzgan, Zabul and Helmand provinces. On 16 July 2006 Taliban guerrillas captured the towns of Garmser and Naway-e Barakzai in Helmand Province, before they were reportedly recaptured a few days later by the Afghan army with the help of US and NATO-led forces.[3] Deputy Interior Minister Abdul Malik Sidiqi had earlier accused Pakistan-based Lashkar-e-Tayyaba and Jamiat Ulema-e-Islam of assisting the Taliban in taking over Garmser. There have been many reports about the Taliban capturing district headquarters, raiding government buildings, killing government officials, Afghan police and army men, burning schools, and killing teachers and tribal elders in the restive southern and eastern parts of the country.

In February 2007 a six-week-long intense battle took place between NATO forces and the Taliban guerrillas in Kajaki District of Helmand Province where an important hydroelectric dam was being restored. Continuing with their raids on urban areas, the Taliban claimed to have captured Nawzad District in Helmand in March 2007, and Giro District (a mere 176 kilometres from the capital Kabul) in Ghazni Province in April 2007. Similarly, the Taliban briefly held a crucial highway in Tagab District (64 kilometres from Kabul) in Kapisa Province. In a discernible pattern in their offensive during 2006-07, the Taliban overrun towns in the rural areas and also focus their assaults in areas close to Kabul.

Suicide attacks and roadside bombings are a new phenomenon in Afghan insurgency. It is said that more than 115 suicide attacks occurred during the year, which accounted for killing of 270 Afghan civilians and 17 international soldiers. In addition, about 110 schools across southern and eastern parts of the country were reportedly

---

2. Borchgrave, Arnaud De (2006). "Middle Ages on Comeback Trail?", 29 June, *http://www.upi.com/InternationalIntelligence/view.php?StoryID=20060629-092541-7764r*. General Barry R. McCaffrey (retd.) is a Professor of International Affairs at West Point, the US military academy.

3. See "Combined Forces Command—Afghanistan Statement", 18 July, 2006, at *http://www.cfc-a.centcom.mil/News%20Release/2006/07-July/Combined%20Forces%20Command%20–%20Afghanistan%20Statement.htm*.

burned down.[4] According to another report quoting a US military intelligence officer:

> Suicide attacks in 2006 totalled 139, up from 27 in 2005 and the number of attacks with roadside bombs more than doubled, from 783 in 2005 to 1677 last year. The number of what the military calls 'direct attacks,' meaning attacks by insurgents using small arms, grenades and other weapons, surged from 1558 in 2005 to 4542 last year.[5]

The US invasion of Iraq in 2003 not only provided the Taliban with enough opportunity to collate on the fringes of Afghanistan and in the tribal areas of Pakistan, it also led to deepening of its linkages with al-Qaeda and other Arab Islamist militant groups. In an interview to *Al-Jazeera* aired on 31 May 2006, Taliban commander Mullah Dadullah described al-Qaeda as "a friendly and brotherly organisation, which shares our ideology and concepts." He asserted that the Taliban "have close ties and constant contacts with it", and that their "cooperation is ideal." On military cooperation with al-Qaeda he said,

> ... when we need them, we ask for their help. For example, the bombings we carry out—we learned it from them. We learn other types of operations from them as well. We have give-and-take relations with the mujahideen of Iraq. We cooperate and help each other.[6]

The rise of former mujahideen commander Jalal-ud Din Haqqani, a known sympathiser of the Arab mujahideen since the days of the anti-Soviet war in the military structure of the Taliban, and the Taliban's adoption of techniques of urban warfare from the Iraqi militants, are proof of the involvement of a larger Arab component in the resurrected Taliban.

Afghan Armed Forces: Low in the Order of Priority

According to Defence Minister Abdul Rahim Wardak, an army of 150,000 to 200,000 soldiers would be needed to secure the country.

---

4. See "2006: Year of Bloodshed in Afghanistan", 26 December, 2006, at *http://www.hindustantimes.com/news/7598_1880566,000500020005.htm*
5. Burns, Robert (2007). "Sharp Increase in Taliban Attacks", 16 January, at *http://www.time.com/time/world/article/0,8599,1578214,00.html*
6. See "Taliban Military Commander Mullah Dadallah: We are in Contact with Iraq Mujahideen. Non-Islamic Countries offered help in Defeating the Americans", 31 May, 2006, at *http://www.memritv.org/Transcript.asp?P1=1156*

The current strength of the Afghan National Army (ANA), which is expected to be 70,000 by 2009, is unverifiable. According to Afghan official sources, the ANA comprised 36,000 soldiers as of January 2007. Desertions and severe logistical problems beset the nascent army. According to the ANA Commander of the 205th Corps, Gen. Rahmatullah Raufi, about 80 per cent of the soldiers and 50 per cent of the officers in his corps are illiterate. Only 20 per cent of soldiers have a professional army background, the rest being former militia fighters or young recruits.[7]

General McCaffrey's report, cited earlier, describes ANA as "miserably under-resourced" which "is now a major morale factor for their soldiers." He adds:

> They have shoddy small arms—described by Defense Minister Wardak as much worse than he had as a Mujahideen fighting the Soviets twenty years ago. Afghan field commanders told me they try to seize weapons from the Taliban who they believe are much better armed ...(They) have little ammo... no mortars, few machine guns, no MK19 grenade guns, and no artillery...no helicopter or fixed transport or attack aviation now or planned...no body armor...no Kelvar helmets ...no light armored wheeled vehicles.

As for the Afghan National Police (ANP), whose US-sponsored training programme is running three years behind schedule, McCaffrey's report observed that "They are in a disastrous condition, badly equipped, corrupt, incompetent, poorly led and trained, riddled by drug use and lacking any semblance of...infrastructure."[8]

NATO's Half-hearted Expansion

> "We would be perfectly happy to leave (Afghanistan) in three years and without firing one shot because our job is to protect the reconstruction."
>
> —John Reid, former British Defence Secretary, 23 April 2006[9]

Apprehensions, contradictions and logistical shortcomings have

7. Baldauf, Scott (2006). "A 'half full' Afghan Army", 10 February, at *http://www.csmonitor.com/2006/0210/p06s02-wosc.html?s=widep*
8. Borchgrave, n.2.
9. Reid said this during his visit to the British forces in Afghanistan, See "UK Troops 'to target terrorists'", 24 April, 2006, at *http://news.bbc.co.uk/2/hi/uk_news/politics/4935532.stm*

characterised NATO's Afghan mission. Lack of clarity among member-states over the rules of engagement have remained its biggest weakness. Lt. Gen. David Richards, the British commander of the NATO-led forces, observed that "Two years ago, when the North Atlantic Council agreed to this plan, they probably didn't know what they were getting into."[10] NATO Secretary General Jaap de Scheffer has been constantly lamenting shortage of troops and lack of required support from member states. Even the ambitious Riga Summit at Latvia on 28-29 November 2006 failed to elicit a greater commitment for the Afghan mission.

The NATO-led International Security Assistance Force (ISAF) took over the military operations from the US Coalition Forces in southern Afghanistan on 31 July and in eastern Afghanistan on 5 October as part of its third and fourth phases of expansion in Afghanistan. With about 12,000 troops, the US remained the single-largest contributor to the approximately 31,000 NATO led forces drawn from nearly 37 countries, including 11 non-NATO countries, during 2006. The remaining 8000 of the nearly 20,000 US troops in Afghanistan continued to be part of the Coalition Forces mainly operating in the eastern provinces bordering Pakistan.

NATO forces were confronted with strong resistance from the Taliban as they moved into southern Afghanistan. There was also growing discrepancy between the security assessment by the commanders in the field and their governments back home. An example is the dichotomy in the assessment of Lt. Gen. David Richards on 21 July and that of Des Browne, the British Defence Secretary, a day earlier. Des Browne stated in the British Parliament that "Neither the Taliban, nor the range of illegally armed groups, currently pose a threat to the long-term stability of Afghanistan."[11] General Richards on the other hand described the situation in Afghanistan as 'close to anarchy' and referred to "the lack of unity

---

10. Graff, Peter (2006). "NATO's Afghan Commander Bemoans Force Shortfalls", July 21, *at http://ca.today.reuters.com/news/newsArticle.aspx?type=topNews&storyID=2006-07-21T135830Z_01_L21755754_RTRIDST_0_NEWS-AFGHAN-NATO-COL.XML*

11. Carlin, Brendan (2006). "Browne in Row Over 'no-threat' Taliban", 20 July, at *http://www.telegraph.co.uk/news/main.jhtml;jsessionid=2SUUMVKE4FOCDQFIQMFCFFWAVCBQYIV0?xml=/news/2006/07/20/wafg20.xml*

between different agencies." He found "poorly regulated private security companies" as unethical and "all too ready to discharge firearms." He also warned that due to continuing logistical shortcomings, the western forces were "running out of time" in terms of fulfilling the expectations of the Afghan people.[12]

In a similar example of dichotomy of perception, NATO's supreme allied commander, Marine Gen. James L. Jones, described in March— rising opium production as the "most serious problem" confronting Afghanistan but denied that the Taliban and al-Qaeda could "restart an insurgency of any size and major scope."[13] A few days earlier the Director of the US Defense Intelligence Agency, Lt. Gen. Michael D. Maples, had stated that "Despite significant progress on the political front, the Taliban-dominated insurgency remains a capable and resilient threat.... We judge that the insurgency appears emboldened by perceived tactical successes and will be active this spring."[14]

As a way out from incessant fighting with the Taliban insurgents and high level of collateral damage, British forces entered into a pact in October with tribal elders in Musa Qala District of Helmand Province. In return for withdrawal of British forces from the district the tribes agreed to maintain their own security and not allow the Taliban to enter the district. In spite of this arrangement, the Taliban reportedly captured the district in February 2007.

Highlights of US-Kabul Relations

On 1 March 2006 President George W. Bush made a 'surprise' five-hour stopover in Afghanistan *en route* to India, the first by a US President in 47 years. President Bush praised President Karzai and his government and reiterated the United States' continued commitment to Afghanistan and the capture of Osama bin Laden. Perhaps a visit by the US President to the first battleground of the war on terror was long

---

12. Norton-Taylor, Richard (2006). "Afghanistan Close to Anarchy, Warns General", 21 July, at *http://www.guardian.co.uk/afghanistan/story/0,,1826303,00.html*
13. Tyson, Ann Scott (2006). "Afghan Threat Played Down", 7 March, at *http://www.washingtonpost.com/wp-dyn/content/article/2006/03/06/AR2006030601571.html*
14. Pincus, Walter (2006). "Growing Threat seen in Afghan Insurgency", 1 March, at *http://www.washingtonpost.com/wp-dyn/content/article/2006/02/28/AR2006022800874.html?referrer=email*

overdue. The visit could also be seen in the backdrop of the United States' proposed reduction in its troop levels by 20 per cent in 2006.

Kabul Demands Reassessment of the War on Terror in Afghanistan

With the Taliban taking battle lines closer to urban areas and key national highways, the US Coalition Forces launched large-scale military operations, especially Operation Mountain Thrust, prior to NATO taking over operations in southern Afghanistan. This led to killing of hundreds of Taliban fighters and often avoidable collateral damage. Given the high level of casualties and worsening security situation in the predominantly Pashtun southern Afghanistan, President Karzai asked for a reassessment of the anti-terror campaign of the US Coalition and NATO forces. In July he stated: "It is not acceptable for us that in all this fighting, Afghans are dying. In the last three to four weeks, 500 to 600 Afghans were killed. (Even) if they are Taliban, they are sons of this land." He urged broadening the scope of the war on terror to address the root causes of the terrorism and suggested, "We must engage strategically in disarming terrorism by stopping the sources of supply of money, training, equipment and motivation" (read Pakistan).[15]

Afghan-Pak Relations: Rickety as Ever

President Karzai's Visit to Islamabad

> "I'm going to Pakistan especially to talk with the President of Pakistan and the government there about the issue of terrorism...I will talk to them about these bombings going on in places like Kandahar, Paktiya Province, Khost, and Mazar-e Sharif."
>
> —President Hamid Karzai, February 2006[16]

During his state visit to Islamabad, (15-17 February) President Karzai gave expression to Kabul's conviction that the Taliban leadership was ensconced in Pakistan. He was reported to have handed over a list of 100-150 Taliban and other militants, along with the

15. Regan, Tom (2006). "Karzai Questions US, NATO Tactics in Afghanistan", 23 June, at *http://www.csmonitor.com/2006/0623/dailyUpdate.html*
16. Synovitz, Ron (2006). "Afghanistan: Karzai to Consult Pakistan about Suicide Bombings", 15 February, at *http://www.rferl.org/featuresarticle/2006/2/A645C166-D11D-48BC-ADBA-454787683128.html*

addresses and telephone numbers of some of them, alleged to be based in the tribal expanse of Pakistan's NWFP (North West Frontier Province) and in the Pashtun-dominated areas in Balochistan Province, and details of supposed Taliban training camps and guerrilla bases located inside Pakistan.

President Musharraf in his interview to CNN on 5 March dismissed the list as outdated and a waste of time, and accused President Karzai of being "totally oblivious of what is happening in his own country."[17] Four days earlier, in an interview to BBC on 1 March he said,

> ... if President Karzai thinks everything is happening from Pakistan, I totally disagree. He should put his own house in order, a lot is happening in Afghanistan also. More is happening in Afghanistan itself, less is happening from Pakistan. We are trying to put our house in order, he should think of his own house, instead of keep blaming Pakistan.[18]

Islamabad also accused Kabul of letting India carry out its subversive activities in Pakistan's restive Balochistan Province and in areas bordering its tribal areas through its consulates in Kandahar and Jalalabad. Karzai responded by emphatically remarking on 15 February that Afghanistan's "relations with India in no way, no way, no way will impact" ties between Kabul and Islamabad.[19] He opposed the idea of fencing the border between Pakistan and Afghanistan and instead proposed an open-border policy as a prelude to other confidence-building measures (CBMs).

On 18 May, while addressing tribal elders during his visit to Kunar Province, Karzai asked Pakistan to forget the days when Pakistan exercised influence over Afghanistan. Describing Mullah Omar, leader of the Taliban, as a coward "hiding in the other country and sending youth to kill our people", he warned that "Pakistan wants that Afghanistan be its military base but that dream will never come

---

17. See "President Musharraf's interview with CNN", 5 March, 2006, at *http://www.presidentofpakistan.gov.pk/FilesPressRoom/Interviews/36200620935AMCNNWolf.pdf*
18. See "Musharraf interview: Full Transcript", 1 March, 2006, at *http://news.bbc.co.uk/2/hi/south_asia/4761338.stm*
19. Tarzi, Amin (2006). "Afghanistan and Pakistan: 'Inseparable Twins' in Need of Separation", *RFE/RL Afghanistan Report*, 5(6) (28 February), at *http://www.rferl.org/featuresarticle/2006/02/eb699008-7c75-4447-bab1-7f6ecb83a9b2.html*

true."[20] On the same day Colonel Chris Vernon, British chief of staff for southern Afghanistan, also told *The Guardian* newspaper that the Taliban leadership was coordinating its campaigns in Afghanistan from the Pakistani city of Quetta.[21] Even after Afghan Foreign Minister Rangin Dadfar Spanta's visit to Islamabad during 22–23 June, the Pak–Afghan discord continued.

Pakistan's North Waziristan Deal

On 5 September the Pakistan Government was reported to have entered into a 'peace pact' with the 45-member tribal 'shura' of North Waziristan. The shura was dominated either by pro-Taliban representatives or by Pakistani Taliban themselves but Islamabad insisted that the 'peace pact' was signed with the tribal elders. The pro-Taliban Jamiat-ul-Ulema-e Islami (JUI) was said to have played an important role in brokering the 'deal'. The 'deal' provided that the Pakistan army would return to its earlier position in the province in return for an undertaking that the Taliban militants would not attack its forces, government installations or carry out attacks across the border into Afghanistan. According to another provision, the foreign students and militants residing in the region would be required to either live peacefully or leave the province.

With the signing of this 'deal', the US war on terror receded from the entire Waziristan region, which has been the cradle of Taliban resurrection. The Taliban found a vast space and a supporting populace in Pakistan's tribal agencies to fall back upon every time they are threatened. It also brought to the fore Pakistan's delicate hold over its vast tribal expanse in its north-west and the institutional weaknesses inherent in the Pakistani polity. The withdrawal of Pakistani forces virtually made Waziristan a free run for the Taliban forces. The US Coalition Force active in Nangarhar and Nuristan provinces bordering Pakistan alleged that the attacks from across the border doubled or trebled since the signing of the 'peace pact.' Even so, the 'deal' could not have been without the backing of the US and Britain. In fact, it

20. See "Pakistan no More a Kingmaker, says Karzai", 19 May, 2006, at *http://www.dailytimes.com.pk/default.asp?page=2006%5C05%5C19%5Cstory_19-5-2006_pg1_3*
21. Walsh, Declan (2006). "Pakistan Sheltering Taliban, says British officer", 19 May, at *http://www.guardian.co.uk/afghanistan/story/0,,1778443,00.html*

was a prelude to British forces replicating the same in the Taliban-infested Musa Qala District in Helmand in October, mentioned earlier. The British Minister of State for Foreign and Commonwealth Affairs, Kim Howells, while terming the North Waziristan pact as "a good example for Afghanistan", and denying allegations of Pakistan as a "source of terrorism" during his visit to Islamabad on 9 September, stated, "We'll have to see how it turns out. It's very much an experiment...but it's got some interesting prospects, one wonders if it could be applied to the other side of the Afghan border."[22] On the same issue, US Vice President Dick Cheney while praising General Musharraf in his interview to NBC News (10 September 2006) stated, "This is a man who has demonstrated great courage under very difficult political circumstances and been a great ally for the United States."[23]

President Musharraf Visits Kabul

> "There are al-Qaeda and Taliban in both Afghanistan and Pakistan, clearly they are crossing from the Pakistan side and causing bomb blasts in Afghanistan."
>
> —President Pervez Musharraf, September 2006, in Kabul[24]

Immediately after signing the North Waziristan 'peace pact', President Musharraf visited Kabul during 6-7 September apparently with the objective of easing tension between the two countries. President Musharraf's statement about al-Qaeda and Taliban elements crossing from Pakistan to Afghanistan was welcomed by Kabul and both sides spoke of reconciliation and joint efforts to combat terrorism. Resident Musharraf also spoke of destroying the Taliban command structure. At the same time, he made it clear that his government was not "behind anything that is happening in Afghanistan." He argued that if Pakistan were to support the Taliban "the coalition would become the enemy of Pakistan and start attacking Pakistan. Would we be so foolish as to do this?"[25] His visit ended with a joint statement

---

22. See "Senior British Diplomat: Pakistan not a 'Source of Terrorism'", 8 September, 2006, at *http://www.iht.com/articles/ap/2006/09/08/asia/AS_GEN_Pakistan_Britain.php*
23. See "Interview of the Vice President by Tim Russert, NBC News, Meet the Press", 10 September, 2006, at *http://www.whitehouse.gov/news/releases/2006/09/20060910.html*
24. Gall, Carlotta (2006). "Pakistani Leader Admits Taliban Cross into Afghanistan", 7 September, at *http://www.nytimes.com/2006/09/07/world/asia/07cnd-afghan.html?ref=asia*
25. Ibid.

in which both governments "agreed that extremism, terrorism and the phenomenon of Talibanisation were a common threat to both Afghanistan and Pakistan", and "reaffirmed their commitment to further intensify their cooperation and coordination in jointly fighting these threats."[26] However, the war of words between Kabul and Islamabad soon resumed as suicide bombings and cross-border terrorism continued unabated.

Musharraf Spoke and Spoke: From Brussels to Washington

> "You'll be brought down to your knees if Pakistan doesn't cooperate with you. That is all that I would like to say. Pakistan is the main ally. If we were not with you, you won't manage anything."
>
> — President Pervez Musharraf to BBC Radio 4[27]

President Musharraf's newfound tirade against the Taliban continued during his subsequent tour to Europe and the US. While addressing the European Union's Foreign Relations Committee at Brussels on 15 September, he remarked that "the centre of gravity of terrorism has shifted from al-Qaeda to Taliban" and "this is a new element which has emerged." He added that the Taliban were a "more dangerous element" than al-Qaeda since they, unlike al-Qaeda, have "roots in the people."

Denying that Mullah Omar ever visited Pakistan after 1995, and referring to him as the centre of gravity of the Taliban forces, he reiterated the long-held Pakistani view that Mullah Omar was in southern Afghanistan. Emphasising for the need to counter both the Taliban and Talibanisation, he argued that "the battle if it is to be one has to address the centre of gravity of the force and centre of gravity lies in Mullah Omar which happens to be in southern Afghanistan."[28] On 25 September, in his address to the US Council on Foreign Relations, Musharraf warned that "...it would be disastrous if the local

26. See "Joint Statement on Visit to Afghanistan by H.E. Pervez Musharraf, President of the Islamic Republic of Pakistan", 7 September, 2006, at *http://www.mofa.gov.pk/Press_Releases/2006/Sep/PR_288_06.htm*
27. See "West 'will fail' without Pakistan", 30 September, 2006, at *http://news.bbc.co.uk/2/hi/south_asia/5394278.stm*
28. See "General Pervez Musharraf's address to European Union's Foreign Relation Committee–Brussels", 15 September, 2006, at *http://www.presidentofpakistan.gov.pk/FilesSpeeches/ForeignVisits/9182006110454PMEU%20Foreign%20Relation%20Committee%20Speech.pdf*

ethnic majority—that is, the Pashtun—were to join the Taliban and convert these Taliban actions into a people's movement against foreign occupations, like whatever happened against the Soviets." President Musharraf also argued in favour of the North Waziristan Pact, saying there are no military solutions to the problem. His remark, in his interview to BBC Radio 4 on 30 September, that the US and the UK have a 'historical debt' towards Pakistan as the latter had helped 'win the Cold War' for the West was considered as controversial.[29]

President Musharraf's increasingly assertive tone, especially during the British leg of his tour, could also be seen in the context of remarks made against him and on Pakistan's role in indirectly abetting terrorism and extremism in a paper by a researcher from the Defence Academy, a British Ministry of Defence think-tank, which was leaked just prior to his visit. The British Government issued a prompt denial and said that the paper did not reflect the views of the government.[30]

And Karzai Too Spoke

> "If I said he (Osama bin Laden) was in Pakistan, my friend Musharraf would be mad at us, but if I said he's in Afghanistan, it would not be true."
>
> — President Karzai, September 2006, in New York[31]

Though President Karzai during his visit to New York in September admitted that "Afghanistan cannot be peaceful and prosperous without the best of relations with Pakistan", at the same time stressed the need to tackle the root causes of terrorism which, in his opinion, lay outside of Afghanistan. Indirectly referring to Pakistan's role, President Karzai observed that "symptoms (of terrorism) are inside Afghanistan but the roots are outside."[32]

---

29. n. 26.
30. For details see "Key Quotes from the Document", 28 September, 2006, at *http://news.bbc.co.uk/1/hi/programmes/newsnight/5388426.stm*; Mark Urban, "Leak Highlights a Complex Relationship", 28 September, 2006, at *http:/news.bbc.co.uk/2/hi/south_asia/5390742.stm*
31. President Hamid Karzai made this remark in his interview to Fareed Zakaria, editor of *Newsweek International*, during his visit to the Council of Foreign Relations, New York. See Lionel Beehner, "Karzai says Pakistan Holds Key to Ending Afghan Violence", 21 September, 2006, at *http://www.cfr.org/publication/11504/*
32. Ibid.

Even the three-way summit by the US President on 27 September with the Afghan and Pakistan presidents failed to reconcile their differences. These differences continued to cast a shadow on the Afghan peace process as the two countries prepare for a Loya Jirga in 2007 comprising tribal representatives from both sides of the Durand Line.

Afghan Opium Survey: Breaking Yet Another Record

> "I don't know if you know this or not, but the Taliban government and al-Qaeda—the evil ones—use heroin trafficking in order to fund their murder. And one of our objectives is to make sure that Afghanistan is never used for that purpose again."
>
> —President George Bush, 15 November 2001[33]

According to the Afghan Opium Survey for 2006 released by the United Nations Office of Drugs & Crime (UNODC), Afghanistan has registered the "highest production level ever recorded", accounting for almost 92 per cent, up from 87 per cent in 2005, of the world's illicit opium production. The link between factional leaders, local commanders, government officials, poppy cultivators and heroin traders continues. Afghan farmers are encouraged to grow poppy both by the mujahideen factions and the Taliban. Many mujahideen leaders and commanders accused of being involved in drug trafficking have held senior positions in government. It was also primarily due to the dependence of the West and the Kabul government on the mujahideen factions in keeping the political process going that little could be done to curb the drug menace.

India Staying the Course in Afghanistan

Sustaining the growing momentum of its relationship with Afghanistan despite several constraints has been the biggest challenge before India, especially as newer threats emerge to destabilise Afghanistan's nascent political process. As the Taliban emerge from the fringe and try to reassert their position in a highly fragmented and unstable Afghan politics, it is time for India to give a fresh look to its Afghanistan policy.

---

33. See "President Bush and President Putin talk to Crawford Students", 15 November, 2001, at *http://www.whitehouse.gov/news/releases/2001/11/20011115-4.html*

India as a neighbour and as the sixth-largest donor to Afghan reconstruction (about US $750 million) is directly affected by the continuing instability in Afghanistan, and therefore has legitimate security concerns. Apart from their traditionally cordial ties India's relations with Afghanistan have been central to both its overall security and its growing economic interests in regions beyond Afghanistan. In times to come, Pakistan, which has been wary of India's growing influence in post-Taliban Afghanistan, will continue to be a notable factor in Afghanistan because of geographic, ethno-political, and economic reasons. Also, as a frontline ally of the US in its war on terror, Pakistan will remain entwined with the United States' larger interests in the South-Central Asia region.

Given the nature of Afghan politics and the regional dynamics, modest defence cooperation between India and Afghanistan is a pragmatic option. Direct military involvement in Afghan wars, known for queer alliances and tribal ebullience, could be perilous, as history shows. Afghan factions have been known to gradually mould their allies and foes alike to their advantage. India could well heed the advice of this Afghan proverb: "Keep your friendships but don't touch the problems of your friends." Perhaps, India will have to continue to plough through a complex and an uncertain Afghan politics, often enmeshed with the interests of extra-regional powers and regional actors.

The year 2006 saw a regular exchange of high-level visits between the two countries. During President Karzai's state visit to India during 9–13 April three MoUs (memorandums of understanding) were signed on education, rural development, and standardisation between the Bureau of Indian Standards and Afghanistan National Standardisation Authority. This was President Karzai's fourth visit to India since December 2001. Prime Minister Manmohan Singh visited Kabul on 28–29 August 2005.

President Karzai's proposal to form "a trilateral structure of cooperation" among the three countries which "would release the best energy of this region and bring quicker progress and economic betterment to it" was seen as consonant with the Indian view on regional cooperation. India hosted the Second Regional Economic

Cooperation Conference (RECC) on Afghanistan at New Delhi on 18-19 November, which President Karzai attended. India also played a significant role in the entry of Afghanistan into SAARC (South Asian Association for Regional Cooperation), and President Karzai attended the 14th SAARC Summit meeting held in New Delhi on 3-4 April 2007, where Afghanistan was formally welcomed as the eighth member of the South Asian grouping. India also conferred the Indira Gandhi Prize for Peace, Disarmament and Development on the Afghan President on 19 November, 2006.

During the visit of External Affairs Minister Pranab Mukherjee to Kabul on 23-24 January, 2007 India announced an additional assistance $100 million, taking the total amount pledged by India towards Afghan reconstruction to $750 million. India and Afghanistan also signed a MoU together with UNDP (United Nations Development Programme) on Capacity Building in Public Administration.

Perspectives

In August 1996, a month before he was put to death by the Taliban, President Mohammad Najibullah said in an interview to an American journalist:

> We have a common task—Afghanistan, the US and the civilised world—to launch a joint struggle against fundamentalism. If fundamentalism comes to Afghanistan, war will continue for many years. Afghanistan will turn into a centre of world smuggling for narcotic drugs. Afghanistan will be turned into a centre for terrorism.[34]

These words have proved prophetic. Five years after the events of 11 September 2001, the Taliban stands resurrected and opium poppy cultivation in Afghanistan has broken previous records. New battle lines appear to be shaping up in the three decades old Afghan civil war. The call by President Karzai to the West to re-strategise the war on terror and his reported proposal to arm the tribes carry the trappings of the failing war on terror in Afghanistan. With the Taliban and their allies pushing hard into the Pashtun heartland, one finds the

34. See Michael Griffin, "The Unwelcome Guest", 19 September 2001, at *http://www.guardian.co.uk/afghanistan/story/0,1284,554239,00.html*

Western forces grappling to retain control over the urban areas, as was the case with the Soviet and Afghan government forces in the 1980s.

With the 'central front' of the war on terror having shifted to Iraq, and the failure of the Bonn process to prioritise institution building in Afghanistan, the resurrection of the Taliban and the increased assertion by Pakistan in Afghan affairs were anticipated.

NATO's endless lamentations over shortage of troops and necessary logistics, and with the Pakistan Army having gradually extricated itself from the Waziristan region, the Afghan war seems to be coming full circle. With a narrow counter-terrorism and a narrower counter-narcotics policy, the war on terror in Afghanistan has undermined Kabul's quest for stability and authority, and has contributed to the resurrection of the Taliban. The persistent incongruity in the reform-oriented objectives of the political process and the alQaeda-centric militaristic agenda of the war on terror bodes ill for the future of Afghanistan.

12

Naxalism/Left-wing Extremism in India

Purpose and Strategy

NAMRATA GOSWAMI

Introduction

Left-wing extremism in India has gradually metamorphosed from posing a limited 'threat potential' in its first phase of violent manifestation in the 1960s and 1970s into a serious internal security concern in recent years. Known popularly as Naxalites, after the district of Naxalbari in West Bengal where the first group of rebels staged an uprising in 1967, the rebel movement has regrouped, rearmed, and re-strategised to spread to strategically located Indian states, namely, Andhra Pradesh, Bihar, Chhattisgarh, Jharkhand, Karnataka, Madhya Pradesh, Maharashtra, Uttar Pradesh, and West Bengal. Headquartered in Dantewada and Bastar districts of Chhattisgarh, the movement affected nearly 170 of India's 602 districts in 2006.[1] Reports in 2006 also indicated that the Naxalites possessed an armed force of 10,000 men and women, 6500 firearms, and cadre strength of 40,000.[2] In this context, an analysis of the Naxal movement in 2006 to diagnose trends and provide certain alternative policy choices towards effective management of the conflict is in order.

Rationale for the Naxalite Movement

Lewis A. Coser argues that "minority communities react violently to announce their unwillingness to accept a *status quo* of differential treatment since no other channels of communication seemed open to

---

1. Naxal Monitor (2006). A Quarterly Newsletter of the Asian Centre for Human Rights 11 (April-June).
2. See "A Spectre Haunting India", *The Economist* (London), 17 August 2006. Also Phillip Bowring, "Maoists who Menace India", *International Herald Tribune*, 8 April 2006.

them."[3] The rationale for the Naxalite movement's expansion and consolidation is rooted in the inability of the legitimate political authority in India to provide avenues for structural uplift to the deprived sections of society in the affected states. The tribal population in these states views the Naxal movement as providing a viable alternative to its desperate social and economic conditions.[4] Naxalism, through its violent manifestation, has successfully drawn attention to the dismal conditions of the tribals in many of these states.

According to the 2001 census, about three quarters of Dantewada district (most affected by Naxal violence) consists of 1220 tribal villages. Of these, 1161 have no medical facility, 214 have no primary school, and the literacy rate is a meagre 29 per cent for men and 14 per cent for women.[5] Similarly, two other Naxalite-affected states, Bihar and Jharkhand, among the poorest states in India, have a literacy rate of 47 per cent and 54 per cent respectively, far behind Kerala with a 93 per cent literacy rate and the national average of 65 per cent. Consequently, tribals and lower castes, amongst India's poorest communities, form the Naxals' cadre base. Ironically, there are Naxalite-affected areas like Abujmarh in Chhattisgarh which remain unsurveyed and lack any civil administration.[6]

The Status Paper on the Naxal Problem, tabled in Parliament by the Union Home Minister Shivraj Patil on 13 March 2006, also stated that:

> The naxalites operate in vacuum created by absence of administrative and political institutions, espouse the local demands and take advantage of the disenchantment prevalent among the exploited segments of the population and seek to offer an alternative system of governance which promises emancipation of these segments from the clutches of 'exploiter' classes through the barrel of a gun.[7]

---

3. Coser, Lewis A. (1967). *Continuities in the Study of Social Conflict*. New York: Free Press 103. See also Coser (1956). *The Functions of Social Conflict*. New York: Free Press.
4. See Independent Citizens Initiative, *War in the Heart of India: An Enquiry into the Ground Situation in Dantewada District, Chhattisgarh*, 20 July 2006. See also Naxal Monitor, n. 1.
5. See 2001 Census at *http://www.censusindia.net* (accessed 5 December 2006).
6. Guha, Ramachandra (2006). "Revolutionaries", *The Telegraph* (Kolkata), 26 June.
7. *http://www.satp.org/satporgtp/countries/india/document/papers/06Mar13_Naxal%20Problem%20.htm (accessed on 12 December 2006).*

A similar view was expressed by Prime Minister Manmohan Singh in the meeting of the Chief Ministers of Naxalite-affected states on 13 April, 2006. He stated that it was a matter of grave concern that the Naxalites provided a sense of empowerment to the deprived sections of society through violent means because of the absence of civil administration and police in some of the affected areas.[8]

Stated Purpose of the Naxal Movement

The Naxalites state their main political purpose as establishing an alternative state structure in India by creating a 'red corridor' in Naxalite-affected states, stretching from the border of Nepal to central India to Karnataka in the south through violent struggle[9] (See Figure 12.1). To achieve this political objective, which requires local support, Naxalite rebel leaders take up causes like protecting people's rights of *Jal, Jangal and Jamin* (water, forest, and land) and providing justice through their committees like the Sangam and Jan Adalat (people's court).[10] Local support is crucial for the Naxalites for cadre recruitment, intelligence, logistics, and territorial control.

In August 2006 Ganesh Ueike, secretary of the West Bastar Divisional Committee of the Communist Party of India (Maoist) (CPI-(M)) stated that the Naxalite movement will expand to Kashmir and India's north-east, already plagued by violent secessionist movements.[11] Thuingaleng Muivah, general secretary of the National Socialist Council of *Nagalim* (Isak-Muivah) (NSCN-IM), also declared the formation of a United Front to forge unity among various revolutionary forces in India. He stated that "United Front is an

8. Prime Minister's Speech at the Chief Ministers' Meet on Naxalism, 13 April 2006, *at http://pmindia.nic.in/speech/content4print.asp?id=311* (accessed on 14 December 2006).

9. See *The Economist*, n. 2. Press Release of the CPI-Maoist on the 9th Congress, January-February 2007, at *http://www.satp.org/satporgtp/countries/india/maoist/documents/papers/19feb07.htm* (accessed on 23 March 2007). Also "The People's Guerrilla Army", at *http://www.satp.org/satporgtp/countries/india/maoist/documents/papers/PGA-Constitution.htm* (accessed on 23 March 2007).

10. The Naxalite organisational structure is headed by the Central Committee, followed by state or zonal committees, divisional committees, range committees, and village committees. See Independent Citizens Initiative, n. 4: 5. Also Rabindra Ray. *The Naxalites and their Ideology*. New Delhi: Oxford University Press, 2002.

11. See Guha, Ramachandra (2006). "How not to Fight Naxalism", mailed to the author in 2006; and Ramachandra Guha (2006). "The Battle for Bastar", *The Telegraph*, 28 June. Also see *The Economist*, n. 2.

Figure 12.1

Naxal-affected Areas in India

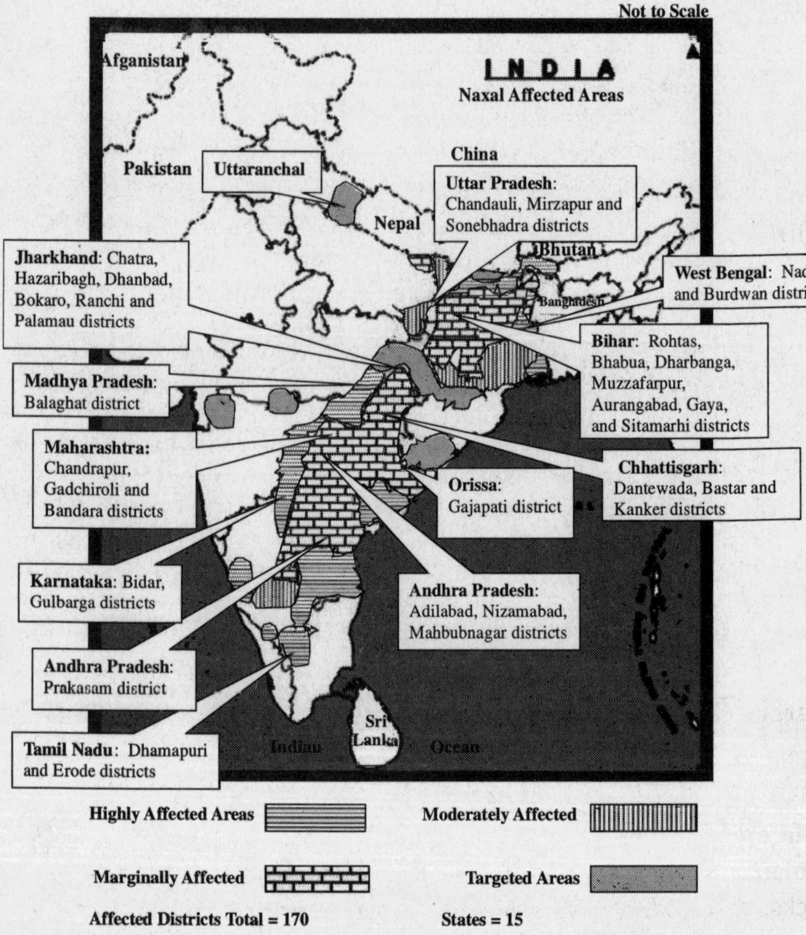

Source: Prepared by the author.

effective strategy in confronting the adversary of superior power."[12] Both rebel groups advocate protracted conflict given the limited resources at their disposal.[13]

The strategy of 'United Front' throws up three challenges. These are:

(i) The political objective that guides the strategy of the two groups is dissimilar. The Naxalites' political goal is to change the present state structure in India whereas the NSCN (IM) demands territorial unification and sovereignty for Naga areas. The resources required for their diverse political objectives will be of a radically different character and dimension.

(ii) The Naxalites are a class-based movement; the NSCN (IM) is mostly an ethnic resistance movement. Developing a coherent unified strategy will prove hazardous for them on the ground. The dissimilar cadre composition, social factors, the politics, motivation levels, and recruitment patterns will create obstacles incomprehensible to the rebel leaders.

(iii) The phenomenon of 'friction' cannot be ignored in rebel strategy.[14] Friction—which entails real obstacles like unfamiliar terrain and population bases, difficult weather, differences in planning, command and control structures and decision making—will hinder smooth inter-communication between the rebel groups.

Strategy of the Naxal Movement

The Naxalite movement engages in guerrilla warfare against the Indian security forces. Mao Tse-tung in *Yu Chi Chan* ('Guerrilla Warfare', 1937) delineated factors such as terrain, communications, popular support, quality of cadres, base areas, technical aid, surprise attacks, and relative military capability of the opposing side as crucial for victory.[15] Leon Trotsky, T.E. Lawrence, Josif Broz Tito, Ho Chi Minh, Nguyen Von Giap and Che Guevara also argued that clearly

---

12. Shimray, A.S. (2005). *Let Freedom Ring Story of Naga Nationalism*. (New Delhi: Promilla): 177-81.
13. See "The People's Guerrilla Army", n. 9. Also Shimray, n. 12.
14. Luttwak, Edward (1987). *Strategy: The Logic of War and Peace*. Cambridge, Mass.: Harvard University Press: 10-15.
15. Griffith, Samuel B. (1961). *On Guerilla Warfare*. New York: Praeger: 39.

stated political objectives and strong local support were linchpins of the people's armed struggle.

The theory and practice of revolutionary warfare has three distinctive phases. These are:

Phase I: Organisation, consolidation, and preservation of regional base areas situated in isolated and difficult terrain.

Phase II: Progressive expansion, which includes attacks on police stations, sabotage, terror tactics, elimination of persons with alternate viewpoints, and procurement of arms and ammunition from the enemy.

Phase III: Destruction of the enemy through conventional battles including mobile warfare, protracted conflicts, negotiations, and unified command and control structures.[16]

In practice, transition between phases might take years or decades. Moreover, 'friction', as identified earlier, will create obstacles for the rebel groups, perhaps even regressing from the second to the first phase more than once. The objective of guerrilla strategy is gradual control of territory and increased perceived local legitimacy of rebel ideology. Once that occurs, there is relative loss of legitimacy for state forces.

Extrapolating the three Phases in the Naxal Movement

This section offers an analysis of the Naxal movement by placing it in the context of the three phases.

Phase I: Organisation, Consolidation, and Preservation of Regional Base Areas

The Naxalites have established base areas in Chhattisgarh, which falls under their Dandakaranya region; Chandrapur, Gadchiroli, and Bhandara districts in Maharashtra; the northern districts of Andhra Pradesh; and Balaghat in Madhya Pradesh.[17] The two worst affected districts of Chhattisgarh—Bastar and Dantewada—comprise hilly

16. Ibid.: 20-22.

17. Guha, n. 6. Chhattisgarh has two Naxalite state committees, for north Chhattisgarh and south Chhattisgarh. The latter is called the Dandakaranya Special Zonal Committee, which further has divisional, range, and village committees.

terrain, ideal for guerrilla warfare. Most of the areas in these two districts are contiguous with Andhra Pradesh and Maharashtra and their forest cover facilitates clandestine interstate movement.

Phase II: Progressive Expansion, Attacks on Police Stations, Sabotage, Terror Tactics, Elimination of Persons with Alternate Viewpoints, and Procurement of Arms and Ammunition from the Enemy

Attacks on Police Stations

Adept at guerrilla warfare and possessing superior local intelligence, the Naxalites have offset the weaponry advantage of the regular police and paramilitary forces in Naxal-affected states. According to the *Annual Report of the Union Ministry of Home Affairs for 2005-06*, 509 police stations across eleven states reported Naxal violence in 2005. In 2006 the number had risen to 1427 police stations. The worst attack on a police station occurred in the early hours of 15 March 2007, when around 600 Naxal cadres attacked the Rani Bodli police station in Dantewada district, in which 55 out of the 79 police personnel present were killed and a large amount of ammunition was looted.[18]

Terror Tactics

An emerging trend in Naxalite violence, which marks a significant point of departure from older revolutionary groups, is attacks on civilians. For earlier revolutionary groups ideology was aimed at real transformation of societies. Inferring from recent Naxalite activities, their movement is not aimed at transformation of society; their 'label' is more of a means to gain territorial control by population 'displacement' rather than support.[19]

Naxal violence in Chhattisgarh reflects this aspect. The Naxalites have attacked and killed civilians in camps manned by Salwa Judum (anti-Naxal movement)[20] in Dantewada: for example, in Darbhaguda where 27 civilians were killed, and in Errabore, where 31 villagers

---

18. "Attack could have been Anticipated", *Times of India* (New Delhi), 22 March 2007: 18.
19. Kaldor, Mary (2006). *New and Old Wars: Organized Violence in a Global Era*. Cambridge: Polity Press: 104. Kaldor points out that this is an emerging characteristic of most contemporary so-called people's movements across the world.
20. The Salwa Judum movement is discussed in a later sub-section.

were killed.[21] In 2006, 749 persons were killed in Naxal-related violence (363 of them in Chhattisgarh). Among the killed, 285 were civilians, 135 security personnel, and 329 alleged Naxalites in counter-revolutionary operations.[22] Prime Minister Manmohan Singh in his Independence Day speech on 15 August 2006 said that "India is facing two major threats to its internal security—Terrorism and Naxalism."[23]

Procurement of Arms

The Naxalite arsenal is becoming consistently sophisticated. For instance, on 8 September 2006 the Andhra Pradesh police recovered 875 rockets, 27 rocket launchers, 70 gelatine sticks, and other explosive material belonging to the CPI (M) from Mahbubnagar and Prakasam districts. Police at Vijayawada also recovered 297 rocket shells and six rocket launchers from Autonagar on 11 September 2006. According to intelligence reports, the Naxalites are also procuring weapons from illegal weapon factories in Chhattisgarh, Maharashtra, Jharkhand, and Bihar.

Phase III: Destruction of the Enemy through Conventional Battles, including Mobile Warfare, Protracted Conflicts, Negotiations, and Unified Command and Control Structures

Unified Command and Control Structure

The Naxalite strategy has become more coordinated with the merger of the People's War Group (PWG) and the Maoist Communist Centre (MCC) into the CPI(M) in 2004. The merger was declared by PWG's Andhra Pradesh state secretary Ramakrishna after peace negotiations on 15–16 October 2004 failed between the Andhra Government and the PWG.[24] This merger brought significant strategic benefits to the Naxalites in cadre recruitment, training, resource management, and military tactics. For instance, on 13 November 2005, 150–200 armed cadres of the CPI(M) along with 800 sympathisers

21. See *Naxal Conflict in 2006*. New Delhi: Asian Centre for Human Rights, 2006: 3.
22. Ibid.: 2.
23. *http://pmindia.nic.in/speech/content.asp?id=365* (accessed on 23 November 2006).
24. Press Statement on "CPI (ML) (PW) and MCCI Merged—Communist Party of India (Maoist) Emerged", at *http://naxalwatch.blogspot.com/2004_12_01_archive.html* (accessed on 13 December 2006).

attacked Jehanabad jail in Bihar, freeing 341 prisoners and looting a huge quantity of arms and ammunition. Simultaneously, attacks were also launched on the District Court, District Armoury, and a paramilitary camp.[25] On 24 March, 2006 CPI(M) cadres simultaneously attacked the local police station, jail, treasury, tehsil office, and State Armed Police camp in Udayagiri town, Gajapati district of Orissa, killing three policemen, freeing 40 prisoners, and looting arms and ammunition.[26] The success of these attacks exposed the incompetence of the state intelligence apparatus. In 2006, Prime Minister Manmohan Singh also indicated that the Naxals had become a highly effective organisation with better trained cadres and efficient coordination.[27]

Cross-border Linkages

The Prime Minister even warned in an Annual Conference of Directors General of Police and heads of Police Organisations in New Delhi on 4 November 2004 that cross-border linkages of the Naxalites constituted "an even greater threat to India than militancy in Jammu and Kashmir and the North East."[28] He repeated the warning in the Chief Ministers' meeting on 13 April 2006. The formation of the Coordination Committee of the Maoist Parties and Organisations in South Asia (CCOMPOSA) in 2001, which includes ten Maoist groups from Bangladesh, India, Nepal, and Sri Lanka, is a matter of concern. In a joint statement issued on 1 July 2001, followed by a subsequent declaration in August 2002, the CCOMPOSA cited its chief aims as resisting not only US imperialism and globalisation, but also the 'centralised' Indian state and its internal repression of minority people through the Naxalite people's War and India's expansionist designs backed by US imperialism in South Asia.[29] In August 2006

25. Balchand, K. (2005). "Naxalites Lay Siege to Jehanabad, free Cadre from Jail", *The Hindu* (New Delhi), 14 November.
26. The Hindu (2006). "Maoists Storm Jail in Orissa, free 40 Prisoners", *The Hindu*, 25 March.
27. "Macist Assessment 2007", at *http://www.satp.org/satporgtp/countries/india/maoist/Assessment/index.html* (accessed on 16 January 2007).
28. Ibid.
29. See "Declaration of CCOMPOSA", at *http://cpnm.org/new/ccomposa/cco/cco_dclr.htm* (accessed on 9 April 2007). For the joint statement see *http://www.satp.org/satporgtp/southasia/documents/papers/CCOMPOSA.htm* (accessed on 9 April 2007).

CCOMPOSA at its Fourth Conference in Nepal reiterated its anti-India stand and reaffirmed its commitment to spread protracted people's war to capture state power through violent means in South Asia.[30]

Counter-Measures to Deter Naxalism

Political Measures

The Prime Minister in his speech at the second meeting of the Standing Committee of Chief Ministers of Naxalite-affected States on 13 April 2006 advocated a coordinated effort under a Unified Command structure to deter Naxalism. He stated that "a lot of responses require coordination among states—in intelligence gathering, in information sharing, in police responses."[31] Indian political leaders have also realised that Naxalism is not just a law-and-order problem but is a result of low levels of development in tribal areas.[32] Consequently, the central government under the National Rural Employment Guarantee Act and the Backward Regions Grant Fund has provided adequate funds to the states to cover all poor families in Naxal-affected areas under the poverty alleviation schemes.[33]

In 2006 a high-level coordination centre was also set up, headed by the Union Home Secretary, with the Chief Secretaries and Directors General of Police of Naxalite-affected states as its members. This coordination centre meets regularly to chart a unified politico-military response to deal with Naxalism. Obstacles to such a unified response are, however, many. First, the political context of the affected states differs. States that are ruled by political parties with political ideologies and loyalties different from those of the ruling party at the Centre may impede smooth coordination. This disjuncture strengthens the Naxalites, who are guided by a unified political purpose.

Secondly, turf battles between the local police and paramilitary forces in an affected area hamper an effective military response. Cases

---

30. Chandrashekharan, S. (2007). "Maoist Fourth Conference of CCOMPOSA Continues with Anti-India Resolutions", at *http://naxalwatch.biogspot.com/2006_09_01_archive.html* (accessed on 9 April 2007).
31. n. 8.
32. Ibid.
33. Ibid.

in point are the ego clashes between the Mizo and Naga Battalions and the police in Chhattisgarh. Thirdly, the tribal populations in the affected states constitute a vital political constituency for state politicians. They are wary of endorsing a unified politico-military policy of dealing with Naxalism for fear that it might lead to disproportionate use of force by state authorities in tribal areas, resulting in tribal alienation.

Counter-revolutionary Operations

Location, isolation, and eradication form the basis of countering rebel groups militarily.[34] 'Location' entails identifying the rebel groups' base areas, which are mostly in thick jungle terrain, through reconnaissance; 'isolation' indicates separation of the Naxal cadres from their support base, involving movement and resettlement of local communities; 'eradication' is based on sound intelligence and operational flexibility of the counter military operations with high degree of mobility to preempt rebel strategy.

Location of Base Areas

The central and state governments have undertaken security measures to locate the base areas. For instance, Dantewada, Kanker, and Bastar districts of Chhattisgarh have been identified as the key base areas. The Andhra Pradesh Director General of Police, Swaranjit Sen, has identified the northern districts of Andhra Pradesh as a Naxal base area; on 20 January 2005 he disclosed that Naxalites had planted 2000 kilograms of gelatine-based mines in this region. In the Dandakaranya region the Naxalites are functioning through 18 dalams (guerrilla squads) divided into four divisional committees.[35]

Isolating the Naxalites from the Support Base

Isolation does not simply mean physically segregating the rebels from the local population. The state must also actively strive to discredit the political message of people's emancipation that the rebels

34. Griffith, n. 15: 32–33. Also see James D. Kiras (2002). "Terrorism and Irregular Warfare", in John Baylis *et al.*, *Strategy in the Contemporary World: An Introduction to Strategic Studies*. Oxford: Oxford University Press: 208-32.
35. IDSA Consultation-Workshop, Maoist Violence in India: Resolution and Prevention, 25 August 2006. New Delhi: Institute for Defence Studies and Analyses, 2006.

espouse.[36] In this direction the Chhattisgarh government launched in June 2005 a so-called people's movement named Salwa Judum, meaning 'peace hunt' in the local Gondi tribal dialect. The movement was launched by a few villagers in Kutru angered by Naxal interference in the local trade of *tendu* leaves (used for making *bidis*/cigarettes).[37] Maintaining law and order in Dantewada and Bastar have been outsourced to the Salwa Judum cadres, some of them as young as 15–16 years in age. Some 5000 such cadres have been made Special Police Officers (SPOs), given a rifle each and paid Rs. 1500-2000 a month. Poorly trained, ill equipped and immature, some of the Salwa Judum cadres themselves have looted many tribal villages. Most of the cadres join merely for mercenary motives. The leader of the Opposition in Chhattisgarh, Mahendra Karma of the Congress party, has made this movement his political platform. In the process, the leadership of the movement has lost its tribal face (all leaders are now non-tribal). According to Dr. K.S. Subramanian, former Director General of Police, Chhattisgarh:

> While official sources maintain that the campaign, led by a local legislator is spontaneous with tribal people joining in large numbers, local enquiries revealed a different picture...In the name of Salwa Judum, the tribal people are forced to join a far from spontaneous mobilisation. Hundreds of people are being killed and corruption is high in the rank and file of the movement.[38]

In 2006, the government and the Salwa Judum also displaced nearly 43,740 tribal villagers in Bastar and Dantewada and placed them in 17 ramshackle roadside camps.[39]

Eradication of Naxalites

Security Measures. In 2006, the central government deployed nearly 37,000 central security forces in Chhattisgarh and 30 companies in Jharkhand. In August 2006 the Centre announced the possible use of

---

36. Kiras, n. 34.
37. See Independent Citizens Initiative, n. 4: 9. Also Guha, Ramachandra (2006). "Counter-Revolutionaries", *The Telegraph*, 27 June.
38. See Cherian, Saji (2007). "Chhattisgarh Populist Follies, Confounded State", at *http://www.satp.org/satporgtp/sair/Archives/4_33.htm* (accessed on 21 March 2007).
39. See *Naxal Conflict in 2006*, n. 21: 3. Also Thompson, Robert G. (1966). *Defeating Communist Insurgency: The Lessons of Malaya and Vietnam*. New York: Praeger.

air power in thirteen Naxal-affected districts for transporting security personnel, food and medical supplies if not for hardcore military operations. It also contemplated the use of unmanned aerial vehicles (UAV) in Chhattisgarh for intelligence gathering.[40] Individual states have also raised their special police forces, drawing recruits from Naxal-affected areas.[41] Mine-protected vehicles (MPVs) have also been provided to these states under the Police Modernisation Scheme. Additional 'India Reserve Battalions' with an estimated cost of Rs. 20.75 crore per battalion have been sanctioned for the Naxal-affected states.[42]

Surrender Policies. Naxal-affected states have also announced surrender policies. The Jharkhand government offered Rs. 50,000 to surrendered Naxalites plus a monthly allowance of Rs. 2000, one acre of agricultural land, and educational and health benefits to their children. The Chhattisgarh government offered up to Rs. 3 lakh for weapon surrender. The Orissa government announced Rs. 10,000 for surrender, Rs. 20,000 for arms surrender, and Rs. 2 lakh of bank loan without interest for two years.[43] But there is no effective intelligence mechanism to identify Naxal cadres. Often, tribal youths surrender as Naxal cadres; many of them even join the Naxal movement to reap these benefits.

Socio-economic Measures. The Planning Commission set up a sixteen-member expert group in July 2006 to study the root causes of Naxalism. The expert group studied the causes of severe displacement, forest-related issues, loss of tribal land, and extreme low levels of human development in Naxal-affected areas.[44] The Ministry of Tribal Affairs also asserted in its National Tribal Policy draft of 21 July 2006 that scheduled tribes were suffering from a deep sense of deprivation

---

40. See "Naxalite Antidote Ten Troopers for a Rebel", *The Telegraph*, 24 April 2006.
41. See "Special Forces for Naxal-hit States Mooted", *Deccan Chronicle* (Hyderabad), 4 September 2006.
42. n. 7.
43. "Jharkhand offers sops to Naxals to surrender", *The Asian Age* (New Delhi), 22 April 2006. Also, "Naxalite can take Home Rewards on his Head: Chhattisgarh's New Plan", *Indian Express* (New Delhi), 23 September 2006.
44. "Govt. Sets up Expert Group to Look into Menace of Naxalism", at *http://www.outlookindia.com/pti_news.asp?id=390453* (accessed on 14 April 2007).

and alienation on account of social, political, and economic factors resulting in acute poverty and lack of adequate opportunities, which manifested in violent resistance.[45] As a follow-up, the Ministry of Home Affairs allocated Rs. 23,000 crore in 2006 for Naxal-affected states.

The Planning Commission's evaluation of the Integrated Tribal Development Project 2006 identified the lack of institutional mechanisms to oversee implementation and hold persons/institutions accountable for misuse of funds.[46] This lacuna persists. Funds allocated for the tribals have been diverted elsewhere, bypassing their intended beneficiaries, and thus fuelling the Naxalite cause.

Legislative Myopia. On 21 March 2006 the Chhattisgarh government enacted a draconian legislation, formally known as the Chhattisgarh Special Public Security Act 2005 (CSPSA). The CSPSA's main objective is to deter individuals and organisations from engaging in disruptive activities in Chhattisgarh. It allows persons to be held on mere suspicion and imprisoned for two to three years without any system of appeal. The non-democratic nature of this legislation looks likely to alienate the local population further.

The *Panchayats* (Extension to the Scheduled Areas) Act, 1996 (PESA), recognises the tribal communities' right of self-rule through local institutions. The tribal areas of the Naxal-affected states come under its ambit. However, PESA has not been implemented in letter and spirit in many of these states. Rather than empowering the tribal, existing power structures try to assimilate tribal societies into a so-called mainstream, refusing in the process to recognise their distinct culture and lifestyles.[47] The Fifth Schedule of the Constitution also protects the tribals' land and natural resources from non-tribals in nine states: Andhra Pradesh, Bihar, Chhattisgarh, Jharkhand, Karnataka, Kerala, Madhya Pradesh, Maharashtra, and Orissa. However, most of these states have come up with policies that

45. See "Draft National Tribal Policy Released", at *http://www.empowerpoor.com/relatednews.asp?report=332* (accessed on 18 January 2007).
46. *Naxal Monitor*, n. 1.
47. Kothari, Smriti (2007). "To be Governed or be Self Governed", at *http://www.hinduonnet.com/folio/fo0007/00070180.htm* (accessed on 23 March 2007).

facilitate the use of tribal land for industrial and commercial purposes.[48]

Policy Recommendations

The Naxalite challenge is daunting but there is still scope for certain imaginative and insightful policies. Four policy recommendations are outlined here.

First, Naxalism predominates in areas that lack basic infrastructure. Civil liberty and the basic right to life implies the state facilitating the fulfilment of people's basic needs such as land rights, medical facilities, primary schools, shelter, security, and freedom from routine police checks. Else, the state machinery loses its legitimacy.

Second, conventional military strategy based on force concentration cannot meet the challenge of guerrilla warfare. The latter thrives on decentralised force dispersal and avoids frontal attacks. Guerrilla units in general are highly mobile, lightly armed, and adept at the tactics of deception, surprise, and speed. Therefore, it is crucial that regular forces skilled in guerrilla warfare are raised. They must continuously challenge the Naxalite armed cadres to put psychological pressure. Both offensive and defensive tactics must be utilised and night patrolling encouraged in these areas. For success, local tribal support and intelligence is crucial.

Third, the Salwa Judum has turned out to be an ill-considered brainchild. According to official estimates, 644 out of 1153 villages in Chhattisgarh are involved in the Salwa Judum campaign. To counter it the Naxalites have organised their cadres from irregular guerrilla squads into an integrated standing army, the People's Liberation Guerrilla Army (PLGA).[49] The Naxalites are using the tactics of terror and intimidation by largely targeting civilians in Salwa Judum camps.[50] The PLGA–Salwa Judum conflict has also increased inter-tribal fissures. Consequently, the conflict in Chhattisgarh has taken on a life

---

48. *http://www.cseindia.org/programme/nrml/policy_watch1.htm* (accessed on 22 March 2007). Also Louise Tillin, "Unity in Diversity? Asymmetry in Indian Federalism", at *http://publius.oxfordjournals.org/cgi/content/full/37/1/45* (accessed on 18 March 2007).
49. Ibid.: 17.
50. Independent Citizens Initiative, n.4: 5.

of its own, threatening to further polarise the affected people. The Chhattisgarh government needs to disband the Salwa Judum cadres and also provide the demobilised cadres alternative avenues of employment lest they join the Naxal movement as a means of livelihood.

Fourth, talking to Naxal leaders is an important policy option as it controls violence and creates space for civil society groups. The beneficial consequent effects of the peace dialogue between the Government of India and the NSCN (IM) on Naga civil society is a case in point. However, talks need to factor in the probability of Naxal rebels de-escalating violence as part of a strategic design to buy time and boost their cadre and weapon base. Hence, it is crucial that the affected states' authorities open alternative channels of communication with important civil society groups like tribal councils and women's groups. Such an alternative engagement will limit the ability of Naxal leaders to mobilise support and unleash violence, once they desert the peace table.

The Naxal conflict feeds on the structured constraints of social, political, and economic deprivations. Therefore, the resolution process must factor in an identification procedure of basic needs and elaborate ways of finding solutions within a limited resource base. Unless such an approach is built into the social, economic, and political structure of Indian democracy, resistance groups like Naxalism will sprout in other deprived regions of the country as well, complicating India's rise to prominence in an emerging new world order.

III

Dynamism and Flux in Asia-Pacific

13

East Asia in 2006

Economic Dynamism and Political Flux

G.V.C. NAIDU

Given the economic dynamism sweeping East Asia and its enormous potential, developments in the region will have far-reaching effect on global economy, politics, and security. The investment bank Goldman Sachs forecasts that India and China will surpass the size of the US economy by 2050,[1] which means three of the world's four largest economies will be in this region. The region also holds nearly $3 trillion of foreign exchange reserves, nearly two-thirds of the worlds' total. The regional consumption patterns are changing with rapid expansion of markets and, more importantly, the region has an unparalleled demographic advantage. Further, already the region is trading within itself more than with the rest of the world—from 35 per cent in 1980 to 55 per cent by 2005, and that is progressively increasing.[2] Similar trends are also seen indirect investments. While market dynamics is promoting greater intra-regional economic interaction, the region itself is transforming. On the negative side, the economic vulnerability of many countries apart, there are important political issues driven by a variety of factors—historical issues, unresolved border and territorial problems, and domestic instabilities, for instance.

Developments in 2006

Economically, besides continued impressive growth rates averaging 8 per cent (excluding Japan) in 2006, the trend towards greater intra-

1. Giridharadas, Anand (2007). "India Projected to Join China in Surpassing Size of the US Economy by 2050", *International Herald Tribune*, 24 January, *http://www.iht.com/articles/2007/01/24/business/rupee.php*.

2. *http://www.adb.org/Documents/Speeches/2006/ms2006016.asp*.

regional trade has intensified. For some countries the region has become critical for their external trade, replacing traditional markets such as the US and the EU (European Union). Another notable feature is the rush to finalise free trade area agreements (FTAs) of various kinds, which would add momentum to intra-regional trade. Much of this economic dynamics is market-driven than by a conscious political understanding or by an overarching region-wide mechanism. Going by this logic, it makes enormous sense to actively promote greater economic cooperation and regional economic integration under the auspices of a multilateral framework. APEC (Asia-Pacific Economic Cooperation), ASEAN Plus Three (Association of South East Asian Nations plus China, Japan, and Republic of Korea) and the EAS (East Asian Summit) have been talking about enhanced regional cooperation leading to integration and possibly creating even an East Asian community, a highly ambitious goal indeed.

The year 2006 was marked by the North Korean nuclear brinkmanship by way of a test, the Japanese quest for 'normal' power status becoming more substantial, ASEAN's momentous decision to push for economic integration in the face of the rise of China and India and its own declining importance, the changing attitude of the great powers towards regional multilateral efforts which face an uncertain future, and further consolidation of India's forays into East Asia.

Emerging Strategic Equations

Taking full advantage of the American preoccupation with wars in Afghanistan and Iraq, North Korea carried out a series of ballistic missile tests, including long-range Taepodong in July, followed by the big bang of a nuclear explosion on 9 October. This led to UN-mandated sanctions and resumption of the stalled Six-Party talks involving the US, China, Republic of Korea, North Korea, Japan, and Russia. The most prominent impact of North Korea's testing on the rest of East Asia is the debate on how soon Japan would acquire nuclear weapons. A leading Japanese daily, *Sakei Shinbun*, brought to light details about an internal study purported to have been done for the government that opined that Japan had the technical capability to build atomic weapons along with a delivery system but it was not 'a-couple-of-screwdriver-turns away' and could take three to five years. The government, especially the prime minister, has repeatedly ruled out going nuclear; but to talk about the nuclear option, including by high-ranking cabinet ministers, is no more taboo.

In 2006, consequent to a decision by the Diet, the Japan Defence Agency was elevate to the status of a full-fledged ministry. Further, policy pronouncements of the Abe administration indicate that Japan is determined to play a larger political role. Its contribution to global security in the form of sending troops to UN peacekeeping operations may intensify further, with more robust articulation not just about its rightful place in the world as a permanent member of the UN Security Council but, more importantly, in stating its security concerns rather explicitly. That way Abe may turn out to be more radical than even his predecessor Junichiro Koizumi. The other significant decision Japan took was to expedite the deployment of the ballistic missile defence (BMD) systems, which is likely to be much more comprehensive than envisaged earlier. Simultaneously, following the US–Japan Security Consultative Committee's agreement, in May 2006 the roadmap for realignment of US forces in Japan was announced, which is also a significant development.[3] Thanks to Koizumi, the uncertainties that dogged the US–Japan alliance starting from the end of the cold war but more recently since the events of 11 September 2001, with fears about its relevance mounting, were dispelled. Further consolidation of strategic partnership with the US will become possible once the Constitution is amended, as promised by Abe. Yet it appears there may be gradual reduction in American troop presence while laying emphasis on deployment of technologically advanced systems.

In response to a series of developments around Japan, not least China's anti-satellite test of 11 January 2007, Prime Minister Abe has initiated steps to create new decision making structures, such as the revamped National Security Council and an external spy agency that can better respond to crises, underscoring Japan's growing concerns on the security front. The Abe administration has also started exploring other possibilities, for example, forging a 'strategic

3. *For details, see http://www.state.gov/r/pa/prs/ps/2006/65517.htm.*

partnership' with India, to bolster Japan's security. This in particular has to be seen in the larger context of enhancing India's role in the regional balance of power in East Asia. India is the only country other than the US with which Japan has been using the phrase 'strategic partnership', implying shared concerns and interests. The process of gradual unshackling of Japan from self-imposed constraints, both formal and informal, has seen a definitive beginning in 2006. How much 'strategic autonomy' Japan would like to achieve and how far it will go to realise this objective in the coming years remains to be seen.

For the US, its alliance with Japan, despite some uncertainties consequent to the Rumsfeld Doctrine (which sought to move American troops where they were required for rapid deployment than concentrate at one or two places), has become important, especially with the unravelling of its alliance with another close partner, South Korea. This unravelling became conspicuous in 2006 with fundamental differences on a range of issues related to North Korea, the control of American troops in South Korea, etc. The US–South Korea alliance, under strain since the onset of Seoul's 'sunshine' policy towards the North, is unlikely to be the same despite the North Korean antics on weapons of mass destruction (WMD) and a possible settlement. As a result, the year 2006 may turn out to be a turning point in US policy towards East Asia. The effects of China's rise are seen in the gradual marginalisation of not just Japan but also the US. Consequently, the US, apart from strengthening its alliances with Japan and Australia, is working towards incorporating 'friends' like India and Singapore in the management of regional security by forging newer partnerships, as envisaged in the March 2006 National Security Strategy by the US President.[4] It appears the name of the new game is 'hedging' *vis-à-vis* China as well as other uncertainties.[5]

---

4. *http://usinfo.state.gov/xarchives/display.html?p=washfile-english&y=2006&m=March&x=20060316170527idybeekcm0.2458155&t=livefeeds/wf-latest.html.*

5. According to Evelyn Goh: "Hedging is defined here as a set of strategies aimed at avoiding (or planning for contingencies in) a situation in which states cannot decide upon more straightforward alternatives such as balancing, bandwagoning, or neutrality. Instead they cultivate a middle position that forestalls or avoids having to choose one side at the obvious expense of another." *Meeting the China Challenge: The U.S. in Southeast Asian Strategies*, East-West Center Policy Studies No 16, *http://www.eastwestcenter.org/res-rp-publicationdetails.asp?pub_ID=1618.*

In the backdrop of these developments and concerns about the future of the East Asian regional security architecture, the year 2006 saw newer attempts among 'like-minded' countries that share certain values and interests, such as the US, Japan, and India, to evolve a *modus vivendi* to deal with challenges that face the region. In March 2006, a Trilateral Strategic Dialogue was initiated, comprising the US, Japan, and Australia. There are indications that India would be willing to join as the fourth member,[6] one of these being the Indian Navy's participation in the US-led Pacific exercises in late April 2007. A balance of power in the classic sense is lacking in East Asia. An effort in that direction will contribute to regional stability. But this development puts a big question mark on the future of security multilateralism, especially the already marginalised ASEAN Regional Forum (ARF).

Concomitantly, the Sino–Russian 'strategic partnership' is getting strengthened especially in advanced arms and military technology transfers. They also closely cooperate on a range of global issues. However, it is unlikely to be a major player in the foreseeable future.

Great-power relations, as the events in 2006 have shown, are likely to remain complex since a rising power tends to aspire for a larger and more assertive role but is constrained by the exigencies of growing economic interdependence. Shinzo Abe could not ignore the impact of estrangement with China on the Japanese economy nor can China afford to antagonise Japan for long. Abe undertook fence mending trips to China and South Korea soon after assuming office from Koizumi in October 2006. At the same time, he is strongly advocating both a new security role for Japan as well as a new coalition with India and the US. China's recent anti-satellite test is seen as a signal to the world of its growing military might. Also, China's avowed resistance to a larger Indian role in East Asian multilateral fora is a part of this great-power dynamic. It is true that India–China relations have improved considerably in the recent past and the booming bilateral trade may have touched US$24 billion by the end of 2006. Mutual investments are also steadily increasing. Nonetheless, neither the

6. Baruah, Amit (2007). "India Likely to Take Part in 4-Nation Talks", *The Hindu*, 17 January, *http://www.hindu.com/2007/01/17/stories/2007011706991200.htm*.

competitive aspects between the two, nor the lingering suspicions of each other's actions can be brushed aside. They compete not only for markets and capital but also for political influence. India's rise is beginning to be felt in Beijing most prominently in the context of East Asia.

Regional Multilateralism

Even as the year 2006 saw the first clear signs of realignment of forces among the great powers, the management of relations among them with competing interests, persistent historical suspicions, and mounting rivalries is going to be a major challenge for East Asia in the coming years. It has been contended that regional multilateralism can help mitigate political concerns and forge better understanding among the great powers; but the experience of multilateralism in the region has not been particularly encouraging. The East Asian region did not have the benefit of operating under multilateralism during the cold war era and the record of multilateral frameworks, both economic and security that have been in existence since the early 1990s does not inspire much hope. The ARF has remained merely a talk shop. It was helpless in any crisis, such as the East Timor issue or the North Korean problem.

Given, the current trends and enormous potential, regionalism should have been flourishing under economic multilateralism, but much of the current regional economic dynamics is market-driven. The EAS has been ineffective in furthering regional economic integration or in pushing the creation of an East Asian Community. The only notable highlight of the second EAS declaration was on energy security—to increase the use of biofuels, promote renewable energy resources, and reduce dependence on fossil fuels, but without any deadlines or goals (unlike a EU decision on energy, for example), and apparently found a prominent place since the Japanese were willing to commit US$2 billion for the cause of energy efficiency and security.

The divisions that undermined the first EAS remained unresolved. Japan, India, and a few other South East Asian countries sought to promote the EAS as the principal mechanism to propel economic integration whereas China, South Korea, and Malaysia were unrelenting on the centrality of ASEAN Plus Three. Once again, thanks to the US $100 million that Japan had pledged to fund a research centre in South East Asia that could undertake the task of studying the prospects for a pan-East Asian FTA and economic cooperation, the Tokyo proposal was accepted, despite Chinese resistance.

Simultaneously, the US also advocated an Asia-Pacific FTA during the November 2006 APEC meeting in Vietnam, but there did not seem to be many takers for this idea. Starting as the most ambitious economic cooperation and integration plan in the early 1990s and especially since the East Asian financial crisis, APEC has failed to make headway either in promoting regional economic integration or in addressing political problems.

The year 2006 was critical for ASEAN. Amidst growing scepticism about its future and role in East Asian affairs, ASEAN had to reinvent itself. It has to cope with a variety of challenges, such as the impact of the rise of new power centres in China and India alongside the intensifying competition among the great powers. South East Asia's overall economic and strategic significance is waning and recent domestic events among the countries of the region will further undermine ASEAN's ability to play the leadership role. For instance, President Gloria Macapagal-Arroyo's declaration of a state of emergency in the Philippines in February 2006 after claims by her government that it had foiled a coup attempt by a section of renegade military officers, and in Thailand the September 2006 military coup by the army commander-in-chief Sondhi Boonyaratkalin, ousting the government of Prime Minister Thaksin Sinawatra while he was away in New York, came as a severe jolt to those who had assumed that the era of military coups was over. Political problems in Indonesia forced President Susilo Bambang Yudhoyono to skip the EAS meet in Cebu (Philippines) and rush back home. There are no signs either in Myanmar or in the Indochina countries that political reforms will be introduced any time soon. The impact of such grave domestic stability issues on ASEAN cannot be overstated.

ASEAN also has had to grapple with the rise of China and India; the North East Asian region hogging the political limelight with issues such as North Korea and Taiwan; transformation of Japan's security policies; China–Japan relations; and China's military modernisation. ASEAN is running out of time unless it charts a concrete plan for integration. The lure of the idea of an economic community may help stem the waning attraction of South East Asia to some extent, but the region is nowhere near the kind of integration the EU is attempting. Many, including Lee Kuan Yew of Singapore, have expressed doubts about the feasibility of creating a borderless region with a common currency. The cracks and underlying tensions in interstate relations among the ASEAN member countries have not shown any sign of abating.

Two significant decisions were taken in the ASEAN summit meeting at Cebu: to create an economic community by 2015 and to adopt an ASEAN Charter based on a blueprint prepared by an Eminent Persons Group, which is expected to make ASEAN a more legalised, rule-based structure so that its decisions are binding. If accepted, it would be a radical departure from the present consensus-based decisions. Will it lead to expulsion of a recalcitrant member, especially if it is a large country, is a big question mark. Myanmar is the most talked about case, especially for its lack of progress on democracy. Can the coup by the Thai generals be condoned? Can certain authoritarian regimes of Indochina be exempted? These are issues likely to haunt ASEAN.

South East Asia as a region is plagued by a variety of problems. The most prominent are telling economic disparities—from US $26,000 per capita in Singapore to US $200 in Laos. Neither are the political systems reasonably uniform. The social, cultural, linguistic, and religious differences are also pretty wide. Moreover, ASEAN's leadership role has been under a cloud since the late 1990s financial crisis. The democratic structures are weak and there is an urgent need to create a whole range of institutions for a variety of activities not only to deal with issues within the region but in the larger Asia-Pacific.

India–Japan Ties

China's unrelenting diplomatic offensive towards South East Asia continued in 2006 and the latest was the successful conclusion of the remaining aspects of the FTA with ASEAN on services and investment, making it the largest FTA in the world. ASEAN's FTA talks with Japan and India have been lagging but India's eastward thrust continues to be robust.

Prime Minister Manmohan Singh made two trips to this region—to Japan for the annual summit meeting and to Cebu for the India–ASEAN and EAS meetings. The visit to Japan attracted considerable attention, with further consolidation of 'strategic and global partnership' between the two countries. The 16-page bilateral declaration signed by the two prime ministers is a comprehensive statement on how the relationship will be developed in the coming years. Prime Minister Abe, a known Indophile (strongly backed by senior cabinet colleagues and Indophile like Foreign Minister Taro Aso) has reportedly expressed the view that the Japan–India relations will soon emerge as the most important bilateral relationship. The joint statement calls for regular, annual bilateral meetings not just between top leaders but at least six other ministries, a unique arrangement for both countries. The joint statement also mentions qualitatively upgraded defence cooperation, including joint exercises, regular exchange of personnel, and annual security dialogues.

To address the weakest link, the low level of economic relations, concerted efforts have been made by both sides. While the Japanese government has been actively promoting the Indian case with the private sector, India's Ministry of Commerce and Industry has created a special cell to attract Japanese investments, the only country to which such a status has been accorded. Simultaneously, the two countries have also started negotiations based on the recommendation of the India–Japan Joint Study Group, submitted in 2006, to finalise an FTA before 2008. Bilateral trade, that had been virtually stagnant for over a decade, is going up from US$5.6 billion in 2004-05 to US $6.5 billion in 2005-06. Japan has immense potential to contribute to India's economic development, given Japan's nearly US$8 trillion savings and mastery over large number of advanced dual-use technologies. India–Japan relations are going to be a major feature of East Asian international relations in the future.

With regard to ASEAN, the Indian prime minister assured the Cebu summit that an India–ASEAN FTA would be finalised by July 2007 after resolving the differences. The Indian defence minister in a speech in Singapore in June 2006 also offered to assist the India–Malaysia–Singapore initiative through 'Compulsory Pilotage' project to monitor shipping in the straits of South East Asia.[7]

Conclusion

The year 2006 was momentous for East Asia, reflecting its numerous political and security problems, notwithstanding the buoyant economic outlook for the foreseeable future. The year also saw the crystallisation of certain developments that will have considerable impact on the nature of the East Asian security order, such as Japan's proactive diplomacy and assertive defence in the wake of mounting security challenges, and China's continued economic and military growth.

India's intensifying thrust towards the East, and multilateralism struggling to make its presence felt were also in evidence. The year also saw the idea of US–Japan–India trilateral cooperation beginning to take shape with intensified dialogues and the first planned trilateral naval exercises. While these developments are seen suspiciously in China, they may also lead to a better regional balance of power. At the same time, despite underlying suspicions, great power relations are far more congenial today than before, especially now that both China and Japan have realised the limits to which they can push their dislike of each other and how important China is to resolve the North Korean imbroglio. Great power realignment is often born out of growing competition and clash of interests.

Regional multilateralism appears to be still on shaky ground. The ARF as a mechanism to promote not just 'predictable patterns of relations' but also to undertake confidence-building measures (CBMs), preventive diplomacy and evolve into an effective framework to resolve disputes, seems farfetched. If the six-party talks that helped to resolve

---

7. See Defence Minister Pranab Mukherjee's speech at *the Fifth IISS Asia Security Summit* (Shangri La Dialogue) on 3 June 2006, *http://www.iiss.org/conferences/the-shangri-la-dialogue/2006-plenary-session-speeches/second-plenary-session-pranab-mukherjee.*

the North Korean nuclear issue were to become a permanent feature to deal with the Northeast Asian security problems, the ARF's importance will further decline. Even economic multilateralism has not made much progress in terms of concrete, implementable decisions. ASEAN's ability to successfully steer this regional multilateral mechanism has also come under doubt.

The year 2006 witnessed domestic instability resurfacing in Southeast Asia, among which were coup rumours in the Philippines, a military coup in Thailand, and terrorism in several parts of the region. Yet, ASEAN has taken a historic decision to economically integrate Southeast Asia by 2015. It has also taken a decision to adopt a new Charter to make itself more rules-based rather than consensus-driven and thus become more effective. The consequences of such a departure for ASEAN remains to be seen.

The year also saw further consolidation of India's engagement with East Asia with the two trips the Indian prime minister made to Japan and to Cebu for summit meetings with ASEAN and the EAS. Deepening of India–US relations and India–Japan relations that were witnessed in 2006 is likely to have considerable impact on the evolving East Asian regional security and economic order.

14

Sino–Indian Engagement?

RAVIPRASAD NARAYANAN

Sino–Indian relations are fundamentally guided by two drivers—'political security' and 'economic cooperation.' These were in evidence during the visit of President Hu Jintao of China to India from 20 to 23 November 2006, a decade after his predecessor Jiang Zemin in 1996. The first leg of President Hu's tour was to Vietnam to attend the 14th APEC (Asia-Pacific Economic Cooperation) Economic Leaders' Meeting, 17-19 November. Laos was his second stop. From India, he was to visit Pakistan.

The 'political security' driver is largely determined by the global vision of the two countries and their increasing stakes in a rapidly changing global system. Resolution of the boundary stalemate—which is the most visible 'political security' issue—is an ongoing process in line with China's pragmatic preference for a negotiated settlement on the basis of "mutual respect, mutual understanding" and, most importantly, "mutually acceptable adjustments."[1] The joint declaration, signed on 21 November during President Hu's visit, stated that:

> The Special Representatives shall complete at an early date the task of finalising an appropriate framework for a final package settlement of the India-China boundary. Pending the resolution of the boundary question, both sides shall maintain peace and tranquillity in the border areas in accordance with the agreements of 1993, 1996 and 2005.[2]

1. See "Agreement between the Government of the Republic of India and the Government of the People's Republic of China on the Political Parameters and Guiding Principles for the Settlement of the India–China Boundary Question", Article 3, available at *http://meaindia.nic.in/*. Accessed on 20 December, 2006.
2. See "Seeking Early Settlement of Outstanding Issues" in the "Joint Declaration by the Republic of India and the People's Republic of China" during President Hu Jintao's visit,

Contd...

Prime Minister Manmohan Singh and President Hu Jintao agreed that an early resolution of the boundary issue would advance the basic interests of the two countries and invest their strategic partnership with further strength and dynamism. They wanted this to be pursued as a "strategic objective."

The emerging comprehensive engagement between the two countries, however, has progressively reduced the exclusivity of the boundary dispute. The joint declaration committed the two countries to pursue a "ten-pronged strategy" for the future development of bilateral relations. The ten prongs are: ensuring comprehensive development of bilateral relations; strengthening institutional linkages and dialogue mechanisms; consolidating commercial and economic exchanges; expanding all-round mutually beneficial cooperation; instilling mutual trust and confidence through defence cooperation; seeking early settlement of outstanding issues; promoting transborder connectivity and cooperation; boosting cooperation in science and technology; revitalising cultural ties and nurturing people-to-people exchanges; and expanding cooperation on the regional and international stage.[3]

The joint statement aspires to raise the volume of India–China trade to US $40 billion by 2010. A bilateral investment protection and promotion agreement has been signed to boost the trade ties. There has been emphasis on multiplying transborder traffic and going beyond Nathu La and opening some more trading points on the border. The joint statement also makes a rudimentary reference to the possibility of civilian nuclear cooperation as part of joint strategic

---

..contd...

21 November 2006, Article 6. Earlier agreements on the matter were the "Agreement on the Maintenance of Peace and Tranquillity along the Line of Actual Control in the India–China Border Areas" signed on 7 September, 1993 by R.L. Bhatia, India's Minister of State for External Affairs, and his Chinese counterpart Vice-Foreign Minister Tang Jiaxuan; the "Agreement between the Government of the Republic of India and the Government of the People's Republic of China on Confidence-Building Measures in the Military Field along the Line of Actual Control in the India–China Border Areas", signed on 29 November, 1996 during President Jiang Zemin's visit; and the "Agreement between the Government of the Republic of India and the Government of the People's Republic of China on the Political Parameters and Guiding Principles for the Settlement of the India-China Boundary Question", signed on 11 April, 2005 in New Delhi during the visit of Prime Minister Wen Jiabao.

3. See Joint Declaration by the Republic of India and the People's Republic of China. Available at *http://meaindia.nic.in/jdhome.htm*. Accessed on 12 February, 2007.

cooperative relationship the two countries have envisioned for themselves. India and China are committed to non-proliferation objectives and agreed to expand their dialogue on related issues, in bilateral and international fora. The declaration stated that

> global energy systems should take into account and meet the energy needs of both the countries, as part and parcel of a stable, predictable, secure and clean energy future. In this context, international civilian nuclear cooperation should be advanced through innovative and forward-looking approaches, while safeguarding the effectiveness of international non-proliferation principles.

China's position is that it is willing to cooperate in the peaceful uses of nuclear energy with all countries on the precondition that all parties honour their international obligations. The Indian Foreign Secretary, commenting on the talks, expressed his satisfaction at the direction and pace of the talks but cautioned the media against over-interpreting the nuclear talks. China remains noncommittal about its position on the Indo–US deal in the Nuclear Suppliers Group meeting.

Prior to President Hu Jintao's visit, in May 2006 Defence Minister Pranab Mukherjee and his Chinese counterpart Cao Gangchuan signed a memorandum of understanding (MoU) for exchanges and cooperation in the field of defence.[4] Following are the highlights of this MoU:

1. Maintain frequent exchanges between the leaders and high-level functionaries of the Defence Ministries and the armed forces of the two countries.
2. Convene an Annual Defence Dialogue at a mutually agreed level, to be hosted alternately by the two sides.
3. Endeavour to hold joint military exercises and/or training programmes in the fields of search and rescue, anti-piracy, counter-terrorism, and other areas of mutual interest.
4. Establish a mechanism of study tours for each other's senior and middle-level military officers and relevant civilian officials,

---

4. "Memorandum of Understanding between the Ministry of Defence of the Republic of India and the Ministry of National Defence of the People's Republic of China for Exchanges and Cooperation in the field of Defence", signed on 28 May, 2006. Available at *http://meaindia.nic.in/*Accessed on 11 January, 2007.

in order to facilitate better understanding of foreign, defence and national development policies of the host side.

5. Establish a mechanism for military officers to study in the military academies of either side.

'Political Security' and the Boundary Dispute

Despite the growing and tangible 'political engagement' by the two sides over the past decade, the Hu Jintao visit was clouded by the untimely remarks over the boundary issue made by the Chinese Ambassador to India, Sun Yuxi, during an interview with a television channel, that "the whole of Arunachal Pradesh is Chinese territory and Tawang is only one place in it."[5] Sun's repeated 'utterances' were met by a robust response from External Affairs Minister Pranab Mukherjee, who said that "the whole of Arunachal Pradesh is an integral part of India."[6]

Article I of the agreement on the Political Parameters and Guiding Principles for the Settlement of the India–China Boundary Question, signed during the visit of Chinese Premier Wen Jiabao to New Delhi in April 2005,[7] specifically states that "the differences on the boundary question should not be allowed to affect the overall development of bilateral relations. The two sides will resolve the boundary question through peaceful and friendly consultations."[8] Article V further states that "the two sides will take into account, *inter alia*, historical evidence, national sentiments, practical difficulties and reasonable concerns and sensitivities of both sides, and the 'actual state of border areas' (emphasis added)."[9] Sun Yuxi's remarks reflect China's methodology in handling

5. Sun Yuxi's verbatim remarks, made to the television news channel CNN-IBN, were: "In our position, the whole of the state of Arunachal Pradesh is Chinese territory. And Tawang is only one of the places in it. We are claiming all of that. That is our position." See *www.rediff.com/news/2006/nov/14china.htm*. Accessed on 14 November 2006.

6. See *http://www.hindustantimes.com/news/181_1843381,0008.htm*. External Affairs Minister Pranab Mukherjee said this in reply to reporters' questions after the ground-breaking ceremony of Jawaharlal Nehru Bhavan, the proposed new headquarters of the Ministry of External Affairs.

7. "Agreement between the Government of the Republic of India and the Government of the People's Republic of China on the Political Parameters and Guiding Principles for the Settlement of the India–China Boundary Question", at *http://www.mea.gov.in/*. Accessed on 9 January, 2007.

8. Ibid.

9. Ibid.

territorial disputes. Was India's resolve on the eventual settlement of the boundary issue being tested? Or were the remarks an outcome of certain dissonant voices in China's foreign policy establishment?

The 'Economics' Dimension of Sino–Indian Relations

The 'economics cooperation' driver in Sino–Indian relations is poised to overshadow and even perhaps significantly influence the 'political security' content of the relationship in the years to come. The prime reason for optimism is the robust expansion of trade. Premier Zhu Rongji on a visit to India in early 2002 had called for Sino–Indian trade to reach US $10 billion by 2007. The Joint Study Group, formed in 2004 to identify bilateral economic complementarities and opportunities had predicted a trade figure of US$20 billion by 2008.[10] Current indications are that both these expectations were modest. In 2006 bilateral trade touched US$24.9 billion, making China India's second-largest trading partner after the United States. For China, India is its tenth-largest trading partner.[11] In 2005 bilateral trade was worth US$18.7 billion.[12] An emerging point of concern, however, is that despite an annual average growth in trade of around 44 per cent for the last five years, the quality and composition are very basic, concentrated in a narrow range to include primary and semifinished steel, iron ore, plastic and linoleum products, and other ores and minerals. At the same time, the two countries are expanding their horizons in sourcing IT hardware goods and software services from each other.

One-time rivals for control of oil and gas fields in Angola, Nigeria, Kazakhstan, and Ecuador, India and China agreed in January 2006 to cooperate on overseas acquisitions. The agreement grew out of their co-ownership of a Sudanese field and a cooperative bid for fields in Syria.[13] The agreement includes upstream exploration and refining in

---

10. Report of the Sino–Indian Joint Study Group on Trade and Economic Cooperation. The joint study group was formed in March 2004.
11. *Xinhua* News Agency (Beijing), 27 January, 2007.
12. See "Sino–Indian trade to top US $20b this year", at *http://www.chinadaily.com.cn/china/2006-04/17/content_569793.htm*. Accessed on 28 November 2006. Also see Ginn Weblog at *http://blogs.fletcher.tufts.edu/ginnblog/archives/000659.html*.
13. Richard McGregor, Jo Johnson and Carola Hoyos (2006). "China and India Forge Alliance on Oil", *Financial Times* (London), 12 January.

the oil sector, the laying of national and transnational oil and gas pipelines, frontier and cutting-edge research and development, as well as a joint energy efficiency programme. The two countries will also tap the potential for working together on biofuels, such as vegetable oils blending with diesel and ethanol blending with gasoline. A working group will meet at least once a year to keep track of the cooperation.

India and China have also agreed to coordinate their strategies in supporting developing countries within the World Trade Organization (WTO). A key aspect of this cooperation and consultation will be the search for special safeguard mechanisms for developing countries in agriculture. This is in recognition of a basic fact for both countries. Despite reforms and their success, a majority of the productive workforce of both India and China still earns its livelihood by cultivating land. With large populations to support, introducing market forces hastily in this crucial sector would undo the relative gains accrued from years of 'fine-tuning' the economy to face the challenges of globalisation. Other areas of potential Sino–Indian cooperation within the WTO framework relate to TRIPS (Trade Related Intellectual Property Rights) with reference to public health issues, in the explicit context of paragraph 6 of the Doha Declaration, besides investment policy and the related issue of dispute settlement.

Analysis

Being 'security seekers' and alternately 'power seekers', China and India are highly conscious of relative gains made bilaterally. By pursuing great-power diplomacy—the July 2005 India–US nuclear deal being a case in point—to secure its vital national interests and raise its profile on the global stage, India's desire to be recognised as a major power beyond South Asia does at various levels pose a challenge to China's interests in the region. From the current Chinese perspective the world's states, particularly the large states, share common approaches to a large spectrum of international problems. Therefore, they must cooperate in their common interest. China has discarded its earlier rigid assumptions of inevitable large-scale world war and adopted a premise that 'peace and development' are the guidelines of the modern world. It has acknowledged the diversity prevalent in the contemporary world with every one of its components composed of 'internal contradictions', on the one hand, and striving for self-reliance, on the other. The evolving Sino-Indian relations reflect this disposition.

President Hu Jintao's public statements during his visit reflected equanimity and temperance. Upon arrival at New Delhi, he complimented India as being "a great nation that has created a time-honoured civilisation and splendid culture."[14] China and India were close neighbours, and the friendly exchanges between the two peoples dated back to ancient times. In recent years, he said, China-India relations had maintained sound momentum of all-round growth, marked by strengthened mutual political trust, expanded mutually beneficial cooperation, broadened friendly exchanges, and good coordination in international and regional affairs.

Within India, there is consensus across the political spectrum on improving and developing relations with China. There is also recognition that the India–China relationship is not to be typecast with antiquated formulations of 'balance of power' and 'clash of interests.' As two continental-size economies and established political entities they are too big to contain each other or be contained by any other country. The issue of Tibet seemed to have receded into the background with the joint declaration mentioning that India recognises the Tibet Autonomous Region as part of the territory of the People's Republic of China and that it does not allow Tibetans to engage in anti-China political activities in India. The Chinese side expressed its appreciation of the Indian position.

As regards Sun Yuxi's 'utterances' about China's territorial claims, these should be seen as the adoption of a 'maximalist approach' aimed at influencing the negotiations between the Special Representatives dealing with the boundary issue. These meetings would infuse dynamism to the entire process of delineating the Line of Actual Control (LAC) and establish the contours of a firm, permanent, mutually acceptable boundary between the two countries. The Special Representatives (M.K. Narayanan and Dai Bingguo) held their ninth round of consultations on 18–19 January 2007. As a matter of policy, their deliberations are not open to public disclosure.

---

14. See *http://www.fmprc.gov.cn/eng/zxxx/t281558.htm*. Accessed on 7 January, 2007.

It could be argued that India's new-found confidence in promoting bilateral political and economic relations with China stems from its improved economic performance. With exports steadily increasing and economic growth at over 9 per cent in 2006, India has become China's largest trading partner in South Asia. China's 'observer' status in the South Asian Association for Regional Cooperation (SAARC) will further intensify and diversify India-China trade. A comparable aspect has been India's entry into the Shanghai Cooperation Organization (SCO) as an observer. India also became a member of the East Asia Summit (EAS) in December 2005, despite China's initial opposition. The recognition and recent reopening of Nathu La[15] as the pass for entry and exit after forty-four years could be interpreted as China's subtle gesture in acknowledging India's sovereignty over Sikkim. The opening of Nathu La and the setting up of two customs posts on either side (Renqinggang in the Tibetan Autonomous Region of China and Sherathang in Sikkim, India) will benefit local communities.

15. Nathu-La, meaning "Listening Ear" and standing at 15,000 ft, was closed in 1962 after China's brief invasion of India.

15

Sino-Japanese Strategic Relations

ABANTI BHATTACHARYA

Sino-Japanese relations have long been a hostage to historical acrimony and power politics. While the Cold War era saw tensions between the two on the legacies of Japanese invasion of China, the Taiwan issue, and the disputed sovereign claims over Senkaku/Diaoyu Islands, the post-Cold War and post-9/11 era saw new tensions over exclusive economic zones (EEZ) and drilling rights, the Japanese Prime Minister's Yasukuni Shrine visits, the textbook issue, the Japanese quest for a permanent seat in the United Nations Security Council, and the illegal Chinese surveys of waters adjacent to Japan.

These tensions have cast a bitter shadow over the relations. However, two major developments in 2006—the election of Shinzo Abe as the Japanese Prime Minister in September and North Korea's nuclear test in October—have altered the Asian balance of power and ushered in hopes of improved relations, with Prime Minister Abe's visit to China in October being hailed as a turning point. This essay reviews how these developments impact Sino-Japanese relations, Asian security structure, and India.

Background: Enmeshing of History and Power Competition

Over the last few years Sino-Japanese relations have soured as a result of the complex enmeshing of two broad issues: history and power competition. These have fuelled their competing nationalisms and shaped the present bitter contours of their relationship. Chinese and Japanese scholars hold that for the first time in history both countries are rising and "have become powers with equal weight."[1] This has induced uncertainty and instability in the East Asian region. The Japanese are uncomfortable with the rise of China, implying a new great power in the neighbourhood poised to attract long-time American allies to its orbit and thus dominate the region. As Joseph Nye has pointed out, China in many ways is fast emerging as a soft power[2] that is economically becoming attractive and politically generating a spirit of harmonious coexistence. This is gravitating the erstwhile allies of Japan and the United States to China's orbit. The growing Chinese defence spending, with 17.8 per cent rise in 2007, and the recent demonstration of its potential to engage in the 'Star Wars' with its anti-satellite weapon test have made Japan even more nervous about the rise of China.

In response, the Japanese are increasingly defining their state policies on the basis of nationalism and the Japanese government is fast shedding its pacifist approach to acquire a 'normal' state status. Besides strengthening its alliance with Washington, Japan has also, for the first time (in 2005), recognised Taiwan as a common security concern with the US. This has alarmed China, since reunification of Taiwan is central to Chinese nationalism. China's opposition to Japan's bid for a permanent seat in the Security Council is also indicative of the logic of China's urge to remain the sole great power in the region. Both countries are in the process of redefining their power positions in the international system and this has transformed the Asian balance of power significantly.

Parallel to this power competition is the vexed issue of 'history', which has increasingly come to influence Sino-Japanese relations. China has a deep sense of history and it consciously uses history to achieve its foreign policy objectives. Embedded in this notion of history is the Chinese worldview that projected China as the centre of the world. This worldview, however, collapsed with the Sino-Japanese War of 1894-95, in which Japan defeated China and took over

1. Yingfan, Wang (2006). "Building Trust between China and Japan", *China Daily*, 8 August, at *http://www.Chinadaily.com.cn/opinion/2006-08/08/content_659299.htm*, accessed on 9 September 2006.

2. Nye, Joseph (2005). "The Rise of China's Soft Power", *Wall Street Journal Asia*, 29 December, at *http://www.ksg.harvard.edu/ksgnews/Features/opeds/122905_nye.htm*, accessed 21 August, 2006.

Taiwan.[3] Chinese animosity towards Japan has its roots in this defeat, by which the superior Chinese civilisational state, which had for long treated Japan benevolently as a younger brother within its realm, was defeated by the latter. The loss of Taiwan to Japan marked an "extraordinary humiliation" for China.[4] Reunification of Taiwan, thus, became firmly embedded in the Chinese nationalist agenda. In Japan, the problem of history is twofold: one, how Japan could emerge as a normal power through amendment of its pacifist constitution and expansion of its military capability. Two, how it would reconcile with its militarist past and put to rest the wartime controversies that impinge on its relations with China and Korea. This history factor has dogged Sino-Japanese relations with three major controversies: history textbooks, apologies, and former Prime Minister Junichiro Koizumi's annual visits to the Yasukuni shrine.[5] It refuses to bow out despite the three joint communiqués signed by the two governments in 1972, 1978, and 1998.

Sino-Japanese Relations in 2006: A Year of Recovery

In 2006 two major developments ushered in hopes of a thaw in Sino-Japanese relations. First was the change in Japanese leadership and Prime Minister Shinzo Abe's subsequent 'ice-breaking' China tour on 8 and 9 October; the second, North Korea's nuclear test on 9 October. *Renmin Ribao* hailed 2006 as a year of recovery for China–Japan relations.[6] Shinzo Abe's tour of China within a fortnight of replacing Junichiro Koizumi as Prime Minister was the first visit by a Japanese leader in five years. During his China visit, the two countries issued a joint press communiqué expressing agreement on properly handling the problems that affect their bilateral relations.[7] Abe's new

---

3. Gries, Peter Hays (2004). *China's New Nationalism* (Berkeley: California University Press): 70.
4. Ibid.
5. Chan, Che-po and Brian Bridges (2006). "China, Japan, and the Clash of Nationalism", *Asian Perspective* 30(1): 141.
6. Zhaowen, Ding (2007). "The Chinese Academy of Social Sciences announces Publication of a Yellow Paper on 2006 Global Political and Security Situation", *Xinhua*, 10 January, *FBIS*, *www.dialog.com*, accessed on 12 January 2007.
7. Japan–China Joint Press Statement, The Ministry of Foreign Affairs of Japan (henceforth MOFA), 8 October 2006, at *http://www.mofa.go.jp/region/asia-paci/china/joint0610.html*, accessed 16 January 2007; Lin Chuan, "Shinzo Abe concludes his China visit; his 'ice-breaking tour' presents an opportunity for change in China-Japan relations", *Zhongguo Tongxun She*, 9 October 2006, FBIS, *www.dialog.com*, accessed on 12 January 2007.

strategy towards China has been characterised as "strategic reciprocity" in the media of the two countries.[8]

High-level visits and bilateral exchanges increased significantly following Abe's China visit. At the November 2006 APEC (Asia-Pacific Economic Cooperation) leaders' informal meeting in Hanoi both sides reached "a consensus on building reciprocal strategic relations."[9] On the vexed history issue they decided to reach an agreement through joint historical research, the research being based on the principle of facing history squarely and looking forward to the future. They also agreed to deepen objective understanding of history by studying bilateral exchanges over the past 2000 years, including the unfortunate developments in China–Japan relations of the past sixty years.[10] On the Taiwan issue, Abe reiterated the principles established by the Japan–China Joint Statement and "this stand has remained unchanged."[11] In a further demonstration of goodwill, instead of visiting the Yasukuni shrine Abe visited a Meiji shrine which only honours Emperor Mutsuhito (1868-1912) and his wife.[12]

North Korea's nuclear test of 9 October, 2006 came during Abe's China visit, diverting the two countries from the vexed 'history' issue to focus on achieving stability in the Korean Peninsula. President Hu Jintao said on the occasion that China and Japan should persist in de-nuclearisation of the peninsula and peacefully resolve the Korean nuclear issue through dialogue, so as to safeguard peace and stability of North East Asia.[13] Reciprocating, Abe said that Japan stands for de-nuclearisation of the Korean Peninsula and resolution of the issue through dialogue.[14] Reflecting the change of emphasis on issues

8. Yuasa, Hiroshi (2006). "Japan-China Summit: Skilful Move to 'Strategic Reciprocity'", *Sankei Shimbun*, 12 October, *FBIS*, *www.dialog.com*, accessed on 12 January 2007.

9. Hui, Luo and Chen Hegao (2006). "Hu Jintao Meets Japanese Prime Minister Shinzo Abe", *Xinhua*, 18 November, *FBIS*, *www.dialog.com*, accessed on 12 January 2007.

10. Haimin, Huang and Xu Jianmei (2006). "Chinese and Japanese Foreign Ministers Reach Agreement on China–Japan Joint Historical Research", *Xinhua*, 16 November, *FBIS*, *www.dialog.com*, accessed on 12 January 2007.

11. Luo and Chen, n. 9.

12. "Abe Revives Visit to Tokyo Shrine by Incumbent Prime Minister", *International Herald Tribune*, 6 January 2007, at *http://www.iht.com/articles/ap/2007/01/06/asia/AS-GEN-Japan-Abe.php*, accessed on 16 January 2007.

13. Luo and Chen, n. 9.

14. Ibid.

besetting China–Japan relations the Chinese Premier Wen Jiabao said in a meeting with members of the New Japan–China Friendship Committee for the Twenty-first Century on 23 October, 2006 that "China does not intend to concentrate on historical issues between China and Japan forever."[15] This convergence of the interests of the two countries may, however, turn out to be a passing phase.

Implications

The developments in Sino–Japanese relations in 2006 are assessed here for their implications for Sino–Japanese relations, for Asian Security Structure, and for India.

Impact on Sino–Japanese Relations

In his New Year message for 2007 Shinzo Abe described Sino–Japanese relations as "mutually beneficial, strategic relationship", indicating his government's recognition of China as a priority in its wider foreign policy strategy.[16] His government has pragmatically handled the history issue, where according to the Chinese Japan has so far been "incorrigibly obstinate."[17] The history question is, however, far from resolved. Significant sections in China are opposed to the moderate policies of their government towards Japan and see history as the key issue between the two sides. In any future solution to the territorial disputes, the history factor is likely to emerge as a key contending area.

At the same time, Abe is promoting the cause of assertive Japanese nationalism, much to the discomfort of China. On 15 December, 2006 the Diet passed a bill that upgraded the Japan Defence Agency (JDA) to full ministry status. The same day the government passed a bill approving, along party lines, that schools should teach patriotism.[18]

---

15. Sugiyama, Hiroyuki (2006). "China, Japan Can Look to Future by Facing History Issue, says Wen", *Yomiuri Shimbun*, 25 October, at *http://www.yomiuri.co.jp/dy/national/20061025TDY03003.htm*, accessed on 29 October 2006.
16. Pilling, David (2007). "Abe Puts Relations with China as Priority", *Financial Times*, 1 January, at *http://www.ft.com/cms/s/67bb5f98-99a5-11db-8b6d-0000779e2340.html*, accessed on 16 January 2007.
17. Qing, Yang (2001). "Enough of Japan's 'Theory of Feelings'", *Jiefangjun Bao*, 16 July, *FBIS*, *www.dialog.com*, accessed on 12 January 2007.
18. Fraser, Ron (2006). "Japan on the Rise", 26 December, at *http://www.thetrumpet.com/index.php?page=article&id=2812*, accessed on 16 January 2007.

Although Abe seems to have toned down strong anti-Chinese sentiments, nationalism in Japan is still characterised by a strong assertive tenor.

Teaching patriotism in Japanese schools, with its message of patriotism and 'love of the country', bears striking similarity to China's 'patriotic education' that started in the 1990s. Since the Chinese began the trend, they may not have much to complain about vocally. The Japanese mainly ascribe anti-Japanese sentiment among the Chinese to China's heightened patriotic education.[19] Japan's revised Fundamental Law of Education introduces in its preamble the idea of respect for the public spirit and calls for developing "an attitude which respects tradition and culture and love of the nation and homeland that have fostered them" as a goal of education.[20]

Commenting on Abe's move to upgrade the JDA to cabinet level Zhou Yongsheng, a professor of international relations at the China Institute of Foreign Affairs, Beijing, told *China Daily* that the change demonstrates Japan's substantial efforts to remove the present restraints in intervening in international affairs.[21] It also means factoring of military matters in Japan's foreign policy decision making.[22]

Abe's visit to the NATO headquarters, the first by a Japanese prime minister, augments Japan's role in international affairs. In his speech at the North Atlantic Council Abe said, "My government will develop and carry out a proactive foreign policy, and that Japan should play a meaningful role on the global stage."[23] Abe has also declared that he views the US–Japan alliance as the central pillar of Japan's foreign

---

19. (2005). "Japan's Guilt Imprinted [on Minds of the Chinese] People: Impression Strengthened Further Since Jiang Zemin Era", *Tokyo Shimbun*, 13 April, FBIS, *www.dialog.com*, accessed on 12 January 2007.
20. (2006). "Revised Education Law to Enhance Patriotism goes into Effect", *Japan Today*, 22 December, at *http://www.japantoday.com/jp/news/394195*, accessed on 16 January 2007.
21. Tain, Le (2007). "Japan's Defence Agency Upgraded", *China Daily*, 10 January, at *http://www.chinadaily.com.cn/world/2007-01/10/content_779165.htm*, accessed on 16 January 2007.
22. (2006). "Military Assumes New Role in Japanese Government", *The Trumpet*, 8 December, at *http://www.thetrumpet.com/index.php?page=article&id=2762*, accessed on 16 January 2007.
23. Speech by Prime Minister Shinzo Abe at the North Atlantic Council, "Japan and NATO: Toward Further Collaboration", MOFA, 12 January 2007, at *http://www.mofa.go.jp/region/europe/pmv0701/nato.html*, accessed on 16 January 2007.

policy. He also expressed apprehensions about China's continued increase in defence spending and lack of transparency in military modernisation.[24] On 11 January, 2007 he disapproved of the European Union's lifting of its ban on arms exports to China. For its part, China is concerned about Japan's robust defence policy, deepening US–Japan alliance, and growing Tokyo–Canberra military ties.

Impact on Asian Security Structure

In the post–Cold War and post 9/11 era Asian security structure is characterised by two broad elements: one, a US-based alliance system with its 'hub and spokes' arrangement; and two, multilateral organisations. Japan is one spoke of the US-led alliance system. China is out of it and has increasingly engaged its Asian periphery through a number of regional and multilateral organisations.

Japan is witnessing two paradoxical developments. On the one hand, it considers its alliance with the US as central to its foreign policy strategy; on the other, it is increasingly charting its own path to acquire a 'normal status.' A strong US–Japan alliance, while helping to contain China would inhibit Japan's aspirations for a normal status.

China's primary regional strategy is guided by the need for a stable, secured periphery that would ensure sustained economic development which, in turn, would lay the basis for achieving a great-power status. However, the US-based alliance system and Taiwanese nationalism pose a grave security threat to China. In this context it is in China's interest not to have an anti-China, xenophobic, ultra-nationalist Japan when it can significantly improve its security environment and diplomatic position through Sino–Japanese rapprochement, which possibility Shi Yinhong describes as a diplomatic revolution.[25] He notes: "China has a greater need than Japan to improve the two countries' relationship....If Sino–Japanese relationship improves dramatically and the Sino–Japanese rapprochement becomes a reality,

24. Press conference by Prime Minister Shinzo Abe following his visit to Europe, MOFA, 13 January 2007, at *http://www.kantei.go.jp/foreign/abespeech/2007/01/13press_e.html*, accessed on 12 January 2007.

25. Yinhong, Shi (2003). "Sino-Japanese rapprochement as a 'Diplomatic Revolution' ", originally published in Chinese in *Strategy and Management (zhanlue yu guanli)*, February, at *http://www.uscc.gov/hearings/2003hearings/written_testimonies/031030bios/sing-japrapprochement.htm*, accessed on 17 January 2007.

it will strengthen China's strategic position and China's diplomatic dealings with the US."[26] Besides security considerations, Japan as the second-largest economic power in the world is still important for China's peaceful rise, enabling it to reach a consensus with Japan on various issues of security cooperation and economic integration. For instance, the East Asian Community would be a reality if Sino–Japanese interests converge.

For Japan the challenges to its great-power aspirations emanate primarily from a rising China and a nuclear North Korea. Lacking independent military power, Japan's interest is better served by being entrenched in the US alliance system. Strengthened US–Japan security relations have given Japanese leaders greater self-confidence and assertiveness *vis-à-vis* China,[27] but Japan's ambition of being a country possessing all the factors of power as a nation is also facilitated by greater cooperation with China. Japan also needs investment and trade in China. China is Japan's biggest trade partner and the importance of the Chinese market for Japan is increasing.[28]

Fractious Sino–Japanese relations are also not in US interest. Since the United States' East Asian security strategy is best served by maintaining a balance between China and Japan, that is, by continuing its alliance with Japan and South Korea while upholding a benign relation with China, Sino–Japanese rapprochement is likely to continue in the best interests of all players in the Asian security structure.

The North Korean nuclear test has created a paradoxical impact on the regional balance of power.[29] On the one hand, it has strengthened the US alliance system in Asia and imparted greater relevance to the US as a security manager; on the other, the nuclear crisis has strengthened China's position in East Asia. US dependence on China in resolving the North Korean nuclear crisis is likely to increase, implying a greater Chinese influence in the region. The complex

26. Ibid.

27. Soerensen, Camilla T.N. (2006). "Strategic 'Triangularity' in Northeast Asia: The Sino-Japanese Security Relationship and US Policy", *Asian Perspective* 30(3): 113.

28. Luo, Wang (2007). "Economic Ties are Changing", *Beijing Review* 50(15) (12 April), at *http://www.bjreview.com.cn/print/txt/2007-04/09/content_61197.htm*, accessed on 1 May 2007.

29. Bhattacharya, Abanti (2006). "North Korean Nuclear Crisis: Challenges and Options for China", *Strategic Analysis* 30(4) (Oct-Dec): 862.

interplay of various elements in the Asian regional order suggests that so long as Sino–Japanese relations remain fundamentally unaltered and the US role remains dominant, the current Asian security structure will hold.[30]

Impact on India

A stable regional order in Asia being contingent on stable Sino–Japanese relations, the present improvement in Sino–Japanese relations is a welcome development for India. It would not only facilitate greater security cooperation and regional integration at the multilateral level but also facilitate strengthening of India's bilateral relations with China and Japan. Robust and meaningful Indo–Japanese relations cannot be developed without cordial relations with China in today's integrated regional political and economic order. India's relations with China are on the upswing and are characterised by strategic partnership. Japan–India ties have also been raised to the level of 'strategic and global partnership' on 15 December 2006.

The changing Asian balance of power has indeed put India in a tight spot. On the one hand, its ties with the US are often viewed as anti-China alliance; on the other, its cooperation with China is imperative to keep Asia peaceful and to facilitate its own rise. Therefore, India's primary diplomatic challenge would be to maintain a balance between the sole superpower and a rising China.

The history factor, which Beijing uses in its foreign policy objectives, especially to assert its territorial and diplomatic claims and which has played a crucial role in determining Sino–Japanese relations, has instructive value for India while dealing with the Chinese on the border issue.

To sum up, given the significance of Sino–Japanese relations in the Asian security structure, a thawing of relations between the two East Asian giants is a welcome development for regional security and economic integration. The twin developments of 2006—the change in the Japanese political leadership and the North Korean nuclear crisis—

---

30. See Yahuda, Michael (2005). "The Evolving Asian Order: The Accommodation of Rising Chinese Power", in David Shambaugh (ed.), *Power Shift: China and Asia's New Dynamism* (Berkeley: University of California Press): 347–61.

have altered the Asian balance of power and ushered in hopes of improvement in Sino–Japanese relations. Much of the cordiality in the relationship would, however, depend upon how the two East Asian giants handle the underlying strategic differences and how they operate in the fluid context of Asian balance of power.

16

Japan's Leadership Transition

ARPITA MATHUR

The year 2006 witnessed a leadership transition in Japan, with Junichiro Koizumi handing over the reins of power to former Chief Cabinet Secretary Shinzo Abe. With this transition a paradigm shift in the eternally circumscribed Japanese security policy as well as a redefinition of its global role along with political resurrection is evident. An obvious pointer to this trend is Japan's staking a claim for a permanent seat in the UN Security Council. While the Koizumi regime initiated many of these changes, especially in the aftermath of the events of 11 September 2001, the Abe government is accelerating the pace of domestic reform, especially in matters pertaining to the pacifist Constitution and educational reforms, even as attempts are being made to ameliorate strained ties with neighbours.

The first prime minister from the post-war generation and a self-professed nationalist and hawk, Abe came as a relative novice on the political centre stage at a time when Japan's strategic culture is in transformation. The process was set in motion by Koizumi, who initiated the ongoing rethinking on the Constitution, amplification of the role of the Japanese Self-Defence Forces (SDF), US-Japan collaboration on missile defence, and Tokyo's active support to Washington in the 'war on terror.' His regime also took unpopular decisions such as despatching SDF to Iraq and breaking Japan out of the traditionally pacifist mould towards a more realist outlook, however 'reluctant' it may have seemed. Although one of the most charismatic leader of Japan, Koizumi riled his neighbours such as China and South Korea with his repeated visits to the controversial Yasukuni Shrine, which they see as a symbol of Japanese nationalism and militarism. On the other hand, there was palpable invigoration and fortification of the US–Japan Security alliance under US President George W. Bush and Koizumi, who shared an extraordinary rapport, often equated with the Ron-Yasu (Ronald Reagan–Yasuhiro Nakasone) years.

In coming to power in September 2006 Abe rode high on the popularity index, defeating his rivals Foreign Minister Taro Aso and Finance Minister Sadakazu Tanigaki, with polls showing as many as 57 per cent voters supporting his candidacy.[1] The immediate challenge for him was to ably handle the Koizumi legacy of strained ties with neighbours, and internal problems like an ageing population and prickly economic problems. The major issues he promised to address included constitutional amendment, resumption of summit-level talks with neighbours, and educational and economic reforms.[2] He articulated the vision of the 'beautiful country', encompassing four variables:

- a country that values culture, tradition, and history;
- a country underpinned by a free society;
- a country that continues to possess the vitality to grow towards the future; and
- a country that is trusted, respected and loved in the world and demonstrates leadership.[3]

Three broad strands have marked Abe's tenure. One, there is greater focus on countries of Asia like Australia, India, and ASEAN members. He chose to visit these countries on the first trip overseas after taking over as Prime Minister, rather than the customary road to Washington taken by most Japanese prime ministers. Second, there is acceleration in the pace of internal reforms like attempts to revise the Constitution and educational reforms. While he has set a timeline of the next five years to revise the current Constitution, the Fundamental Law of Education has been revised and the Japan Defence Agency

1. (2006). "Survey Shows 57 per cent Support Abe, but his Leadership Abilities are Doubted", *Asahi Shimbun*, 23 September, at *http://www.asahi.com/english/Herald-asahi/TKY200609230139.html*.
2. (2006). "List of Abe's Policies Pledged", *Kyodo News*, 26 September, at *http://home.kyodo.co.jp/modules/fstStory/index.php?storyid=273163*
3. (2006). "Policy Speech by Prime Minister Shinzo Abe to the 165th Session of the Diet", 29 September, at *http://www.kantei.go.jp/foreign/abespeech/2006/09/29speech_e.html*.

(JDA) has been upgraded to ministry level. The Education Law, promulgated in 1947, had remained unaltered. Prime Minister Abe pushed for reform of the law to aim at "cultivating an attitude that respects tradition and culture, loves the nation and homeland that have fostered them, while respecting other countries and contributing to international peace and development."[4] Upgradation of JDA to ministry level and its Director General to a Cabinet Minister level is significant both symbolically and also for its practical implications. The Defence Minister is now permitted to directly submit legislation to the Diet and call for Cabinet meetings. Abe has also shown considerable urgency in moving ahead on the national referendum law, a prerequisite to the proposed revision of the Constitution.

Third, Abe has sagaciously restored damaged relations with neighbouring countries such as China and South Korea. His neighbourhood policy appears to be more pragmatic than his predecessor's even as he actively pursues his domestic agenda of buttressing Japan's strategic culture. His views on trips to the Yasukuni Shrine remain ambiguous, to be considered 'appropriately' when the time comes.

Abe travelled to China and South Korea within a month of taking over as prime minister. Koizumi had travelled to China five years earlier. Abe met Chinese President Hu Jintao, who described the visit as a "turning point" in ties that will "lead Japan–China relations to a higher level."[5] Commending Abe for choosing China as the first destination on his first overseas trip as prime minister, Hu described it as "a sign that you are emphasising improvement and development of China-Japan relations."[6] The two sides spoke of establishing a strong strategic partnership. Other issues which came under the scanner during the visit were setting up of a panel to discuss the history issue and energy and environmental issues.

---

4. Ito, Masami (2006). "Abe's Education Bill Clears Lower House: Opposition Boycotts Floor Vote", *Japan Times*, 17 November, at *http:// search.japantimes.co.jp/cgi-bin/nn20061117a1.html.*
5. Kahn, Joseph (2006). "China and Japan Take Steps to Mend Fences", *New York Times*, 8 October, at *http://www.iht.com/articles/2006/10/09/asia/web.1009abe.php.*
6. Nakata, Hiroko (2006). "Abe, Hu Agree to Push 'Strategic' Ties: North Korea Nuclear Crisis Sparks 'Deep Concern'", *Japan Times*, 9 October, at *http:search.japantimes.co.jp/cgi-bin/nn20061009a1.html.*

Abe's visit to Seoul coincided with the North Korean nuclear test and became the talking point for much of the discussions. The visit, originally aimed at resolving the problem over history, saw a shift in focus, as China, South Korea, and Japan in unison condemned Pyongyang for its "unpardonable act."

Dovetailing Japan's strident moves towards 'normalisation' with current realities, legislation has been enacted delineating participation in peacekeeping operations as a primary duty of Japanese SDFs. The White Paper on Defence 2006 justifies this duty with the following reasons:[7]

- need to respond to emergency situations arising out of the spread of WMDs (weapons of mass destruction), ballistic missiles;
- alterations in the roles of defence forces of the international community beyond preventive measures and respond to contingencies like terrorism and UN peacekeeping;
- to strengthen response to emergencies; and
- ensure Japan's proactive initiatives for peace and stability.

Simultaneously, Japan's response to developments and situations in the regional context like the Taiwan issue and the North Korean nuclear test have also been more vocal and sharper. While the Joint Statement after the US-Japan Security Consultative meeting on 19 February 2005 in Washington D.C. broke new ground by including Taiwan as a 'common security concern', Pyongyang's nuclear test also drew censure from Japan and became yet another test of Abe's diplomatic and political mettle. Japan imposed tough unilateral sanctions on Pyongyang with support from Washington. Magnifying Tokyo's concerns is the unresolved abductees issue with North Korea.[8] Demonstrating his particular concern over the matter Abe has created a special Cabinet post to grapple with it. Pyongyang's test also reignited the Japanese domestic debate over the nuclear issue and

7. *Defense of Japan 2006*, Japan's Ministry of Defense, at *http://www.jda.go.jp/e/publications/wp2006/pdf/2-4-1.pdf*: 134-5.

8. The issue involves Pyongyang's abduction of Japanese citizens for the purpose of using them to tutor North Korean spies in Japanese language and culture. North Korea officially admitted to the abduction of 13 Japanese citizens in 2002.

whether the US nuclear umbrella would suffice in the midst of a critical regional situation, even as public support for Abe's hardliner approach towards Pyongyang lifted his approval ratings to 83 per cent.[9] Encapsulating his vision of a more globally assertive Japan, Abe in his opening speech to the Diet advocated the need for Japan to switch to a more proactive diplomacy to meet the 'quintessential' need for Japan to present its 'country identity' to the world.[10]

Abe's domestic popularity plummeted, however, to 48.6 per cent by the end of the year after he readmitted into the Liberal Democratic Party rebels to the cause of postal privatisation.[11] Koizumi had expelled them in 2005.

Mapping the Realignment of US Forces in Japan

Washington still remains the lynchpin of Tokyo's security construct but there is a plan to realign American forces in Japan. Major features of the document, *United States–Japan Roadmap for Realignment Implementation,*[12] issued in May 2006 and endorsed by the Cabinet soon after, are:

- relocation of the US Marine Corps Futenma Air Station within Okinawa Prefecture;
- move 8000 of the 18,000 US Marines from Okinawa to Guam by 2014;
- Japan to set up a council with Okinawa, Nago and other local authorities to discuss specific realignment plans, environmental issues, etc.;
- headquarters of the 1st Marine Air Wing Headquarters to be moved from Futenma to Guam;
- US Patriot PAC-3 capabilities to be deployed in Japan within existing US facilities and areas;

9. (2006). "Survey: 62 per cent Support Sanctions Against North Korea", *Asahi Shimbun*, 11 October, at *http://www.asahi.com/english/Herald-asahi/TKY200610110291.html.*
10. n. 3.
11. (2006). "Cabinet Support Rate Falls to 48.6 per cent", *Japan Times*, 7 December, at *http://search.japantimes.co.jp/cgi-bin/nn20061207a1.html.*
12. For text of the document see *United States-Japan Roadmap for Realignment Implementation*, 1 May 2006, at *http://www.globalsecurity.org/military/library/news/2006/05/d20060501realign-implement.pdf.*

- bilateral training plans between US forces and Japan's SDF to be drawn out.

The realignment plan is seen as crucial to bolster the security alliance. While the plan focused on reducing the burden on Okinawa, which hosts 75 per cent of the American troops, the Okinawa Prefecture government expressed reservations over certain clauses of the plan, raising questions over its effective implementation.

India–Japan Ties

Under the Abe administration ties between India and Japan have entered a period of significant substance and scope, more than half a century after relations were established in 1952. During Prime Minister Manmohan Singh's visit to Japan in December 2006 Prime Minister Abe termed the bilateral relationship as the "most important" one in the world from the Japanese perspective. In his recently authored book, entitled *Towards a Beautiful Country*, Abe notes that he would not be surprised if the India–Japan relationship overtakes the Japan–China and Japan–US ties in the future. This, of course, would necessitate considerable inputs from both partners to the relationship. The proposed Asia-Oceania Democratic Three-plus-US quadrilateral formula mooted by Abe, to include Japan-India-Australia and the US at the summit or ministerial level is yet another proposed common forum. With infectious enthusiasm Abe told the Diet in his policy speech, "... as a democratic nation in Asia, I will engage in strategic dialogues at the leader's level with countries that share fundamental values such as Australia and India, with a view to widening the circle of free societies in Asia as well as in the world."[13]

The India–Japan Joint Statement envisaging this Global and Strategic Partnership, issued during Prime Minister Manmohan Singh's visit to Japan, has to encompass a wide spectrum of elements—defence, politics, and economics. It clearly builds on the Eight-fold initiative carved out during Prime Minister Koizumi's visit to India in April 2005. The 2006 Joint Statement calls for holding annual summit-level and ministerial meetings, institutionalisation of strategic dialogue at the Foreign minister level, consultations between the Japanese

---

13. n. 3.

Ministry of Foreign Affairs and the Indian Ministry of External Affairs, greater interaction between the Indian Navy and Japanese Maritime SDF, including proposed joint exercises in 2007, cooperation in securing maritime traffic, and a joint working group on terrorism. Placing comprehensive economic engagement as the bedrock of bilateral ties, the statement called for launching of negotiations for the conclusion of a bilateral Economic Partnership Agreement in a span of two years. A Japan-India Special Economic Partnership Initiative to promote investment from Japan has also been envisaged.

To achieve the strategic orientation of the envisioned global partnership both countries will need to effectively implement the charted roadmap under achievable timelines. There is also a need to bridge the gap in thinking on the civilian nuclear issue through more discussion and dialogue. India's not having a historical baggage against Japan will work to promote this relationship as also the fact that Japan's normalisation is not viewed with any emotional baggage unlike some other Asian neighbours.

Conclusion

The year 2006 was a milestone in Japanese political and strategic architecture in myriad ways. Politically, the leadership transition ended a most significant phase of the Koizumi regime. Continuity has been ensured in the fact that Prime Minister Abe was mentored by Koizumi to take on the mantle and shares his nationalistic and hawkish orientation, demonstrated by the fact that within three months of assuming office, Abe's priorities were clearly laid out to focus on educational reforms to instil patriotism, active steps to move towards constitutional revision, and augmentation of the role of the SDFs, among other things. Most of these variables Koizumi initiated. Abe entered the arena with high approval ratings, which soared following his fire-fighting with neighbouring countries, but the sheen wore off by the end of the year, with public opinion sceptical about his ability to deliver as also his ambiguous stance on a number of issues, further compounded by his choosing to reinstate rebel lawmakers. The challenge for Japan just now is not just to maintain ties with neighbours and build on them, but also to bring ambitious domestic reforms to a logical conclusion.

17

Nuclear Brinkmanship in East Asia

Responses and Ramifications

S. SAMUEL C. RAJIV

The nuclear test conducted by the Democratic People's Republic of Korea (DPRK, North Korea) on 9 October 2006, close on the heels of the multiple missile launches of 5 July, impacted negatively on the strategic landscape of East Asia. This chapter attempts to examine the responses to and ramifications of Pyongyang's brinkmanship, directed mainly against the United States.

First, events leading up to DPRK's escalatory actions will be examined briefly. Second, the responses of its immediate neighbours, such as South Korea, Japan, and China will be looked at. Diplomatic and military efforts undertaken by the United States to strengthen its key alliance relationships with Seoul and Tokyo will also be highlighted. Third, the impact on global nuclear non-proliferation efforts will be briefly examined, in the backdrop of the continuing march of Iran towards nuclear capability. Next, India's response in the light of the close relationship between Pyongyang and Islamabad encompassing the missile and nuclear fields will be pointed out. The section will also highlight the negative security implications of the United States' counter-proliferation initiatives. The chapter will conclude with an assessment of the deal put together on 13 February 2007 that promises to verifiably lock down Pyongyang's nuclear assets in a phased manner.

The author wishes to acknowledge the comments of Ambassador Shashank, former Foreign Secretary, Government of India, on this article.

Background: Broken Promises, Stalled Negotiations

If a policy of 'brinkmanship' is "the ability to get to the verge without getting into war", as defined by John Foster Dulles, North Korea seems to have perfected the art. The missile launches of 5 July and the nuclear test of 9 October followed the termination of the Korean Peninsula Energy Development Organization (KEDO) on 1 June.[1] Negotiations were also stalled over the implementation of the agreement reached at the fourth round of the Six-Party Talks, involving the United States, China, Japan, DPRK, Republic of Korea (RoK/South Korea), and Russia at Beijing on 19 September 2005.[2] At the talks, while North Korea agreed to verifiably abandon its nuclear weapon programme in return for economic and energy assistance, the United States pledged that it had no intention to attack or invade the DPRK with nuclear or conventional weapons. The two countries also agreed to "respect each other's sovereignty" and "exist peacefully together."[3]

Even before this round of talks had concluded, matters had worsened. On 15 September 2005 the US Department of Treasury designated the Banco Delta Asia, located in Macau, in which North Korea had invested $24 million, as a "primary money laundering concern" under Section 311 of the USA PATRIOT Act.[4] The bank was

1. KEDO was established in 1995 as part of the October 1994 Agreed Framework (AF) agreement concluded with the United States with a mandate to build two light water reactors (LWR's), having greater proliferation-resistant designs, in exchange for North Korea abandoning its nuclear weapons programme. The work on the reactors was suspended in November 2003 after the DPRK revealed in October 2002 that it had secretly continued its efforts to build nuclear weapons, in contravention of its promises under the 1994 agreement and its obligations as a member of the Nuclear Non-Proliferation Treaty (NPT).
2. The 2002 crisis resulted in the suspension of heavy oil shipments to North Korea by the US, Japan, and South Korea, 500,000 tonnes of which were pledged annually to the North under the terms of the AF agreement. Pyongyang reacted to the suspension of the oil shipments by withdrawing from the NPT, ejecting the inspectors of the International Atomic Energy Agency (IAEA) from the Yongbyon nuclear power plant, and restarted the production of plutonium. In order to find a way out of the impasse, the Six-Party Talks, brokered by China, were initiated in August 2003. Progress was achieved during the fourth round of talks in September 2005.
3. Kerr, Paul (2005). "North Korea Talks Achieve Breakthrough", *Arms Control Today* (henceforth *ACT*) 35(10) (October), at *http://www.armscontrol.org/act/2005_10/OCT-NKBreakthrough.asp*.
4. (2005). "Treasury Designates Banco Delta Asia as Primary Money Laundering Concern under USA PATRIOT Act", US Department of the Treasury, 15 September, at *http://www.ustreas.gov/press/releases/js2720.htm*.

providing financial services to North Korean agencies involved in illicit activities, including distribution of counterfeit US currency, it said.[5] Viewing this as Washington's strategy for regime change and a bargaining tactic to force concessions at the Six-Party Talks, Pyongyang insisted on the lifting of these sanctions to participate in future talks. The US on its part pointed out that the talks were about the verifiable closure of the North Korean nuclear programme.[6]

Pyongyang's Escalatory Actions: Reactive Interlocutors

Missile Tests

The multiple missile launches of 5 July included the firing of the three-stage Taepodong-2 intercontinental ballistic missile (ICBM) with a range exceeding 6000 km, shorter-range Scud-Cs and the medium-range Nodongs. In the aftermath, while Seoul, DPRK's primary aid-giver, further tightened its economic restrictions, Tokyo closed its ports to North Korean vessels, froze its assets in the country, and initiated moves to restrict cash remittances to Pyongyang. The Japanese government also seriously considered the prospect and the need to acquire assets that could be used to preemptively attack missile targets in North Korea.[7] Such assets included Tomahawk land-attack cruise missiles and fighter aircraft like the F-22 Raptor. Tokyo was also acquiring four Boeing airborne warning and control system (AWACS) aircraft for $500 million each.[8]

The US on its part renewed its commitments to provide Seoul and Tokyo with the necessary means to defend their sovereignty. During talks in Washington with representatives of South Korea in September 2006, the two sides agreed to reshape the military alliance to give a bigger decision making role to Seoul, specifically wartime command of

5. A report that details North Korea's counterfeit activities is Stephen Mihm, (2006). "No Ordinary Counterfeit", *New York Times*, 23 July, at *http://www.nytimes.com/2006/07/23/magazine/23counterfeit.html?ei=5088&en=1532e77e2eabea37&ex=1311307200&partner=rssnyt&emc=rss&pagewanted=all*
6. Kerr, Paul (2006). "North Korean Talks Hit Impasse", *ACT* 36(1) (January/February): 29–31.
7. Minnick, Wendell and Sam Jameson (2006). "Japan may Consider Pre-emptive Strike", *Defense News*, 14 August: 1, 6.
8. Lim, Robyn (2006). "Japan Spirals into Insecurity", *Far Eastern Economic Review* 169(7) (September): 17–22; Wendell Minnick (2006). "Japan Seeks F-22s Despite Tech-transfer Hurdles", *Defense News*, 17 July: 1–8.

the RoK forces.[9] Washington and Tokyo had pledged in early May to recast the US–Japan security alliance to make it a "pillar, not just of regional, but of global stability."[10] While agreeing to develop a joint missile shield with Tokyo, Washington also offered up to 80 PAC-3 missiles for nearly $100 million for the year 2007.[11] The PAC3s with Standard Missile 3 (SM 3) interceptors on Aegis-class warships would form an integrated land and sea defence system to protect Japanese and US forces.

The UN Security Council (UNSC) adopted Resolution 1695 on 15 July 2006, which demanded that North Korea suspend its missile programme and urged a return to the Six-Party Talks without precondition. The resolution expressed "grave concern ... given the potential of such systems to be used as a means to deliver nuclear, chemical, or biological payloads".[12]

Nuclear Test

On 9 October DPRK exploded a plutonium device generating a yield that was supposedly less than 1 kiloton. Condemning Pyongyang's action, the UNSC passed Resolution 1718 on 14 October imposing an asset freeze, a travel ban on persons involved with the nuclear weapon programme, and urged the DPRK to abandon its nuclear weapons in a "complete, verifiable, and irreversible manner." The resolution put in place varied measures to punish Pyongyang for its action, under Article 41 of the UN Charter. Russia and China opposed the imposition of sanctions under Chapter VII, which would have been enforceable. The Security Council also established a Sanctions Committee comprising representatives of its members, to monitor the status of the sanctions it had imposed and report back to it every ninety days.[13]

---

9. (2006). "S Korea, US Reach Accord", *Defense News*, 2 October, p. 3.
10. Jameson, Sam (2006). "Japan-US Military Relationship Adds Muscle", *Defense News*, 22 May, p. 36.
11. Minnick, Wendell (2006). "US Offers Japan Additional PAC-3s after N-Korean Tests", *Defense News*, 28 August: 8.
12. "UN Security Council condemns Democratic People's Republic of Korea's missile launches", at *http:/www.state.gov/p/eap/rls/prs/69022.htm.*
13. "Security Council condemns Nuclear Test by Democratic People's Republic of Korea", Security Council SC/8853, 14 October 2006, at *http://www.un.org/News/Press/docs/2006/sc8853.doc.htm.*

Rejecting what it termed the "gangster-like" coercive measures of the Security Council, Pyongyang asserted that it was "compelled to substantially prove its possession of nukes to protect its sovereignty and right to existence from the daily increasing danger of war from the US." The test was a 'positive measure' towards the implementation of the 19 September 2005 agreement, it said.[14] North Korea asserted that it would not give up its nuclear weapons because of the presence of US nuclear weapons in South Korea, a charge that Washington denied.[15]

Denouncing the test, South Korea noted that the action constituted a failure to meet Pyongyang's obligations under the terms of the 19 September 2005 agreement, an outright defiance of the UNSC Resolution 1695, and a unilateral breach of the Joint Declaration of the Denuclearisation of the Korean Peninsula that it signed with the RoK in 1992.[16] With Seoul's Sunshine Policy of Engagement being a failure in that it did not prevent North Korea's belligerent actions, President Roh Moo-Hyun called for 'a strategic mix' of 'strong sanctions' and 'dialogue' to resolve the dispute.[17] Seoul displayed reluctance to squeeze its northern neighbour harder, for fear of regime collapse and the likely resultant problems, including that of handling refugee flows.[18]

Japan condemned the test as a violation of all of North Korea's international obligations, including the Japan-DPRK Pyongyang Declaration of 2002. It banned imports from Pyongyang as well as the entry of North Korean ships at Japanese ports, and denied entry to Japan for North Korean citizens.[19] Tokyo also considered changes to its pacifist constitution.[20]

---

14. (2006). "Statement from Pyongyang: Rationale for a Nuclear Test", *ACT* 36(9) (November): 24.
15. (2006). "N. Korea says US has Nuclear Bomb in South: Tass", *The Washington Post*, 7 December, at *http://www.washingtonpost.com/wp-dyn/content/article/2006/12/07/AR2006120700429_pf.html.*
16. (2006). "Statement of the Government of the Republic of Korea on the North Korean Nuclear Test", 10 October, at *http://www.mofat.go.kr/me/me_a002/me_b004/1211900_971.html.*
17. (2006). "Japan Slaps Sanctions on North Korea", *The Hindu*, 12 October, at *http://www.thehindu.com/2006/10/12/stories/2006101203611400.htm.*
18. Kim, Samuel S. (2006). "The Mirage of a United Korea", *Far Eastern Economic Review* 14(9) (November): 9–14.
19. (2006). "Measures Against North Korea", *Japan Plus* 4 (December): 25.
20. (2006). "Japan PM Mulls Changes to Pacifist Constitution", *Indian Express*, 20 December: 7.

North Korea's closest ally, the People's Republic of China (PRC), seemed to have been caught off-guard by Pyongyang's brinkmanship. Beijing described the test as a move in "flagrant disregard" of international norms.[21] The timing of the test was particularly irksome to China, coinciding with the annual meeting of the Communist Party of China (CPC) and the visit of Japanese Prime Minister Shinzo Abe.[22]

However, while supporting Security Council Resolution 1718 and its provisions of "thorough inspection of cargo to and from the DPRK", Beijing was against an intrusive inspections mechanism, as envisaged under Washington's Proliferation Security Initiative (PSI), to enforce these provisions. At the same time, China stressed on dialogue and negotiations to resolve the issue peacefully.[23] It is worth noting that the Chinese reaction to Resolution 1718 was markedly different from its reaction to Resolution 1695. In the aftermath of the missile tests, it had opposed any action by the Security Council "that may lead to complication and tension on the Peninsula."[24]

Analysts pointed out that China, DPRK's biggest trading partner and its primary source of food, oil, and arms, would be forced to reconsider the parameters of its relationship with its eastern neighbour if its brinkmanship continued. China's biggest concern overflowing from the test was the likelihood of Japan adopting a more militaristic policy, including a possible decision to acquire nuclear weapons, and thus complicating its security posture.[25]

---

21. Aiyar, Pallavi (2006). "The End of a Long Friendship?" *Frontline* 23(21) (21 October–3 November), at *http://www.flonnet.com/fl2321/stories/20061103003401700.htm.*
22. Shirk, Susan L. (2006). "China Gets Tough with North Korea", *Yale Global*, 26 October, at *http://yaleglobal.yale.edu/display.article?id=8341.*
23. "Foreign Ministry spokesman Liu Jianchao makes remarks on the UN Security Council resolution concerning the nuclear test by the DPRK", Ministry of Foreign Affairs of the People's Republic of China, 15 October 2006, at *http://www.fmprc.gov.cn/eng/xwfw/s2510/2535/t277541.htm.*
24. "Foreign Ministry spokeswoman Jiang Yu's remarks on unanimous adoption of the Security Council resolution on DPRK missile launching", Ministry of Foreign Affairs of the People's Republic of China, 19 July 2006, at *http://www.fmprc.gov.cn/eng/xwfw/s2510/2535/t263917.htm.*
25. Shirk, "China gets tough with North Korea", n. 20; see also Carin Zissis, "China's relationship with a nuclear North Korea", Council for Foreign Relations, 24 October 2006, at *http://www.cfr.org/publication/11791.*

Non-proliferation Challenges of the Nuclear Test

Apart from being in contravention of a host of pledges as noted above, North Korea's nuclear test exposed the inherent inadequacies of the verification and enforcement mechanisms of the Nuclear Non-proliferation Treaty (NPT), to which Pyongyang was a signatory from 1985 till 10 January 2003. North Korea's test would also seem to offer an incentive to other nuclear aspirants like Iran to continue to hold out against Western pressure and stall efforts to cap their alleged nuclear ambitions.[26] (Iran has denied reports of nuclear cooperation with Pyongyang[27]) Iran's assertion that it is entitled to harness nuclear technology for 'peaceful' purposes, as guaranteed under the terms of the NPT to which it is a signatory, and the proliferation concerns expressed by the US and others, point out yet again the loopholes of the NPT regime.

Pyongyang's test raised the prospects of its immediate neighbours going down the nuclear route. Seoul had admitted in October 2005 to enriching nuclear material in 2000 in contravention of international nuclear safeguards obligations.[28] In the aftermath of the test, however, President Roh Moo Hyun expressed confidence in the security of the nuclear umbrella being provided by the United States. He maintained that South Korea's conventional strength was sufficient to deter a nuclear North Korea; the North "may inflict fatal damage" with its nuclear weapons but could not hope to win a war, he said.[29]

With an advanced nuclear industry, Japan could opt to build a nuclear weapon, if it doubted the efficacy of the American nuclear umbrella. Domestic constituencies like the Liberal Democratic Party (LDP) chief Shoichi Nakagawa have called for Japan to debate the need

---

26. Lin, Liu (2006). "The North Korean Nuclear Test and its Implications", Silk Road Paper, Central Asia-Caucus and Silk Road Studies Programme, November: 24.
27. (2007). "Iran Denies Nuclear Test help from North Korea", *Defense News*, 31 January, at *http://www.defensenews.com/story.php?F=2522430&C=asiapac.*
28. Foley, James A. (2004). "South Korea Admits to Nuclear Experiments", *Jane's Intelligence Review*, October: 10-11. Cited in S. Samuel C. Rajiv (2006). "Defence Postures of Major Powers", in Satish Kumar (ed.), *India's National Security Annual Review 2006* (New Delhi: Knowledge World).
29. (2006). "S. Korean President undaunted by North", *The Washington Post*, 7 December, at *http://www.washingtonpost.com/wp-dyn/content/article/2006/12/07/AR2006120700393_pf.html.*

of a nuclear arsenal.[30] Prime Minister Shinzo Abe, while repeatedly denying Japanese nuclear intentions, has stated that the constitution does not ban Japan from possessing nuclear weapons for peaceful purposes.[31]

There was also danger that the steps taken by the United States to counter a nuclear Pyongyang would in fact legitimise the utility of nuclear weapons and their delivery systems, thereby undermining global non-proliferation efforts. The Pentagon's Prompt Global Strike Plan (PGSP), for instance, seeks to launch conventional warheads from the Navy's submarine-launched Trident D5 ballistic missiles. Analysts point out that the development and deployment of conventional long-range ballistic missiles would negatively impact on one of the core US security interests, as enshrined in the 2001 Nuclear Posture Review, of preventing the proliferation of weapons of mass destruction (WMD) and their means of delivery.[32] Continual efforts by the US and other nuclear powers to modernise their arsenals and continued refusal to give up their weapons as envisaged under Article VI of the NPT, according to some analysts, legitimise the possession of these weapons and could encourage future 'breakout' states to go down North Korea's route.[33]

The Islamabad-Pyongyang Nuclear/Missile Nexus and India's Response

The Libyan decision in late 2003 to give up its nuclear ambitions had exposed the extent of the proliferation activities of the A.Q. Khan network. Similarly, DPRK's nuclear test brought into international limelight the clandestine cooperation between Islamabad and Pyongyang in the nuclear and missile field. Pyongyang had dismissed as a 'sheer lie' Khan's revelations in February 2004 that he sold nuclear weapon technology to North Korea, imputing to these

30. (2006). "Nakagawa Raises Nukes on US visit", *The Asahi Shimbun*, 30 October, at *http://www.asahi.com/english/Herald-asahi/TKY200610300112.html.*
31. (2006). "Japan Looked into Developing Nuke Warhead", *Times of India*, 26 December: 26.
32. Anderson, Steve (2006). "Off Target? The Bush Administration's Plan to Arm Long-range Ballistic Missiles with Conventional Warheads", *ACT* 36(6) (July/August): 6-11.
33. Ramachandran, R. (2006). "Road to Rubicon", *Frontline* 23(21) (21 October-3 November), at *http://www.flonnet.com/fl2321/stories/20061103005500900.htm*

revelations the motive of being a design to justify an invasion of the country by the United States.[34] It was reported in 2005 that Pakistan had resold to Libya weapon-grade uranium hexafluoride that it had received from North Korea. The US effectively shrugged away the issue in order not to alienate Pakistan which it need as a partner in its 'war' on terror.[35]

It is widely acknowledged that Pakistan played a prominent role in the North Korean nuclear quest, especially in providing enrichment technology, in return for Pyongyang's help in the missile field. When Islamabad could not pay cash for missiles, it is believed that it started bartering nuclear technology.[36] Pakistan, however, condemned the North Korean test as "destabilising" and "regrettable"[37] and denied any Pakistani assistance to it, with President Musharraf pointing out that North Korea's was a plutonium blast whereas Pakistan was pursuing the uranium-based programme.[38]

Commenting on the Pyongyang test, India's Ministry of External Affairs said that such actions reinforced the "dangers of clandestine nuclear proliferation." The statement pointed out that the test jeopardised "peace, stability and security on the Korean Peninsula and in the region."[39] There were also apprehensions that US efforts to erect a National Missile Defence (NMD)/Ballistic Missile Defence (BMD) shield to protect itself from 'rogue' state actions would lead to greater instability. These measures would induce second-tier nuclear powers like China to expand their second-strike arsenal, for fear of

34. (2004). "N Korea says Pakistan Nuclear Confession a Lie", *China Daily*, 10 February, at *http://www.chinadaily.com.cn/english/doc/2004-02/10/content_304824.htm*

35. (2005). "US Misled Allies about Nuclear Export", *The Washington Post*, 19 March, at *http://www.washingtonpost.com/wp-dyn/articles/A50241-2005Mar19.html.*

36. For a brief history, see Gordon Corera (2006). *Shopping for Bombs: Nuclear Proliferation, Global Insecurity and the Rise and Fall of the A.Q. Khan Network* (New Delhi: Foundation Books): 86-102. See also Sharon Squassoni (2006). "Weapons of Mass Destruction: Trade between North Korea and Pakistan", *CRS Report for Congress*, RL 31900, 11 October, at *http://www.fas.org/sgp/crs/nuke/RL31900.pdf.*

37. See Raman, B. (2006). "Nuclear North Korea: Nervousness in Pakistan", South Asia Analysis Group, Paper No. 2004, 26 October, at *http://www.saag.org/%5Cpapers21%5Cpaper2004.html*; "Pakistan Condemns Korea Nuke Test", BBC News, 9 October 2006, at *http://news.bbc.co.uk/go/pr/fr/-/2/hi/south_asia/6032843.stm.*

38. (2006). "Musharraf Denies Pakistan enabled North Korea Test", *Defense News*, 11 October, at *http://www.defensenews.com/story.php?F=2168890&C=asiapac.*

39. (2006). "Remarks by Official Spokesperson on the Reported Nuclear Test by DPRK", Ministry of External Affairs, New Delhi, 9 October, at *http://meaindia.nic.in.*

being overwhelmed by a US first strike on their minuscule nuclear delivery vehicles.[40] Countries like India would then be forced to take corresponding measures to offset the Chinese moves.[41]

Pyongyang's nuclear test also cast a shadow over India's civilian nuclear energy programme. Soon after the test, Australia, containing 40 per cent of the world's uranium reserves, went back on its earlier promise of reconsidering its policy of not selling uranium to non-signatories of the NPT like India.[42] However, based on India's impeccable non-proliferation record and the strength of the bilateral relationship, Prime Minister John Howard has in the recent past expressed his government's willingness to support India's case at the Nuclear Suppliers Group (NSG) and also kept the door open for nuclear trade between the two countries.[43] The United States, however, asserted its commitment to implementing the India–US nuclear deal signed in July 2006. In making this assertion Undersecretary of State Nicholas Burns contrasted the nature of the regime in Pyongyang with that in New Delhi.[44]

The Beijing Deal: Back from the Brink or Back to the Future?

Analysts advocated that the United States take immediate steps to verifiably halt Pyongyang's programme, as it had the potential to irreparably damage "an already beleaguered global non-proliferation system."[45] Engagement with Pyongyang to address its concerns was

---

40. See, for example, "BMD and China", *Nuclear Threat Initiative* (NTI), at *http://www.nti.org/f_wmd411/f2h2_2.html;* see also Li Bin, "The Impact of the US NMD on the Chinese Nuclear Modernisation", at *http://emergingfromconflict.org/readings/bin.pdf.*

41. See, for example, Michael Krepon (2002). "Missile Defence and the Asian Cascade" (Washington DC: The Henry L. Stimson Center); see also Peter Dyvad (2005). "China's Response to the US Missile Defence Programme: National Options and Regional Implications", in Bertel Heurlin and Sten Rynning, *Missile Defence: International, Regional, and National Implications* (New York: Routledge).

42. (2006). "North Korean Test Hits India's Chances of Australian Uranium", *Defense News*, 11 October, at *http://www.defensenews.com/story.php?F=2169255&C=asiapac.*

43. (2007). "Australia Ready to Sell Uranium to India", *The Hindu*, 3 April, at *http://www.thehindu.com/2007/04/03/stories/2007040307421200.htm.*

44. (2006). "US Committed to Nuclear Deal", *The Hindu*, 13 October, at *http://www.thehindu.com/2006/10/13/stories/2006101304841200.htm.*

45. Kimball, Daryl G. (2006). "Number Nine", *ACT* 36(9) (November), at *http://www.armscontrol.org/act/2006_11/focus.asp.*

widely favoured as the best option to get it back to the negotiating table. Echoing this sentiment the Director General of the IAEA (International Atomic Energy Agency), Mohammad El Baradei, advocated the need "to address the security, economic and other concerns of the DPRK" and stressed the inadequacies of sanctions to effectively address the North Korean nuclear problem.[46]

Hopes of a solution to the crisis grew following the first series of one-on-one meetings between representatives of the United States and the DPRK at Berlin in January 2007. Such private meetings with representatives of the so-called 'rogue' regimes were previously looked down upon by the Bush administration, as conferring legitimacy on these regimes.[47] With Washington's willingness to address the irksome issue of financial sanctions, Pyongyang's reported threat to conduct another nuclear test also receded.[48]

The fifth round of the Six-Party Talks began at Beijing on 8 February 2007 and resulted on 13 February in the agreement titled "Initial Actions for the Implementation of the Joint Statement." Pyongyang agreed to shut down its Yongbyon nuclear reactor within sixty days, in return for 50,000 metric tonnes of fuel aid or on the provision of equivalent economic aid. The country would not receive another 950,000 tonnes of heavy fuel oil or equivalent fuel, energy, or humanitarian aid until it disabled the reactor and declared all its nuclear programmes. The United States on its part agreed to remove North Korea's name from the list of terrorism-sponsoring nations and to lift the trade sanctions imposed on it in late 2005. UN Secretary General Ban Ki-moon welcomed the deal as the "first practical stage" toward a nuclear-weapon-free Korean peninsula.

Proponents of the deal, while pointing out the assurances of a verifiable closure of North Korea's nuclear programme, note that the US or the other interlocutors have not promised any new nuclear reactors this time around, as the US did under the AF agreement in

---

46. (2006). "IAEA: Sanctions won't Resolve N Korea Issue", *The Washington Post*, 5 December, at *http://www.washingtonpost.com/wp-dyn/content/article/2006/12/05/AR2006120500052_pf.html*.
47. (2007). "Seed of North Korean Nuclear Deal was Planted in Berlin", *International Herald Tribune*, 13 February, at *http://www.iht.com/articles/2007/02/13/news/nuke.php*.
48. (2007). "North Korea Eyes 2nd Test if Dispute not Resolved", Reuters, 31 January, at *http://in.news.yahoo.com/070131/137/6bo5s.html*.

1994. The current agreement also involved five other countries who were parties to the deal, including China. Moreover, the promise of fuel aid is contingent on North Korea's actions in verifiably dismantling its nuclear programme.[49]

Critics of the deal pointed out, however, that the Bush administration was rewarding the regime in Pyongyang, which was not giving up its nuclear assets with immediate effect, with disproportionate amount of energy aid.[50] Unresolved questions remain over the fate of the nuclear fissile material, the possible warheads that are in Pyongyang's possession, their process of dismantling, and the eventual use of the fissile material. Also, the agreement does not mention the uranium enrichment programme, an alternative route to nuclear weapons, which Washington believes Pyongyang was also pursuing. Doubts were also being raised about the effectiveness of the verification regime to credibly lock out Pyongyang's nuclear capabilities, given the history of broken promises.

Events on the ground seem to support sceptics' suspicions. Pyongyang insisted soon after the agreement that it was effecting only a 'temporary' closure of its nuclear reactor at Yongbyon.[51] Doubts were being expressed about its ability to stick to the sixty-day deadline for the closure of the reactor, failing which the energy aid would not be forthcoming.[52] Delays were also being encountered in the transfer of the $25 million frozen funds to a North Korean account in the Banco Delta Asia, which Pyongyang was insisting had to take place to take the process forward. Japan on its part was initially reluctant to take an active role in providing energy aid. This was due to its displeasure over the slow progress made on the issue of abductions of Japanese citizens by the DPRK during the Cold War.[53] Given these

49. (2007). "Outside Pressures Broke Korean Deadlock", *New York Times*, 14 February, at *http://www.nytimes.com/2007/02/14/world/asia/14assess.html?ref=todayspaper.*

50. (2007). "Pact with North Korea Draws Fire from a Wide Range of Critics in US", *New York Times*, 14 February, at *http://www.nytimes.com/2007/02/14/world/asia/14korea.html?_r=1&oref=login.*

51. (2007). "New Clouds Over the Korean Nuclear Scene", *The Hindu*, 23 February, at *http://www.thehindu.com/2007/02/23/stories/2007022304141100.htm.*

52. (2007). "North Korea unlikely to Meet Nuclear Deadline: Report", *Reuters*, 4 April, at *http://in.news.yahoo.com/070404/137/6e5co.html.*

53. (2007). "South Korea and Japan Split on North Korea Pact", *New York Times*, 15 February, *http://www.nytimes.com/2007/02/15/world/asia/15japan.html?_r=1&oref=login.*

hard and uncomfortable realities, the implementation of the 13 February deal would be closely watched by everyone interested in the peaceful resolution of the North Korean nuclear conundrum.

18

Meeting Threats to Sea-Lines Collectively

Emerging Contours in the Indian Ocean

GURPREET S. KHURANA

Introduction

Maritime communications across the Indian Ocean have always been of immense significance for global trade and commerce. Until a decade ago, barely one-fifth of the trade transiting these waters was intra-regional,[1] but this proportion is increasing rapidly, with the trajectory of Asia's own economic growth. In the surge of seaborne transportation involving regional states, the most remarkable is their increasing demand for energy resources—an essential ingredient of industrial development. Hence, the safety/security of general cargo shipping, container vessels, cruise liners, and particularly oil tankers and LNG (liquefied natural gas) carriers, has become a major component of national security reckoning in Asia. India has been a player of consequence in the process. Its reliance on sea-lines has increased remarkably in recent years due to its high economic growth, and also owing to its 'insular' characteristics in overland communications.[2]

In the past few years, security risks to commercial shipping transiting the Indian Ocean are growing. The changing contours of sea piracy are far from propitious, which poses the potential of terrorism diversifying to the ocean realm. Insecurity is particularly high for infrastructure and transportation of energy resources, aggravated by

1. Vohra, N.N. (1997). "Security in the Indian Ocean: An Overview", in Jasjit Singh (ed.), *Bridges Across the Indian Ocean* (New Delhi: IDSA): 20.
2. This is due to the barriers to overland trade due to natural topography and India's political dissonance with Pakistan and Bangladesh.

growing vulnerabilities of the global trading system. Unlawful acts at sea like smuggling of drugs and weapons, which nourish non-state violence, also impinge on the security of the sea-lines of communication (SLOC), albeit indirectly.

This has led the major powers and key stakeholders in the Indian Ocean sea-lines to contemplate cooperative security mechanisms. At times, such ventures implicitly further their respective strategic and geopolitical ends as well. Given India's geostrategic location astride these key sea-lines and its growing comprehensive eminence, it has become a 'common denominator' in such potential bilateral and multilateral ventures.

This essay attempts to analyse the current trends of piracy and terrorism, the two principal non-state threats to the sea-lines in the Indian Ocean and the adjoining waters. It also examines the cooperative response to these insecurities, the strategic compulsions of major powers like the US and China, and India's policy options.

The Risk to Shipping: A Trend Analysis

The regional trends of piracy since 2003 are given in Table 18.1, with figures in parentheses noting the particular contribution made to this phenomenon by some countries in their region.[3] The 'piracy curve' has oscillated widely in the past. The region as a whole witnessed a decline in the episodes of piracy from the peak in 2003, but since 2005, episodes of piracy have been associated with greater violence and more casualties. Also, 'Asian piracy', traditionally associated with South East Asia, has spread to other areas.

Off East Africa and West Asia

In contrast to the declining regional trend, piracy off Somalia increased substantially in 2005, wherein sophisticated weapons were used. In November 2005 a US-flagged cruise liner, *Sea-bourn Spirit*, was attacked using machine-guns and rocket-propelled grenades,[4] leading

---

3. Data sourced from the International Maritime Bureau (IMB) piracy reporting centre, at *http://www.icc-ccs.org/prc/piracyreport.php*;. and "Worldwide threats to shipping", United States Office of Naval Intelligence (henceforth, ONI) reports, at *http://www.nga.mil/portal/site/maritime/?epi_menuItemID=3e37041ec7a4546e36890127d32020a0&epi_menuID=e106a3b5e50edce1fec24fd73927a759&epi_baseMenuID=e106a3b5e50edce1fec24fd73927a759*

Table 18.1

Piracy Trends in the Indian Ocean and Adjoining Seas

	East Africa and West Asia (only Somalia)	*Indian Subcontinent (only Bangladesh)*	*South East Asia (only Indonesia)*	*Total*
2003	31 (0)	87 (58)	189 (151)	307
2004	18 (2)	33 (17)	169 (138)	220
2005	62 (35)	36 (21)	122 (98)	220
2006	32 (10)	55 (44)	86 (60)	173

some analysts to call it terrorism. In end-February 2006, the Indian vessel *Bhaktisagar* was hijacked by Somali warlords and its 22 crewmen held for ransom.[5] The International Maritime Bureau (IMB) warned ships to stay at least 75 miles from the Somali coast.[6] Absence of an effective government in Somalia encourages this rampant piracy. Off Iraq, 10 attacks were reported in 2005 compared with none in 2004, and the area was declared a new piracy hot-spot in January 2006.[7]

In 2006, piracy in both areas dropped (10 in Somalia and 2 off Iraq), probably because in Iraq the presence of US-led coalition naval forces increased and in Somalia the Islamic Courts Union (ICU), in *de facto* control of the country, took anti-piracy measures in the closing months of 2006.[8] In end-December 2006, however, the Ethiopian forces routed the ICU to bring a US-backed transitional government to Mogadishu. Piracy may increase in Somalia if the ICU resorts to insurgency; and in Iraq as well, where insurgency is gathering pace.

Ever since the hijack of MV *Achille Lauro* in 1985[9] the only occasion

---

4. Statement issued by *Securewest International* on 7 November 2005, cited by Cargo Security International, at http://www.cargosecurityinternational.com/channeldetail.asp?cid=9&caid=5865, 7 November 2005.
5. Patranobis, Sutirtho (2006). "Plan in Place to Free Sailors from Somalian Pirates", *Hindustan Times*, 10 March, at *http://www.hindustantimes.com/news/181_1646780,0008.htm.*
6. IMB report, as quoted by Cargo Security International, at *http://www.cargosecurityinternational.com/channeldetail.asp?cid=9&caid=7704*, 1 November 2006.
7. (2006). "Iraq declared new piracy hotspot", IMB report, 31 January, at *http://www.icc-ccs.org/main/news.php?newsid=63.*
8. (2006). "Somali Islamic Courts Crack down on Piracy", *Noonsite.com news*, 23 November, at *http://www.noonsite.com/Members/doina/R2006-11-22-3/view.*
9. The Italian cruise ship, *Achille Lauro*, was hijacked in the Mediterranean Sea in October 1985 by four heavily armed Palestinian terrorists, which led to the killing of an American tourist.

of terrorists targeting a moving vessel worldwide was the bombing in 2002 of the French super-tanker *Limburg* off Yemen by al-Qaeda. Al-Qaeda has also carried out many attacks on energy installations in the Persian Gulf.[10] In October 2006, US intelligence also warned of a possible strike on Saudi Arabia's Ras Tanura oil facilities.[11] This translates into an increased risk to energy transportation as well. Although the rarity of such attacks so far may be attributed to al-Qaeda's lack of nautical expertise, this may be overcome with the help of the LTTE (Liberation Tigers of Tamil Eelam) active in Sri Lanka[12] or the pirates operating off East Africa.[13]

Off the Indian Subcontinent

Piracy off the Indian subcontinent increased in 2006, being primarily attributable to Bangladesh. Two years ago its waters contributed to half of the piracy episodes in the subcontinent; the proportion has now become 80 per cent. The probable reasons are the unsound socio-economic conditions in Bangladesh and its insufficient capacity for law enforcement. In mid-2006, a massive joint operation was launched by the Bangladesh navy and coast guard to crack down on piracy[14] but statistics indicate that it hardly made any difference: of the 44 incidents that occurred in Bangladesh waters in 2006, 22 occurred after the operation.[15]

LTTE-linked violence in Sri Lanka recommenced towards the end

10. These include attacks on Iraqi offshore oil terminals in April 2004. "Suicide Boat Bombers Attack Key Iraqi Oil Terminal", *Jihad Watch*, 24 April 2004, at *http://www.jihadwatch.org/archives/001704.php*.

11. (2005). "Worldwide Threat to Shipping: Mariner Warning Information", ONI Report, 27 July, at *http://www.nga.mil/MSISiteContent/StaticFiles/MISC/wwtts/wwtts_20061025100000.txt*.

12. The explosives-ridden fast-boat used by alQaeda to bomb the *Limburg* (and also *USS Cole*) is a standard tactic of the LTTE, indicating a possible nexus. Also see International Institute for Strategic Studies (October 2005), *The Military Balance 2005-06* (London: Routledge, 2006): 430; and Neville de Silva, "LTTE linked to alQaeda?", *Sunday Times*, 30 October 2005, at Sri Lanka government's official website, *http://www.peaceinsrilanka.org/InsideNews/news.asp?newsID=4735*.

13. A September 2006 report indicated an alQaeda quest to expand its operations to Africa. See, "Is Africa Next Qaida Haven? US Mulls New Command There", *Times of India*, 1 September 2006: 23.

14. (2006). "Worldwide Threat to Shipping", ONI Report, 19 July, at *http://www.nga.mil/MSISiteContent/StaticFiles/MISC/wwtts/wwtts_20060719100000.txt*.

15. Data culled from the ONI weekly reports at *http://www.nga.mil/portal/site/maritime/?epi_menuItemID=3e37041ec7a4546e36890127d32020a0&epi_menuID=e106a3b5e50edce1fec24fd73927a759&epi_baseMenuID=e106a3b5e50edce1fec24fd73927a759*.

of 2005, accompanied by attacks on government naval craft. This led to the waters of Sri Lanka being placed under 'war risk' rating by Lloyd's (London insurance market) in April 2006.[16] In recent months, Tamil separatists have even targeted merchant ships flying foreign flags, which they often did in the past to capture cargo and to use the hijacked vessels for trafficking of drugs and arms.[17] While a US intelligence report of mid-2006 warned of a greater LTTE threat off "Colombo and Trincomalee ports";[18] the risk has lately increased off northern Sri Lanka ("Eelam waters") as well. In December 2006 the LTTE captured and burgled the Jordanian ship MV *Farha-3* off Mullaitivu.[19] In January 2007, MV *City-of-Liverpool* was attacked off Jaffna while on a humanitarian mission.[20] The employment of bomb-laden suicide boats for the attack reiterates the hazy dividing line between piracy and terrorism. The LTTE's tremendous potential to resort to high-intensity violence against shipping is further evidenced by its frequent attacks on Sri Lankan naval craft, including the use of Scuba divers.

Off Archipelagic South East Asia

Piracy in South East Asia has been declining, attributable to the Acehnese insurgents in Indonesia laying down arms. However, the area still contributes to half of regional piracy, which since 2005 has also witnessed an increasing use of heavy weapons like rocket launchers, grenades and machine-guns.[21] This is closely linked to the rampant gun running (and drug trafficking to generate funds) *via* sea routes. In February 2004 and August 2005, the Filipino militant group

16. (2006). "Sri Lanka in the War Risk List Again", *Global Order*, 1 May, at *http://globalorder.wordpress.com/2006/05/01/sri-lanka-in-the-war-risk-list-again.*
17. The ships involved were *Irish Mona* (1995); *Princess Wave* (1996); *Athena, Misen, Morong Bong*, and *Cordiality* in 1997; *Princess Kash* (1988); and *M V Sik Yang* (1999).
18. In June 2006 LTTE frogmen and a boat with mines and explosives were sighted north of Colombo. Local reports said that their mission was to attach mines to merchant ships in the port. "Worldwide threat to shipping", n. 14.
19. The captors burgled the vessel's radar, computers, and communication sets, and the Jordanian authorities confirmed the charge of piracy against the LTTE. Walter Jayawardhana, "Jordan confirms Tamil Tigers pirated ship", *Asian Tribune*, 24 December 2006, at *http://www.asiantribune.com/index.php?q=node/3826.*
20. (2007). "Sri Lanka Military Catches LTTE in Another Act of Piracy", *Sri Lankan Daily*, 21 January, at *http://www.colombopage.com/archive_07/January21140512CH.html.*
21. Bateman, Sam, C.Z. Raymond, and Joshua Ho (2006). "Safety and Security in the Malacca and Singapore Straits: An Agenda for Action", IDSS Policy Paper, May 2006: 25.

Abu Sayyaf bombed passenger ferries in the area by pre-positioning explosives onboard.[22] The combination of maritime crime, Islamic fundamentalism, and separatism in the area leads to a high potential of such attacks on moving vessels as well.

The Malacca Straits had been under Lloyd's "war risk" rating since July 2005. Since by August 2006 there were only six incidents, Lloyd's removed the area from the list,[23] citing "a significant improvement in security." This indicates that the enhanced security measures implemented by the littoral states have not been very effective. Terrorism risk in the Straits is clearly rising, the navigationally constrained waterway becoming more vulnerable with the increased density of shipping, particularly oil tankers, LNG carriers, and cruise liners.

The Cooperative Response: An Assessment

Off East Africa and West Asia

Effectively, the only multilateral security construct in the area at present is through the US-led multinational naval presence. In West Asia, the Gulf Cooperation Council (GCC) has hardly been effective due to the non-inclusion of Iran and Iraq. It is difficult to predict when a truly regional mechanism would replace the US-led coalition. Since the end of 2004, the International Institute for Strategic Studies (IISS) has been convening Regional Security Summits annually at Track-2 level for informal interactions among the security establishments of regional states and key stakeholders. During the third summit held in December 2006 (The Manama Dialogue), China, India and the US were among the eleven extra-regional states represented.[24] Though it would take time for the deliberations at the

22. Cruz, Arlyn de la (2004). "We Bombed Ferry, Claims Abu Sayyaf", *The Nation*, 1 March, at *http://www.inq7.net/nat/2004/mar/01/nat_4-1.htm*; and "Bomb Blast Hits Philippines Ferry", BBC news report, 28 August 2005, at *http://news.bbc.co.uk/1/hi/world/asia-pacific/4192102.stm*.

23. (2006). "Market Removes Malacca Straits from the List", Lloyd's website, 11 August, at *http://www.lloyds.com/News_Centre/Features_from_Lloyds/Market_removes_Malacca_Straits_from_the_List.htm*.

24. The forum is modelled on the highly successful Shangri La Dialogue. The other stakeholders were Australia, France, Germany, Japan, Pakistan, Russia, Singapore, and the UK. While the Indian delegation was led by the National Security Adviser, the Commander-in-Chief of India's Eastern Naval Command participated in the maritime security deliberations. "The Manama Dialogue: The Third IISS Regional Security Summit", *IISS Newsletter*, Winter 2006: 5, at http://www.iiss.org/conferences/the-iiss-regional-security-summit

IISS-sponsored meetings to influence policymaking, this forum is a step in the right direction. Its wide representation and the profile of its participants (belying its Track-2 status) are noteworthy, providing a valuable platform for exchange of perspectives.

The waters off West Asia, and to a relatively lesser extent East Africa, bear energy 'lifelines' of the Asia-Pacific states, including China and India. With the distance of the area to Indian shores ranging from 400 to 1500 nautical miles, India could play a significant security role, but it has opted not to participate in the US-led coalition operations. Notwithstanding, India may need to search for alternatives for such participation in multilateral fora and bilateral engagements with regional states. Iran is a power of consequence in the Persian Gulf, whose naval ties with India have traditionally been strong. Notwithstanding the growing stakes in its relations with the USA, it may be necessary for New Delhi to maintain these links with Tehran.

China also is banking on its close ties with Iran to secure its strategic imports in the short-to-medium term. In the medium-to-long term, however, Beijing is likely to extend its naval reach to the area. Its assistance to develop the Pakistani port of Gwadar, sited close to the mouth of the Persian Gulf (Straits of Hormuz), is likely to be used for increasing the staying power of Chinese naval forces. If India and China could build sufficient political trust and cooperate within multilateral arrangements that may be instituted in the future, could it mitigate China's compulsion of 'self-help' in terms of Gwadar?

The current US strategic objective in the area is, besides maintaining its influence, to eliminate terrorism, which has lately become more critical with al-Qaeda operations steadily expanding from West Asia to East Africa. The coalition forces thus find themselves stretched. In December 2006, the US deployed its own warships off Somalia to prevent al-Qaeda elements escaping by sea.[25] Through Track-2 channels, the US has lately been trying to gauge India's willingness to police these waters, if invited by the Somali government.[26] This probably stems from its awareness of the Indian

25. Gedda, George (2007). "US Patrols Somalia for Terrorist Watch", *The State*, 3 January, at *http://www.thestate.com/mld/thestate/news/nation/16375896.htm*.

26. Based on the author's interaction with the US Deputy Naval Attaché at New Delhi on 10 January 2007.

Navy's security assistance to Mozambique in 2004 during the African Union Summit. It may be in India's larger and longer-term interest to assist Somalia to curb piracy, after considering various operational factors such as the availability and suitability of assets for the task.

Off the Indian Subcontinent

Low-intensity maritime threats off the Indian subcontinent impinge on the vital interests of not only the countries directly affected but also the stakeholders in the Indian Ocean, and particularly the states in eastern Asia critically dependent on the security of its sea-lines for their energy supplies. While strategic considerations bear more heavily on the Chinese security calculus off the subcontinent, Beijing does take cognisance of non-state threats to its growing stakes in sea-lines to maintain its robust economic growth. The US also has stakes in these waters such as in terms of safeguarding the critical imports of its allies like Japan. Another stake is to contain terrorism—to prevent the subcontinent serving as a bridge between West Asia/East Africa and South East Asia (the two fronts of the US "war on terror"). This becomes critical considering the LTTE's possible symbiotic bonds with al-Qaeda and thereby with the Qaeda-linked terrorist groups in South East Asia;[27] and here lies a clear Indo–US convergence.

Given that the Sri Lankan peace process has virtually failed and LTTE-linked violence is likely to increase, the cardinal question is whether the Sri Lankan Navy has sufficient wherewithal to choke the LTTE's military logistics and blunt the capability of its Sea Tigers. Even if it does, Sri Lanka is undoubtedly looking for Indian assistance to hasten the process. Notwithstanding its geographically confined agenda, the LTTE's growing naval capabilities pose a serious threat to India's maritime interests due to geographic proximity. The potential threat to shipping that will transit the Sethusamudram canal also cannot be ignored.

India and Sri Lanka began 'coordinated'[28] naval patrols in February 2006 for ensuring safety of fishermen and to prevent criminals from

27. IISS (October 2005), *The Military Balance, 2005-06* (London: Routledge, 2006): 430. Also see, de Silva, "LTTE linked to al-Qaeda?" n. 12.

28. In a 'coordinated' patrol the patrol units of two countries operate independently on their side of the common maritime boundary, while coordinating their effort through constant communications.

crossing the maritime boundary.[29] In August 2006, the Sri Lanka government sought India's assistance to enforce a sea blockade of the LTTE's military supplies,[30] which implies upgrading the existing arrangement to 'joint'[31] patrols. In November 2006, India declined this proposal, though it assented to supply 'non-lethal' military hardware to Sri Lanka.[32] India's reluctance for joint patrols would appear to be to avoid direct involvement in the conflict and keeping in view the sensitivities of the political leadership in Tamil Nadu. But while preventing human rights violations by government forces in Sri Lanka on Tamils is necessary, more proactive measures may be required to disarm the LTTE to catalyse the peace process and future stability in the area.

The increasing insecurity in Bangladesh waters severely impinges on India's maritime security indirectly, but it constitutes a greater threat to Bangladesh. The significant reduction of piracy in Indian waters has not gone unnoticed, and the US wants India's neighbours to use the Indian case as a template to secure their own waters. The Bangladesh government has shown disinclination to cooperate with India in this regard. If, for example, the US can catalyse such cooperation, it could lead the way for cooperative responses to other threats as well, such as insurgency and terrorism. A US role in South Asia could be useful considering that the SAARC has yet to prove that it can succeed as a multilateral security forum. Its deliberations on counter-terrorism are yet to yield any meaningful results; maritime security has not even been discussed.

The Regional Cooperative Agreement for Anti-Piracy (ReCAAP) in Asia has been the most significant multilateral arrangement of recent times. It links three countries of the subcontinent (Bangladesh, India, and Sri Lanka) with thirteen other states in eastern Asia. On 4 June 2006, India became the tenth country to ratify the agreement, leading

29. Radhakrishnan, R.K. (2006). "Coordinated Naval Patrolling Formalised", *The Hindu*, 25 February, at *http://www.hindu.com/2006/02/25/stories/2006022509630100.htm.*

30. Times of India (2006). "Sri Lanka Seeks Military Support from India", *Times of India*, 10 August, at *http://timesofindia.indiatimes.com/articleshow/1879540.cms.*

31. As opposed to a 'coordinated' patrol, in a 'joint' patrol the patrol units of two countries operate together in the designated area under a joint command and control structure.

32. Tamil Net (2006). "India Rejects Rajapakse's Call for Joint Naval Patrols: Hindu", *Tamil Net*, 29 November, at *http://www.tamilnet.com/art.html?catid=13&artid=20438.*

to its entry into force three months later.[33] The agreement aims at responding to piracy through exchange of information among participating countries, for which an Information Sharing Centre (ISC) has been established in November 2006 at Singapore.[34] The arrangement ensures compilation and dissemination of more accurate data than currently available, thus enabling better policy decisions by regional states. However, its effectiveness may be marred in case of spatial voids, either due to non-participation of Indonesia and Malaysia (discussed later), or if a participating state contributes incorrect information due to its vested interests.

Malacca Straits

Securing the Malacca Straits has been a vexed issue in the past half decade, due not only to piracy and fears of maritime terrorism since the events of 11 September 2001, but also geopolitical factors. The attempt by major powers to monitor the strategic choke-point is best exemplified by the US move in April 2004 to have the Straits patrolled by its forces under its Regional Maritime Security Initiative (RMSI). China has often articulated its opposition to what it perceives as an attempt by major powers to 'control' the waterway.[35] To avoid being drawn into the big-power tussle, Indonesia and Malaysia rejected the proposed RMSI, stating that the responsibility of security in the Straits lies solely with the three littoral states (Indonesia, Malaysia, and Singapore). The stand was justified under the United Nations Convention on the Law of the Sea, 1982 (UNCLOS-3),[36] since much of the Straits constitutes their territorial waters.

The rejection of RMSI and vociferous resistance to any extra-littoral military 'assistance' is also due to the well-known sensitivities of Indonesia and Malaysia over issues of national sovereignty. This has also been an impediment for the two states' accession to multilateral

33. Japan Ministry of Foreign Affairs (MOFA) press release, 4 September 2006, at *http://www.mofa.go.jp/announce/announce/2006/9/0904.html*; and ReCAAP Information Sharing Centre, at *http://www.recaap.org/publish/recaap/index.html*.

34. Ministry of Transport (Singapore) press release, 20 November 2006, at *http://app.mot.gov.sg/data/pr_06_11_29.htm*.

35. Storey, Ian (2006). "China's Malacca Dilemma", The Jamestown Foundation, *China Brief* 6(8) (12 April): 4. Also available at *http://www.jamestown.org/images/pdf/cb_006_008.pdf*.

36. UNCLOS-3 entered into force in November 1994.

legal regimes that seek to enhance cooperative security, such as the Search and Rescue Convention (SAR-79),[37] the Convention for Suppression of Unlawful Acts at sea (SUA-88),[38] and ReCAAP-2006. Such sensitivities have even impeded cooperation amongst the littorals themselves, such as for hot pursuit of criminals into the territorial waters of the adjacent state.

The anxieties over a possible military intervention by a major power compelled the Straits littorals to institute 'visible' security measures, such as the trilateral coordinated patrol (MALSINDO, involving Malaysia, Singapore, and Indonesia) in July 2004 and the combined aerial surveillance effort named "Eyes in the Sky" in September 2005. However, due to inadequacy of assets and the resulting low deployment rate, the risks to shipping in the Straits have persisted.

Since the end of 2005 the Straits littorals have displayed an increasing flexibility to enhance security. These moves have included the invitation to Thailand to be part of MALSINDO (Bangkok, however, decided on being an observer)[39], invitation for international assistance for air surveillance,[40] and the bilateral 'hot pursuit' agreements between littorals.[41] However, the continuing sensitivity of Indonesia and Malaysia about their sovereignty is evident in their non-ratification of the recent ReCAAP (2006).

The Straits littorals have been insistent that user states must share the costs of securing the waterway.[42] 'Compulsory pilotage' and 'toll

37. SAR-79 aimed at delineating the spatial responsibilities for search and rescue at sea and its coordination.

38. SUA-88 came into being to deal with violence against ships. It aimed at delineating the jurisdiction of states over such offences, which was hitherto complex due to the transnational nature of shipping, for example, in case of an act committed by a national of State A, against a ship belonging to State B, and in territorial waters of State C.

39. The Bangkok Post (2006). "Thailand Delays Strait Security Plan", *The Bangkok Post*, 22 April, at *http://www.parliament.go.th/news/news_detail.php?prid=446*.

40. Bendeich, Mark and Chaitanya Kalbag (2005). "Malaysia Says Foreign Planes may help Hunt Pirates", Maritime Institute of Malaysia (MIMA) news flash, June, at *http://www.mima.gov.my/mima/htmls/mimarc/news/newsflash_files/news-cut/jun05.htm*.

41. Channel News Asia (2006). "Singapore, Malaysia, Indonesia Sign Pact on Malacca Strait Patrols", *Channel News Asia*, 21 April, at *http://www.channelnewsasia.com/stories/singaporelocal news/view/204221/1/.html*.

42. See, People's Daily (2006). "Malaysia urges Malacca Straits users to Share Security Cost", *People's Daily* online, 2 June, at *http://english.peopledaily.com.cn/200606/02/eng20060602_270365.html*.

tax' for transiting vessels have been proposed, but user states have opposed the move on the ground that it will amount to curtailing freedom of navigation, which forms the bedrock of UNCLOS-3. The littorals have intensified their efforts to seek such contribution under Article 43 of UNCLOS-3, which provides for cooperation with stakeholders for navigational safety and protection of marine environment in international straits. The underlying rationale is that this will help mitigate the focus on 'hard' security while enhancing 'security', which significantly overlaps with 'safety.' This has led to three IMO-facilitated meetings since September 2005 to 'push' user states to fund related projects[43] in the Straits. Only China has so far consented to fund projects (Japan has also made such contributions in the past), undoubtedly for ensuring the safety and security of its own shipping; particularly its energy imports. China's consent may also be driven by its strategic imperatives (mentioned below).

A symbolic divide between the Straits littorals and user states has also become palpable since February 2006, when the US convened a meeting of seven user states (including India) in Alameda (California).[44] The aim was to preserve their common interests while making contributions. The littorals, however, saw this as an effort by user states to assume the initiative in Straits security and internationalise the issue.[45]

China, an important stakeholder in the Straits, was also invited to the Alameda meet but declined. This was hardly a difficult choice for Beijing, and the dividends were clear. Coupled with its consent to fund projects, this would have enabled China to increase its influence (at the expense of the US) among the littorals of the strategic waterway that is a critical conduit for its energy imports.

Given the geopolitical complexities pertaining to the Straits, any multilateral security arrangement involving more than one major

43. These projects involved wreck removal, automatic identification system (AIS) for small ships, and systems for nautical data measurement systems/aids to navigation. See Japanese Ocean Policy Research Foundation (OPRF) monthly report (September 2006): 5, at *http://www.sof.or.jp/ocean/report_e/pdf/200609.pdf.*

44. Pandit, Rajat (2006). "India Joins US War on Maritime Terror", *Times of India*, 15 February: 8. The other states were UK, Germany, Japan, South Korea, Australia, and Russia.

45. As per inputs of a security analyst from Malaysia.

power may be inconceivable in the foreseeable future. The scenario seems more like a 'competitive bidding' amongst the powers for inclusion in a cooperative security framework, and thus be in a position to influence events in the strategic waterway. However, this may not apply to India, which is a major stakeholder in the Straits and not a mere user state. India's maritime zone (like that of Thailand) being contiguous to the waterway, its maritime (and even internal) security is closely enmeshed with 'good order' in the waterway, secure against piracy, drug trafficking, or smuggling of weapons (which often reach the insurgents in India's north-eastern states).

It was thus not surprising that during the Alameda conference India preferred to call it a "prospective donor states' conference" instead of a "user state conference",[46] probably since it did not want to be identified solely in the latter category. Also, contrary to the general sense of the draft resolution of the conference, India insisted that any proposal for security of the Malacca Straits must be with the unanimous consent of the Straits littorals. The same spirit was evident during the Indian Defence Minister's address at the Fifth IISS-sponsored Asia Security Summit (Shangri La Dialogue) at Singapore.[47]

Considering the geographic location of its Nicobar Islands virtually at the northern entrance to the Straits, India can make a significant contribution. Besides, its bilateral coordinated naval patrols with Indonesia and Thailand in close proximity (intended to counter transnational maritime crimes) could be integrated with MALSINDO. However, in any cooperative mechanism, India will need to address not only 'capacity augmentation' of the littorals but also their 'capacity building', reduction of vulnerabilities of shipping, and also responding to the aftermath of mishaps and disasters.

Also, two key issues need active consideration by Indian policymakers. First, notwithstanding the security convergence with the US, must India continue to participate in 'user state' conferences that accentuate the symbolic divide between 'users' and 'littorals'? While

---

46. Based on the author's discourse with Dr. P. Paleri, Indian Coast Guard Inspector-General (now retired), who led the Indian delegation at the Conference.
47. Ministry of Defence (MoD), Government of India press release, 3 June 2006, at *http://pib.nic.in/release/release.asp?relid=18213*.

on the one hand, such participation may be counterproductive in terms of building political trust with the Straits littorals, on the other hand, through its representation, India could preserve the vital interests of the littorals. Furthermore, should India participate as a delegate member or just an observer? The answers need a better understanding of the littorals' perceptions through more interactions. Second, must India endorse the move by the littorals to impose compulsory pilotage and toll tax in the Straits, considering that it contradicts the essence of UNCLOS-3, the only global maritime legal regime representing near-universal consensus?

Conclusion

Insecurities for legitimate shipping activity in the Indian Ocean are increasing with the emerging contours of low-intensity threats, particularly in the tenor and scope of piracy and the likelihood of terrorism at sea, more so since the security and law enforcement mechanism of many regional states is inadequate. The major powers, which are also the principal stakeholders, therefore advocate the exigency of a cooperative response. While these powers are often driven by conflicting *inter se* geo-political and strategic calculus, the smaller littoral states continue to seek security through equations that prevent the overwhelming domination of any one power.

As a major stakeholder in the Indian Ocean sea-lines, India's interest lies in cooperative security within the region. Its geographic location and peninsular disposition make it a 'common factor' in any such multilateral arrangement. India's approach will need to be specific to the area/'hot-spot' since each of these is characterised by a distinct geopolitical and security issue. In the Persian Gulf, India will need to continue to participate in multilateral fora, and forge bilateral bonds with the Gulf states, including Iran. It will also be in India's interest to assist East Africa's coastal states in maritime security, if requested. In the Indian subcontinent, while India's role will be crucial in de-capacitating the LTTE, greater political trust will first need to be generated between India and Bangladesh for a bilateral mechanism to counter piracy and other crimes in the northern Bay of Bengal. Owing to the geographical contiguity of the Malacca Straits with its own maritime zone, India will need to prepare itself to address not only 'hard security' issues, but also navigational safety, environmental protection, and disaster relief. Much greater interaction with the Straits littorals will be necessary for a better understanding of their perceptions before it proposes any cooperative arrangement.

India's cause would be best served if it could successfully identify the convergence of its interests with those of other major powers. The emerging Indo–US congruence is aimed at this. The key challenge for New Delhi will, however, lie in balancing its national interests, if its cooperative relationship with the US were to come in conflict with its cooperative relationship with a regional state or another major power.

IV

Engagements and Conflict in West and Central Asia

19

Indo–Saudi Engagement

Breaking New Ground

GULSHAN DIETL

The year 2006 marks a high point in Indo–Saudi engagement. King Abdullah was invited to be the official guest at India's Republic Day parade. It was the King's first trip outside the region. The earlier visit by a Saudi king to India was half a century earlier, by King Saud in 1955. From the Indian side, Prime Ministers Jawaharlal Nehru and Indira Gandhi visited the kingdom in 1956 and 1982 respectively.

Saudi Arabia is a unique country at least in three specific details. One, it possesses more than a quarter of the global oil reserves, has been the largest oil producer for over half a century, and is the only producer with a spare production capacity. Two, the holiest Islamic shrines are located in Makkah and Medina, placing the country in the epicentre of the Muslim sacred space. Three, it is one of the last surviving ruling monarchies and the only one that has named the country after its own family name. The country is located on the Arabian Peninsula between Africa and Asia. It covers nearly 80 per cent of the peninsula, with an area of roughly 2.2 million square kilometres, with the Red Sea on the west, the Indian Ocean on the south, and the Gulf on the east. It shares 4500 km-long land border with Iraq, Jordan, Kuwait, Oman, Qatar, United Arab Emirates, and Yemen. It has roughly 1800 kilometres of shoreline on the Red Sea on its west, and 800 kilometres on the Gulf on its east.

Saudi Arabia possesses oil reserves estimated at 260 billion barrels, the world's largest, and some 6.3 trillion cubic metres of natural gas, the fourth-largest after Russia, Iran, and Qatar. The Saudi population is estimated at 26.5 million. In addition, there are some 5.5 million foreigners working in the country. Ninety per cent of the people are

Arabs; the rest of Afro-Asian descent. On the east coast, there is an Iranian racial influence.

Saudi Arabia–India Relations: An Overview

Two of the earliest and greatest civilisations—Mesopotamia and Dilmun—sprang in the vicinity of the Gulf. The Mesopotamian civilisation in today's Iraq and the Indus Valley civilisations were roughly contemporaneous, in contact with each other and enriching each other across the Gulf. The Dilmun civilisation that flourished in today's Saudi territory and the archipelago of Bahrain is still in the process of discovery and must bide its time till a final verdict is pronounced on its antiquity, expanse, and achievements. Maritime networks across the western Indian Ocean date as early as the third millennium BC. Notable ports of the time were Dilmun around the Bahrain archipelago, Magan on the Oman peninsula, and Malukkha on the Indian coast.

After the emergence of Islam and a relatively peaceful period over vast stretches of the territory where the Islamic dispensation ruled, trade and shipping flourished. Pearls from the Gulf; spices, textiles, and swords from India; silk, slaves, monkeys, and ivory from China; gold from Africa, and much more passed through Arabia. By the eighth century shipping in the Gulf had entered its golden age. The Arabs traded between all the major civilisations of the medieval world.

Vasco da Gama's arrival heralded the European era in the Gulf. The Dutch, the French, and the British followed the Portuguese. The British stayed to protect the area as a halfway house between the British Empire and its prized possession, India. During the era of Pax Britannica from the early nineteenth to the mid-twentieth century, the Gulf was virtually a British Lake.

When Prime Minister Nehru visited Saudi Arabia in 1956, the Saudis greeted him enthusiastically, with the slogan "*Marhaba, Rasool al-Salam*", that is, "Welcome, O Messenger of Peace." When the Pakistanis took offence at the greeting, the Saudi Embassy in Pakistan explained that *Rasool al-Salam* was not the same as *Rasool al-Islam*, which is "Messenger of Islam", the term used exclusively for Prophet Muhammad.

Saudi Arabia was a founder member of the Non-Aligned Movement, in a period of aberration in Saudi foreign policy. During the Cold War, India chose to remain non-aligned, whereas Saudi Arabia was firmly in the US-led bloc. It did not however formally join the US-led multilateral treaties like the Baghdad Pact or CENTO. India's closeness to Egypt and the Saudi–Egyptian cold war within the Arab world did not help either. India, though, refrained from criticising the Saudi special relationship with and security dependence on the US. During the India–Pakistan conflicts of 1967 and 1971, Saudi policy was clearly against the Indian position.

The divergent views and policies of the two countries were most clearly evident on Afghanistan during the Soviet occupation. The Saudis were supportive of the Afghan mujahideen groups and resented India's refusal to criticise the Soviets. The Soviet withdrawal resulted in strife among the varied groups, eventually leading to the emergence of the Taliban who swept through most of the country. Saudi Arabia, Pakistan, and the United Arab Emirates were the only countries to accord recognition to the Taliban-ruled state while India continued to support the Northern Alliance.

The Saudi-led OPEC (Organization of Petroleum Exporting Countries) and OAPEC (Organization of Arab Petroleum Exporting Countries) displayed a considerate policy towards India during the oil crisis of 1973. There was no embargo against India. The bilateral relations have been on a steady upswing since then. Prime Minister Indira Gandhi visited the country in 1982 in a friendly and positive atmosphere.

India's Minister for External Affairs, Jaswant Singh, visited Saudi Arabia in early 2001. The visit marked the beginning of a process in the political-security sphere. A memorandum of understanding on Foreign Office consultation was signed to facilitate frequent interaction. Saudi Arabia is currently the largest supplier of oil to India at nearly 24 million tonnes annually. Imports are expected to reach 50 million tonnes in twenty years. The Saudis have assured India about meeting its full oil requirement for the next two decades. Though the system of annual term contracts will continue, these would remain evergreen despite sharp increase in the expected demand. India exports tea, coffee, basmati rice, tobacco, spices, cashews and consumer durables to Saudi Arabia. The total trade between the two countries stood at $3.4 billion in 2005-06, according to the Indian Commerce Ministry. Unofficial trade estimates indicate that India has emerged as Saudi Arabia's fourth largest export destination with $9.8 billion worth of exports. Oil accounts for 94 per cent of these exports. Saudi imports from India are, however, much lower at $1.6 billion. Trade deficit is set to widen as the price of oil is going up.

Currently, there is a 20 per cent annual growth in telecommunication, personal computers and Internet sectors in Riyadh, which is being planned as a hub for information technology (IT) in the region. The Confederation of Indian Industry (CII) has, in the meanwhile, identified IT as the most important sector for business in Saudi Arabia.

Since mid-2000, Saudi Arabia has issued fifty-eight licences to Indian companies to set up joint ventures or wholly owned subsidiary companies. India ranks sixth in investments in Saudi Arabia, after the US, Japan, France, United Kingdom, and Syria. The two have also agreed in principle on mutual investments in each other's energy sectors. The kingdom has been offered investment opportunities in exploration in India; and India has expressed interest in investing in pipeline and refinery installations in Saudi Arabia.

Roughly 1.3 million Indians are working in the kingdom, who remit $2 billion annually back home. More professionals in energy and IT sectors are joining the traditional labour force. Every year, thousands of Indian pilgrims visit Saudi Arabia to perform Hajj or Umra. India gets loans from the Saudi Development Fund for power projects, Nhava Sheva port, refineries, railways, etc. The Saudi ARAMCO–Hindustan Petroleum joint venture refinery in Philo Khari in Punjab, set up at a cost of $2.5 billion, has the capacity to refine nine million tonnes of crude oil a year. The kingdom was also the first to send substantial aid after the earthquake in Gujarat in January 2001.

The King's Visit: An Assessment

The King's visit is best understood in a wider context than being a merely bilateral affair. Since the terrorist attacks of 11 September 2001 in New York, the Saudis are no longer the closest US allies in the Gulf. There are frequent calls for a regime change in Saudi Arabia, with the human rights, women, and pro-Israeli lobbies being the most vocal Saudi baiters. The US-led war on terrorism has resulted in an ever increasing demand on the regional countries to cooperate and assist American wars in Afghanistan and Iraq by cutting off foreign aid and charities that might be diverted to terrorist groups by monitoring domestic financial transactions, and initiating democratic transformation. The Saudis have been subjected to the most intense and persistent demands on these counts.

After Abdullah took over as King in August 2005, he initiated changes on several significant issues at home. In foreign affairs, his visits to China and India marked a departure from earlier times, a clear choice to expand and diversify his circle of friends. The King's initiative was variously referred to as an "Asian Alternative", a "New Look East Policy", a "Strategic Shift", a "Rebalancing", and so on.

The Indian decision to engage Saudi Arabia was also motivated by its desire to expand and diversify its circle of friends in the Gulf. In September 2005 India had voted in line with the US position on the Iranian nuclear issue at a meeting of the International Atomic Energy Agency (IAEA). After a second vote in February 2006, with India again voting for it, the Iranian nuclear file was sent to the United Nations Security Council. Even as Russia, China, and members of the Non-Aligned Movement abstained from voting, the repeated Indian votes sent out a clear signal of a rethink in India's policy towards the Gulf in general and Iran in particular. In an obvious exercise in 'balancing', the Indian Minister for External Affairs, Pranab Mukherjee, visited Iran within ten days of the Saudi King's visit.

The King's visit concluded with the signing of the "Delhi Declaration", the first agreement that the King himself signed. Terrorism and energy security are identified in the document as two strategic issues. On terrorism the two sides would make concerted efforts for an early realisation of a Comprehensive Convention on

International Terrorism, which has been on the agenda of the United Nations General Assembly for decades. India has agreed to the Saudi King's proposal, made at an international conference on Counter-Terrorism held in Riyadh in February 2005, to set up an International Counter-Terrorism Centre. It may be noted that Saudi Arabia was the first country to have categorically condemned the attack on the Indian Parliament House as an act of terrorism.

The Declaration reiterated the two sides' resolve to develop a strategic partnership in the energy sector based on complementarities and interdependence. The specified elements of the partnership incorporated in the Declaration are: reliable, stable, and increased volume of crude oil supplies, through 'evergreen' long-term contracts; cooperative and joint ventures, both in the public and private sectors, in the upstream and downstream oil and gas sectors in India and Saudi Arabia as well as in third countries; Saudi investments in oil refining, marketing and storage in India, subject to commercial viability; and setting up of India–Saudi ventures for gas-based fertiliser plants in Saudi Arabia.

In the political sphere, the two sides registered their common perspectives on a number of issues concerning West and South Asia. The Declaration emphasised the importance of and complementarity between the Beirut Arab Peace Initiative and the Road Map, and expressed hope that they would invigorate the peace process and lead to the establishment of a viable and independent state of Palestine living in peace and prosperity side by side with Israel. The Beirut Arab Peace Initiative was proposed by Saudi Arabia and was unanimously approved by the Arab League Summit meeting in Beirut in March 2002. It proposed that Israel should withdraw from all territories occupied since the 1967 Arab–Israel war, provide a just solution to the Palestine refugee problem, and recognise the establishment of a sovereign, independent state of Palestine in the West Bank and Gaza Strip. In 2003 US President George W. Bush presented the Road Map under the auspices of the Quartet (US, UK, UN, and Russia) that aimed at the final, comprehensive solution to the Palestine issue with the creation of an independent state of Palestine.

On Iraq, the two sides expressed hope that the country would attain its security, unity, territorial integrity and prosperity, and respect for its sovereignty and independence. Saudi Arabia welcomed the ongoing dialogue between India and Pakistan and their continued efforts aimed at settling bilateral outstanding issues. The Saudis have long since given up their pro-Pakistan position and gradually occupied a middle ground on the Kashmir issue. Indo–Pakistan relations, to that extent, may not be a decisive factor in Indo–Saudi interaction.

In the economic sphere, the two sides noted with satisfaction the signing of agreements regarding promotion and protection of investments and avoidance of double taxation that would help expand and diversify mutual trade and investments. The Declaration also called for the exploration of investment opportunities in all sectors, including infrastructure, in both countries. Even as the 'Saudiasation' policy is set to adversely affect the Indian migrant workers in the kingdom, Indo–Saudi joint ventures and wholly owned subsidiaries are likely to offer new openings to Indian job seekers there.

The health sector was identified as of special interest, where possibilities for enhancing cooperation in health services, exchange of health personnel, health education, and pharmaceuticals could be explored. Intensified cooperation in science and technology, tourism, youth affairs and sport, agricultural research and education, technical and vocational training, and cultural exchanges was also agreed to. During King Abdullah's visit, the Indian quota for Hajj pilgrims was raised from 137,000 to 147,000.

Follow-up and the Future

The King was accompanied by a large delegation of Saudi dignitaries. They visited and interacted with their Indian counterparts. Additionally, it was agreed to form a Saudi–India Joint Business Council to provide an institutional framework for economic activities among the businessmen and entrepreneurs.

Several follow-up actions have been taken since then. The Reliance Company would invest in a refinery and petrochemical projects in Saudi Arabia. Engineers India Limited would open an office to engage in the Saudi infrastructure activities. The Indian Council of Cultural Relations would send delegations to Saudi Arabia and work out an exchange programme for writers, literary figures, artists, and others in cultural field. Indo–Saudi co-operation in the areas of health and medical treatment seems set to improve in future. More Saudis are visiting Kerala for medical treatment and rejuvenation at the Ayurvedic clinics and hospitals. The Apollo Hospitals Group has signed an agreement with the Fawaz al-Hokair group of Saudi Arabia to set up three 250-bed hospitals and twenty clinics in the kingdom. The project is estimated to cost $100 million. The Saudi group will make the investments and the Indian group will provide the complete technical knowhow, for a one-time fee of $1.8 million.

The Rajiv Gandhi Institute of Youth Development would establish institutional contacts with corresponding institutions in Saudi Arabia. An exchange programme involving students, youth, and sports persons will be instituted. In sports, football, volleyball, basketball, handball, athletics, and equestrian sports would be given priority. Since India has become an attractive tourist destination for the Saudis, special tourist brochures have been published in Arabic for them.

No bilateral relationship is immune to developments in the neighbourhood. The Indo–Saudi engagement would, similarly, be influenced by developments in South and West Asia and in the world. Peace in Iraq and Afghanistan, resolution of the Palestine issue, developments on the Kashmir problem, and the evolution of the global system in general will continue to colour and shape the Indo–Saudi engagement. The Iranian nuclear issue, if not amicably resolved, will have unpredictable consequences; and not just on Indo–Saudi engagement.

The Chinese factor also weighs in this equation. The King visited China and India in the same trip. Three months later, when President Hu Jintao paid a return visit to Saudi Arabia he was accorded a rare honour of addressing the Saudi Majlis. A return visit by the Indian leadership is still pending. China is the largest single oil importer from Saudi Arabia. India is the fourth-largest, after China, the US, and Japan. Will there be a scramble for Saudi oil between India and China? Or will there be enough for both?

20

Iran's Nuclear Defiance

RAJESH KUMAR MISHRA

In response to the UN Security Council's repeated calls for halting Iran's uranium enrichment activities, President Mahmud Ahmedinejad said: "After the first resolution, we undertook the nuclear fuel cycle; after the second one, we began the industrial phase of nuclear fuel; and if another resolution is issued, new capabilities of the Iranian nation will surface."[1] Iran denies allegations of developing a nuclear weapon programme under cover of peaceful uses. In the face of external opposition and continuing demand for suspension, Iran seems determined to exercise its right under the NPT (Nuclear Non-Proliferation Treaty) to develop and use nuclear fuel cycle abilities for general industrial energy.

Since August 2005, when Iran resumed uranium conversion, the current standoff has emerged out of Iran's refusal to adequately cooperate with the demands of the IAEA (International Atomic Energy Agency) and the requirements of the UN Security Council resolutions as stipulated by P-5+1 (US, Britain, France, China and Russia plus Germany). The confidence deficit between Iran and the IAEA has been considerably widened, which led to the reporting of Iran's nuclear case to the Security Council.

External Imperatives: US–Iran Relations

Ever since the Iranian revolution of 1979, the US has looked upon the Iranian regimes with suspicion and animosity. In 1984 the Reagan administration designated Iran as a state sponsoring international

---

1. Karimi, Nasser (2007). "Iran: Sanctions could Push Nuclear Drive", *Indian Express*, 17 April 2007, at *http://hosted.ap.org/dynamic/stories/I/IRAN_NUCLEAR?SITE=IXPRS&SECTION=HOME& TEMPLATE=DEFAULT.*

terrorism. In 1987 the American government imposed prohibition of all Iranian imports and kept on adding various military and economic sanctions against Tehran. It also resisted Iran's integration with international organisations such as the World Trade Organization (WTO). In 1996 Iran was clubbed with Libya when the US Congress approved the Iran-Libya Sanctions Act (ILSA). In 2002 the current Bush administration labelled Iran as part of the 'axis of evil' along with Iraq (under Saddam Hussein) and North Korea. The focus of US policy of sanctions against Tehran "has shifted from containment to behaviour change and, at times, regime change."[2]

Before the Iranian revolution the Shah had the backing of the US over an ambitious plan of producing electricity from nuclear energy by setting up twenty power reactors. Partly constructed reactors in Bushehr got damaged during the Iraq–Iran War, 1983–88. Advocates of tougher US moves against Iran believe that for more than two decades Iran has been encouraging and supporting armed radical groups in West Asia/Middle East to adversely affect the United States' geopolitical and economic interests in the region. They argue that a nuclear Iran would destabilise the current regional security architecture.

Media reports disclosed in March 2005 that, as part of European offers of incentives to Iran, the US agreed to tone down opposition to Iran's membership in the WTO and to allow some spare parts for civil aviation in exchange of Iranian commitment to freeze its enrichment plan. This formula did not work.

On its part, Iran believes that economic incentives should not be linked to the demand of Iran's rights under the NPT and perceives the US-led political push on matters nuclear to be historically rooted in their uneven bilateral relationship. Despite numerous US-imposed sanctions, Iran continued expanding its oil and gas trade with major international actors such as France, Russia, Japan, and China and broadened its economic engagements with them. By raising the economic stakes, Iran has made it difficult for others to impose tougher measures against it in case the Security Council mood turns uglier

---

2. Perkovich, George and Silvia Manzanero (2004). "Plan B: Using Sanctions to End Iran's Nuclear Program", *Arms Control Today*, May, at *http://www.armscontrol.org/act/2004_05/PerkovichManzanero.asp*.

under US pressures. At the same time, it is becoming increasingly challenging for major international actors how to deal with the issue of discrepancies reported by the IAEA in Iran's nuclear programme. The gaps in Iran's declarations, as reported by the IAEA, provide enough scope for the US and its allies to mobilise international support for asking Iran to stop enrichment and related activities.

Domestic Imperatives

The nuclear row emerged during the presidency of Ali-Akbar Hashemi Rafsanjani. As soon as President Ahmedinejad assumed office in August 2005, he went ahead with the decision of resuming uranium conversion which had been voluntarily suspended since October 2003. Conservative clerics and the Revolutionary Guards, who had backed Ahmedinejad's candidature in the elections, are two pillars of Iran's polity and they firmly support Iran's right to develop nuclear technology for peaceful purposes. In tough posturing, Ahmedinejad also expressed Iran's readiness to share nuclear know-how with Islamic states.[3]

Regarding Iran's right to develop nuclear infrastructure for peaceful purposes President Ahmedinejad enjoys overwhelming support in the country. In expression of this support the Majlis adopted a legislation to recognise and continue with the country's right to develop and use nuclear technology for peaceful purposes. At the same time, the spokesman of the Majlis' Foreign Policy and National Security Commission, Kazem Jalali, has been quoted saying that the sources of jurisprudence "have made it religiously forbidden to manufacture, stockpile, or use the atomic bombs."[4] It has been reported that Iran's supreme leader Ali Khamenei also holds a strong view that Iran should not back down from its confrontation with the West over Tehran's nuclear ambitions.[5] In an attempt to send strong signals that the US and the West cannot isolate Iran with tools of sanctions the government of President Ahmedinejad has proposed that Russia and

3. Dareini, Ali Akbar (2006). "Iran Offers to Transfer Nuke Technology", *The Guardian*, 16 December, at *http://www.guardian.co.uk/worldlatest/story/0,,-6285584,00.html*.
4. (2006). "MP: Nuclear Weapons not in Iran's Defense Doctrine", *Islamic Republic News Agency* (henceforth IRNA), 3 April, at *http://www.irna.ir/en/news/view/line-17/0604037747235107.htm*.
5. Penketh, Anne (2007). "Israel Raises Nuclear Stakes with Iran", *The Independent* (London), 25 January, at *http://news.independent.co.uk/world/middle_east/article2183872.ece*.

Iran should form a gas OPEC-like cartel. The two countries together possess almost half of the natural gas resources of the world.[6]

Even before Ahmedinejad took over the reins of power, former President Khatami had argued:

> It is ironic that those who are concerned about saving humanity from nuclear weapons fully support Israel which is a nuclear power... these (NPT, IAEA safeguards) are all pretexts for imposing certain policies on Iran and the region and to create panic and mistrust.[7]

When the UN Security Council passed Resolution 1737 on 23 December 2006, the permanent representative of Iran to the UN, Javad Zarif, stated in his address to the Security Council:

> Today is a sad day for the non-proliferation regime....the Security Council is imposing sanctions on a member of the NPT that—unlike Israel....The same Governments, which have pushed this Council to take groundless punitive measures against Iran's peaceful nuclear program, have systematically prevented it from taking any action to nudge the Israeli regime towards submitting itself to the rules governing the nuclear non-proliferation regime.[8]

In reaction to the Security Council resolution, a member of the Majlis National Security and Foreign Policy Commission, Heshmatollah Falahat-Pisheh, was quoted as saying that Iran's nuclear programme was virtually under sanctions ever since 1990 and that "this resolution has only legitimised previous sanctions" of the IAEA.[9] The government has also expressed its support for a bill proposed by parliamentarians to review Iran's relations with the IAEA.[10]

---

6. "Iran's Ayatollah Khamenei Calls on Russia to form a 'Gas OPEC'", *Vedomosti, reproduced in RIA Novosti*, 30 January 2007, at *http://en.rian.ru/analysis/20070130/59954267.html*, accessed 30 January 2007.
7. Schake, Kori N. and Judith S. Yaphe (2001). "The Strategic Implications of a Nuclear-armed Iran", McNair Paper (Washington, D.C.: Institute for National Strategic Studies, National Defence University, May): pp.37–8.
8. "Iran Strongly Condemns Security Council Resolution Against Iran", IRNA, 24 December 2006, at *http://www.irna.ir/en/news/view/menu-234/0612241362011244.htm.*
9. (2006). "MPs Introduce Double-urgency Motion on Suspension of IAEA Inspections", IRNA, 24 December, at *http://www.irna.com/en/news/view/line-24/0612242656161014.htm.*
10. (2006). "Gov't Backs Bill on Revising Relations with IAEA: FM", IRNA, 26 December, at *http://www.irna.com/en/news/view/line-24/0612262355125507.htm*

Background of the Current Standoff

The current standoff began after Iran informed the IAEA on 3 January 2006 that it would resume nuclear research in a week's time, ending a two-year-long voluntary suspension. On 10 January 2006 the IAEA confirmed that Iran started removing IAEA seals on enrichment-related equipment and material at Natanz. In fact, Iran decided in August 2005 to restart uranium conversion against the commitment to suspend "all enrichment-related activities" under the Paris Agreement of 14 November 2004 with the EU-3 (France, Germany, and Britain). Subsequently by resuming work on enrichment, Iran also decided to revoke the assurance given to EU-3 in the Tehran Agreement of 21 October 2003 for voluntary suspension on "all uranium enrichment and reprocessing activities."

The Deputy Director General of Safeguards in his report of 31 January 2006 noted that the IAEA demanded clarifications from Iran on issues such as procurements and activities related to P-1 and P-2 centrifuges; sources of contamination found in the samples collected from enrichment-related facilities; activities at Lavizan-Shian Physics Research Centre; 'Green Salt Project' concerning the conversion of uranium dioxide into UF4 as well as tests related to high explosives and the design of a missile re-entry vehicle; and a few other technical activities related to other aspects of the fuel cycle. The IAEA stated that activities under the Green Salt Project "could have a military nuclear dimension" and also "appear to have administrative interconnection."[11] Iran claims that activities under its nuclear programme are under the authority of the Atomic Energy Organization of Iran (AEOI), which is a civilian agency. In his February 2006 report the IAEA Director General stated:

> It is regrettable, and a matter of concern, that the above uncertainties related to the scope and nature of Iran's nuclear programme have not been clarified after three years of intensive Agency verification. In

11. "Developments in the Implementation of the NPT Safeguards Agreement in the Islamic Republic of Iran and Agency Verification of Iran's Suspension of Enrichment-related and Reprocessing Activities", Update Brief by the Deputy Director General for Safeguards, IAEA, 31 January 2006.

order to clarify these uncertainties, Iran's full transparency is still essential.[12]

On 29 March 2006, in its Presidential Statement, the UN Security Council gave a strong message to Iran to suspend enrichment and reprocessing and to resolve outstanding questions with the IAEA in a month's time paving the way to create an appropriate atmosphere to find a diplomatic solution. But Iran's Shaheb missile test on 31 March 2006 further contributed to international apprehension. The Security Council adopted Resolution 1696 on 31 July 2006, demanding that Iran suspend all enrichment-related and reprocessing activities, including research and development, and cautioned that Iran's non-compliance by 31 August 2006 might lead to exercising appropriate measures under Article 41 of Chapter VII of the UN Charter. Article 41 reads:

> The Security Council may decide what measures not involving the use of armed force are to be employed to give effect to its decisions, and it may call upon the Members of the United Nations to apply such measures. These may include complete or partial interruption of economic relations and of rail, sea, air, postal, telegraphic, radio, and other means of communication, and the severance of diplomatic relations.

The Security Council unanimously adopted Resolution 1737 on 23 December 2006 under Article 41 demanding that Iran, without further delay, suspend proliferation-sensitive nuclear activities such as: all enrichment-related and reprocessing activities, including research and development; and work on all heavy-water related projects, including the construction of a research reactor moderated by heavy water. The halt to those activities is needed to be further verified by the IAEA.[13] Repeating the earlier demand on Iran to cooperate with the IAEA and to voluntarily suspend enrichment activities, the Security Council adopted Resolution 1747 on 24 March 2007 putting sanctions on 13 entities and 15 individuals related to Iran's nuclear and missile programmes.[14]

---

12. "Implementation of the NPT Safeguards Agreement in the Islamic Republic of Iran", Board of Governors Report, IAEA, GOV/2006/15, 27 February 2006, p.11.
13. "Security Council Imposes Sanctions on Iran for Failure to Halt Uranium Enrichment, Unanimously Adopting Resolution 1737 (2006)", Press Release, UN Security Council, SC/8928, 23 December 2006, at *http://www.un.org/News/Press/docs/2006/sc8928.doc.htm.*

Meanwhile, enrichment work in Iran is being carried on to set and operate 3000 centrifuges soon. On 9 April 2007 President Ahmedinejad announced "With great pride...as of today our dear country is among the countries of the world that produces nuclear fuel on an industrial scale."[15] He had been explicit in his remark in April 2006: "our centrifuges are the P1 type, and the next step is the P2, which has a capacity four times greater and on which we are presently conducting research."[16] P1 and P2 are Pakistani nomenclature of centrifuges developed out of URENCO uranium enrichment centrifuge designs of Almelo—P1 consisting of rotors made of aluminium and P2 based on maraging steel. URENCO centrifuge designs were first brought by A.Q. Khan to Pakistan and subsequently were supplied to Iran, Libya, and North Korea, through the clandestine Khan network. The procurements and activities related to P1 and P2 centrifuges have been the crucial aspects of contestation between Iran and the IAEA.

Challenges for the NPT Regime

There are four critical issues related to Tehran's nuclear case as an NPT member-state.

- There have been numerous incidents of 'non-reporting' related to its nuclear programme, and 'contamination' or 'material loss' during the fuel cycle activities, which a member state under the IAEA safeguards is obliged to declare.
- The dwindling confidence of nuclear suppliers in assisting NPT-defined non-nuclear weapon states for possible breaches of international commitments creates mutual suspicion between the demand and supply sides.
- Even the IAEA has incrementally found it difficult to perform its role, as is evident from the disclosures about extensive links of Iran's nuclear programme with the Pakistan-based A.Q. Khan network.

---

14. UN Security Council Resolution 1747, 24 March 2007, S/RES/1747 (2007).
15. Fathi, Nazila (2007). "Iran Claims Progress in Enriching Uranium", *New York Times*, 10 April, at *http://www.nytimes.com/2007/04/09/world/middleeast/09cnd-iran.html?_r=1&hp&oref=slogin.*
16. Fathi, Nazila and Christine Hauser (2006). "U.N. Official Reaches No Clear Outcome in Iran Talks", *New York Times*, 13 April.

- Iran may continue with the denial mode and simultaneously be working towards attainment of nuclear weapon capability.

Uncertain Scientific Assessment

Both the US and Britain maintain that Iran has a covert nuclear weapon programme but they lack credible evidence. US intelligence, while claiming to have information about Iran's unstated weapon ambition, does not have 'clear-cut knowledge' as to how long Iran would take to develop weapon capability.[17] Many western analysts hold an opinion that "judgements about the speed at which Iran is pursuing this capability are highly relevant."[18]

Current estimates by analysts vary from four to ten years when Iran would possibly be able to build the bomb. The Pentagon has for long maintained that if Iran decides, it would take a decade's time to develop a weapon. In an interview with BBC Radio, then Director of the US National Intelligence John Negroponte disclosed that according to his agency's estimate Iran could develop a nuclear weapon by 2010–15[19] but two years ago a US presidential commission reportedly found that US intelligence knew 'disturbingly little' about Tehran's capabilities.[20] The IAEA also has not conclusively proved that Iran is diverting its nuclear resources for military purposes.

Temptation for the Weapon

In the past, the nuclear policies of the Arab states and Iran have often been propelled by their concerns regarding each other's defence capabilities, though their publicly stated threat perceptions have focused inevitably on Israel.[21] Iranian and Arab politicians have perceived American and British persuasion to abandon their nuclear,

---

17. (2006). "Iran Bomb 'Within Next 10 Years'", *BBC News Online*, 2 June, at *http://news.bbc.co.uk/2/hi/middle_east/5039956.stm.*
18. Fitzpatrick, Mark (2006). "Assessing Iran's nuclear programme", *Survival* 48(3) (Autumn), p.5.
19. (2006). "Iran Bomb 'Within Next 10 Years'", *BBC News Online*, 2 June, at *http://news.bbc.co.uk/2/hi/middle_east/5039956.stm.*
20. Linzer, Dafna (2006). "Strong Leads and Dead Ends in Nuclear Case Against Iran", *Washington Post*, 8 February.
21. Feldman, Shai (1997). *Nuclear Weapons and Arms Control in the Middle East* (Cambridge, Mass.: MIT Press), p.121.

chemical, and biological weapons programmes as a move to weaken their position *vis-à-vis* Israel.[22] For Iran, possessing nuclear weapons means "gaining leverage over Israel, the United States, Turkey, and Saudi Arabia in a potential military confrontation or diplomatic crisis."[23] Also, Iran would be the only other country, apart from the US and Russia, in the club of nuclear weapon states to have its nuclear influence bolstered by its economic and strategic leverage over oil.[24]

The following five reasons could induce Iran to decide to become a nuclear weapon power.

- Two of its neighbours, Israel and Pakistan, are nuclear powers. With rich gas and oil resources, it may choose to develop nuclear weapons as a matter of national pride.
- Israel as a strategic partner of the US with undeclared nuclear weapon capability remains Iran's strongest regional adversary after the fall of Saddam's regime in Iraq.
- Iran has always aspired to become the leading regional power in the West Asian region. Development of nuclear weapons may significantly enhance its military capability to match its ambition.
- To strengthen its politico-military position *vis-à-vis* US pressure in any potential crisis, especially in the light of how easily Saddam's government buckled under US aggression.
- US military presence around Iran has become ubiquitous in Afghanistan, Pakistan, Iraq, Central Asia, and Turkey. Therefore, Iran may consider that the nuclear deterrent has become even more urgent.

The Dilemma Continues for Iran

In an attempt to caution the international community, the head of the AEOI has stated, "In the past 27 years we had experienced many

---

22. Perkovich, George and Avner Cohen (2004). "Devaluing Arab WMDs", *Washington Times*, 19 January.
23. Schake and Yaphe, n.7, p.6.
24. El-Labbad, Mustafa (2007). "If Iran gets the bomb", *Al-Ahram Weekly*, No. 828 (18–24 January).

kinds of sanctions. But they should know that the artery of the world energy passes through the straits of Hormuz in the Persian Gulf."[25] It is, however, unlikely that either the US or Iran would like to escalate military tensions in the region, with the US being bogged down in the Iraq quagmire. Iran, too, may proceed cautiously in order not to lose the sympathies of China and Russia, who have hitherto resisted attempts made by the US, Britain, and France to adopt tougher measures against Iran.

Toughening its posture the US recently started massive troop deployment, including the two aircraft carriers in the Gulf.[26] The appointment of a Navy admiral to head the US Central Command (CENTCOM) along with the dispatch of aircraft carriers and minesweepers to the Gulf is being seen by analysts as a move to prevent blockade of the Strait of Hormuz.[27] While conscious of the need to ensure energy supplies, it is not certain how China and Russia will react to the increasing US military presence and influence in and around Central and West Asia.

There is still room for diplomatic manoeuvring. Official US estimates indicate that Iran is still five to ten years away from making the bomb. If indeed Iran has plans of nuclear weaponisation it still needs to do a lot of work on the technology front to start planned industrial-scale enrichment of 50,000 centrifuges. Also, the construction and operation of a nuclear power plant to use weapon-grade nuclear material may take some more time.

Iran has indeed shown some flexibility. Despite the recent row over its disapproval of the entry of some IAEA inspectors into the country, the visits of a large number of IAEA inspectors to Iranian locations are still continuing. Surveillance cameras are still in place at the conversion plant of Isfahan. The IAEA has reportedly also been allowed to install some cameras at new locations in the Natanz complex. These cameras are placed to watch the gas injection and

---

25. (2006). "Iran Injects Gas in Centrifuges, Yet Keeps on Talking Peace", *Times of India* (New Delhi), 18 February.
26. Aneja, Atul (2007). "Warship raises US-Iran Tensions", *The Hindu* (New Delhi), 22 February.
27. Weiss, Leonard and Larry Diamond (2007). "Congress must Stop an Attack on Iran", *Los Angeles Times*, 5 February, at *http://www.latimes.com/news/printedition/asection/la-oe-weiss5feb05,1,6694223.story.*

storehouse parts of the complex. Iran has also expressed its willingness to resolve outstanding issues through negotiations. Significant scope therefore remains for engaging Iran to break the stalemate.

21

Hamas, Israel, and Peace

A.K. PASHA

The State of Israel occupied the Palestinian territories of West Bank (5640 sq. km) and Gaza Strip (360 sq. km) and East Jerusalem in the third Arab–Israel war of June 1967. In return for peace, Israel was required to withdraw from occupied Arab lands as per UN Security Council Resolution 242 of 22 November 1967. But all Israeli governments since then have allowed Jewish settlements in occupied Arab lands. A combination of events starting from Israeli invasions of Lebanon in 1978 and 1982, tough policy by the Israeli military commanders, and oppression by armed Jewish settlers have made life for Palestinians difficult in West Bank and Gaza Strip areas.

The Oslo Peace Process

In this backdrop, the Palestinian Intifada (Uprising), which extended from 1987 to 1993, paved the way for the Oslo Peace Accords of 1993–95 between Israel and the Palestinians. The Oslo Peace intensified rather than mitigated Palestinian "dispossession, deprivation and oppression", reinforcing the unequal power equations between Israel and the Palestinians. This precluded a fair and workable settlement of the Palestinian–Israeli conflict. This soon led to sharp economic decline for the majority of the Palestinians living in the West Bank and Gaza Strip mainly due to the policy of closures. Thus, "Oslo formalised and institutionalised the occupation in a manner that was altogether new."[1]

The Israeli general elections of 1996 brought a hard-liner, Benjamin Netanyahu of the Likud party, as prime minister. He employed all his

1. Roy, Sara (2007). *Falling Peace: Gaza and the Palestinian–Israeli Conflict* (London: Pluto Press): 234, 236, 238, 242.

powers to 'freeze and undermine' the Oslo accords. Netanyahu's obdurate unwillingness to honour negotiated agreements collapsed the Oslo accords. A US neo-conservative report, *Clean Break: A New Strategy for Securing the Realm* by Douglas Feith, Richard Perle, and David Wurmser for the Institute for Advanced Strategic and Political Studies in Jerusalem was published in June 1996. Netanyahu quickly accepted the report on 10 July 1996. The report, among other things, called on Israel to abrogate the Oslo accords, annex West Bank, launch preemptive attack on the Palestinian Authority, and thereby prevent the emergence of a Palestine state.[2] In order to breathe fresh life into the peace process, US President Bill Clinton organised a summit at Camp David in July 2000 between Yasser Arafat, chairman of the Palestine Liberation Organization (PLO) and Israeli Prime Minister Ehud Barak but peace eluded them. Soon alAqsa Intifada (second uprising) led to suicide bombings and Palestinian resistance to Israeli occupation of the West Bank and Gaza Strip resumed in right earnest. In the so-called Operation Defensive Shield launched by Israeli Prime Minister Ariel Sharon against the Palestinians on 29 March 2002 the declared objective was to destroy the infrastructure of Palestinian terrorism; in reality, Israel destroyed almost the entire Palestinian infrastructure.

Collapse of the 2003 Road Map

"The Performance-Based Road Map to a Permanent Two-State Solution to the Israeli-Palestinian Conflict", better known as the Road Map for Peace, was introduced on 30 April 2003. It was hailed as a historic compromise as it made a clear reference to a provisional Palestinian state, although its boundaries are unclear. Unlike the Oslo process, the Road Map referred explicitly to Israeli occupation and asked for ending it at the end of the process. However, it did not call the occupation illegal and that it must be brought to an end as per UN resolutions and international law.

Unfortunately, the Road Map had many structural flaws of the Oslo accords. It called for dismantling of Israeli settlements established only since March 2001, leaving the bulk of the earlier settlements in place,

---

2. A copy of the full text of *Clean Break* can be found on the Institute's web site.

reinforcing the geographic non-contiguity of Palestinian lands. It expected the Palestinians to deliver a great many things but made few demands on Israel.[3] The Road Map failed to take off and with the US attention focused on Iraq, the Palestine issue was largely left to Prime Minister Sharon even though the EU (European Union), the UN, and Russia occasionally took some interest whenever a crisis appeared on the scene.

Sharon accepted the Road Map on 25 May 2003 but raised fourteen objections, which effectively stalemated negotiations and precluded the establishment of a viable Palestinian state.[4] Under this plan, the Palestinians were to have an independent Palestine state by 2005. Instead what they got was unilateral Israeli withdrawal from the Gaza Strip and removal of a few Jewish settlers from the West Bank. Sharon announced in December 2004 his "unilateral disengagement" plan under which Israeli troops and settlers were to withdraw from Gaza and four small West Bank settlements with 526 Jewish settlers by August 2005. Despite stiff opposition Sharon implemented his plan.

Israel even after its withdrawal from Gaza has at will launched deadly attacks deep inside the West Bank and Gaza Strip on the pretext of controlling terrorist attacks and has resorted to indiscriminate targeted killings. In the view of Palestinians all peace plans, Israeli or otherwise, "foresaw Israeli control of significant West Bank territory, a Palestinian existence on minimal territory surrounded, divided and ultimately controlled by Israel, and a Palestinian entity that would assume responsibility for internal policing and civil matters."[5] Palestinians could not freely access the outside world by air, sea or land as Israel continues to control the entry and exit points.[6]

On 9 January 2005 Palestinians elected Mahmood Abbas as President of the Palestinian National Authority (PNA). Many expected him to put the peace process back on track and end the cycle of violence.

---

3. Roy, n.1: 228–9; see also Mearsheimer, John J. and Stephen M. Watt (2006). *The Israeli Lobby and US Foreign Policy,* Faculty RWP's series, John F. Kennedy School of Government, Harvard University, March: 33, 73, 77.
4. Ibid. See also Chomsky, Noam (1999). *The Fateful Triangle: The US, Israel, and the Palestinians.* Cambridge, Mass.: South End Press.
5. Beinin, Joel and Rebecca L. Stein (eds.) (2006). *The Struggle for Sovereignty: Palestine and Israel, 1993–2005* (Stanford: Stanford University Press): 236, 347.
6. See also Pasha, A.K. (2005). "Post-Arafat Palestine", *World Focus* 26(5) (May): 7–10.

Meanwhile, Israel continued with its policy of targeted killings of Palestinian leaders, especially of Hamas. Continued hostile policy from Israel and Abbas' inability to get Israel to withdraw from Palestinian lands steadily increased the popularity of Hamas.

Thus, by the end of 2005, Israel had withdrawn from Gaza and parts of West Bank and released a few hundred Palestinian detainees, but large sections of the Palestinians still remained under Israeli occupation. It was clear that after decades of Israeli occupation and use of lethal force, the Palestinian will to resist could not be crushed. The US and Israel once again called for reforms in the Palestinian Authority and accused President Abbas of not doing enough to contain Hamas and stop suicide bombings as well as the Qassam rockets. President Abbas did control a very difficult security situation and, in all fairness, acted with wisdom and worked slowly to regain confidence and trust of the Palestinian people.[7]

Squeezing the Hamas Government

It was in this background of deprivation, destruction and death that parliamentary elections were held in Palestine in January 2006, which brought Hamas to power for the first time. The Palestinian hope of having an independent state was again dashed in 2005 for a second time after 1998. With the demise of Arafat, the chances of reaching a lasting settlement based on 1967 lines became slim given Sharon's determination to retain much of the West Bank and East Jerusalem. As early as in April 2004 Sharon had stated in an interview with *Ha'aretz*, "The Palestinians understand that this ['disengagement'] plan is, to a great extent, the end of their dreams, and a very heavy blow to them."[8] Much later, his advisor Dor Weisglass confirmed that the idea of an independent Palestinian state was a non-starter.

The election of Hamas by the Palestinians is to be seen as an expression clearly of their frustration at the policies of Israel and continued US support to its illegal actions. The Palestinian National Council (PNC) elected Ismail Haniyeh as Prime Minister of Palestine.

7. Khalidi, Walid (2003). "The Prospects of Peace in the Middle East", *Journal of Palestine Studies* 32(2) (Winter): 50–62.

8. Ibid.: 346. See also Pasha, A.K. (1999). *India and West Asia: Continuity and Change.* Delhi: Gyan Sagar.

Hamas came to dominate the new Palestinian government, although others were invited to join. The election of Hamas government gave Israel a handle to intensify its so-called war on terror and put more pressure on President Abbas to contain Hamas. The US also used the demand of the Quartet negotiating the Road Map, involving United Nations, Russian Federation, the United States, and European Union, that Israel's "right to exist" be recognised as a pretext to challenge the Hamas leaders. Soon the US declared Hamas, like Hezbollah, a terrorist group and boycotted the Hamas government. The EU, Canada, and some others followed suit. To deprive the Hamas government of financial resources money transfer was banned.

Though Hamas has rejected Israel's right to permanent existence on this land on several occasions it has also said it is willing to recognise Israel on the basis of equality and reciprocity. It supports peace talks with Israel conducted by President Abbas, promising to accept the results if approved by a referendum.[9]

President Abbas and the Fatah, still smarting after its defeat in the January 2006 parliamentary elections, rejected the Hamas demand to cede control of the Palestinian security services to Prime Minister Ismail Haniyeh. Soon, clashes erupted on the issue, especially in Gaza, between the Fatah-led Palestinian security forces and the Hamas militia. Gaza was soon heading towards a civil war mainly due to President Abbas' refusal to integrate the Hamas militia either into the regular Palestinian security force or allow the formation of a parallel security force. Ismail Haniyeh on the other hand was keen to see his militia men employed in the revamped security force, in order to ease widespread unemployment in the West Bank and Gaza Strip. This would have also strengthened his position in maintaining law and order.[10]

In order to put pressure on the Hamas government, Israel intensified its policy of indiscriminate arrests, assassinations or targeted killings, indefinite curfews, large-scale house demolitions, incursions, frequent closures of the West Bank and Gaza Strip,

9. Ibid. See also Christison, Kathleen (2001). *Perceptions of Palestine: Their Influence on US Middle East Policy* (Berkeley: University of California Press, 2001).

10. Pasha, A.K. (ed.) (2000). *Arab–Israeli Peace Process: An Indian Perspective*. New Delhi: Manas: 447–53.

humiliating checkpoints (540 in the West Bank), levelling of lands, digging works in Jerusalem, general shut-downs that prevented Palestinians from reaching to work in Israel, and far-reaching restrictions that prevented Palestinians from attending schools, visiting hospitals, and holding down jobs in their villages and towns.[11] The Palestinian economy ceased to function in major areas.

Former US President Jimmy Carter in his book *Palestine Peace Not Apartheid* writes:

> For 39 years Israel has occupied Palestinian land and has confiscated and colonised hundreds of choice sites. Often excluded from their former homes, land and places of worship, protesting Palestinians have been severely dominated and oppressed. There is forced segregation between Israeli settlers and Palestine's citizens, with a complex pass system required for Arabs to traverse Israel's multiple checkpoints.[12]

The huge security wall which Israel has been constructing at astonishing speed in clear violation of international law and against the advice of the International Court of Justice as also UN Security Council resolutions has exposed its colonial expansionist intentions. On its side of the wall Israel has annexed large tracts of fertile Palestinian lands which also contain wells. Thousands of Palestinians are trapped on either side of the wall. It has not only caused them immense suffering, dispossession and impoverishment but has led to an internal refugee problem. A volatile situation was deliberately aggravated by the US and Israel to bring about 'regime change'. According to one writer, "Washington has pulled out all the stops to undermine the Hamas-led government. US media reports that US and Israeli officials have met at the 'highest-level' to discuss 'starving'" the Hamas government.[13]

---

11. Roy, n. 1: 290. See also Shlaim, Avi (2000). *The Iron Wall: Israel and the Arab World.* New Delhi: Penguin; A.K. Pasha (2004). "Why is the Islamic World Important for India"? *Hard News* 1(7) (June): 56–7.
12. Carter, Jimmy (2007). *Palestine Peace Not Apartheid* (New York). See also Pradhan, Bansidhar (2004). "Changing Dynamics of India's West Asia policy", *International Studies* 41(1): 73–84.
13. See Cherian, John (2006). "Threat of Civil War", *Frontline,* (30 June), pp.52–3. See also Pasha, A.K. (1997). "Indo-Israeli Cooperation", *Asian Affairs.* London 1(5) (March): 22–3.

Truce Breaks Down

To compound the Palestinian woes, Israel killed more than ten Palestinians, including six women and three children, in a completely unprovoked act on 9 June 2006 in Gaza. More than forty Palestinians were seriously injured in this attack. A few days earlier, Israel Special Forces (ISF) killed Jamal Abu Samhadana, head of the Hamas-led resistance forces in Gaza. Hamas reacted to the Gaza killings by immediately calling off the 'truce' with Israel and launching Qassam rockets into Israel. It is pertinent to remember that since August 2004 Hamas had respected the cease fire arranged with Abbas and Israel, which had indeed considerably brought down the level of violence. Soon after the Israeli offensive, the spokesman for the popular resistance committee, Abu Abir promised that "rockets would rain into the Zionist entity and our heroes will blow themselves into their dirty bodies."[14]

Articulating the Palestinians' frustration, Khalid Mishal, head of the Hamas political Bureau based in Damascus, wrote,

> Since the elections of January 2006 our people have been boycotted and punished by the international community for exercising their democratic rights. In the meantime, Israel has continued to kill and detain Palestinians on a daily basis, demolishing hundreds of houses and making thousands homeless. Today, Israel has more than 11,000 of our brothers and sisters in jail and continues to deny millions of refugees the right to return to their homeland. It has defied international law by proceeding with the construction of the Apartheid Wall and building settlements in land expropriated from Palestinians.[15]

Not only are Palestinians under pressure from Israel on financial, security, political, and diplomatic fronts, they are also being forced to part with their land. Israel's settlement policy amounts to "ethnic warfare."[16]

---

14. Ibid. See also Neumann, Michael (2005). *The Case Against Israel* (California: Counterpunch).
15. Mishal, Khalid (2007). "Hamas and Fatah Unity can Pave Way for Peace", *The Hindu*, 16 February; see also Haas, Amira (1999). *Drinking the Sea at Gaza: Days and Nights in a Land under Siege*. New York: Henry Holt.
16. Neumann, n.14; Cherian, n.13: 52; see also Kimmerling, Baruch and Joel S. Migdal (2003). *The Palestinian People*. Cambridge, Mass.: Harvard University Press.

In November 2006 Israeli Prime Minister Ehud Olmert announced a new plan for a final settlement of the Palestinian issue. The plan proposes the creation of a Greater Israel by 2010 under which Israel will formally annex the whole of Jerusalem and big chunks of the West Bank, including those taken behind the apartheid wall. In this plan Olmert claimed to follow David Ben Gurion, a former Israeli prime minister.[17] Despite his call for large-scale evacuation of land and settlements in the West Bank, the Israeli settler population in the West Bank (excluding East Jerusalem) increased in 2006. There were 268,379 Israelis living in the West Bank at the end of 2006, according to the Israeli Interior Ministry, compared to 253,748 in 2005, a 5.8 per cent increase.[18]

Palestinians now have even less land than before on which to establish an independent Palestine state. Khalid Mishal says:

> We Palestinians have been the victims of invasion, occupation and oppression for almost a century. Yet we have been constantly blackmailed to make concessions and give up yet more of our legitimate rights. There must be no more blackmail of Palestinians, for there is nothing else they can give away. Global powers should have learned by now that neither sanctions nor any other form of pressure of bribery will force the Palestinians to abandon their struggle for freedom and independence.[19]

For the young in Palestine, life under occupation is seared by violence, occupied by Israel, largely cut off from the world, and segmented by barriers and checkpoints, fostering Nihilism and a loss of hope. One Palestinian said, "We never see anything good in our lives."[20] Generations of young Palestinians have grown up stateless, seething at Israel as the visible agent of oppression and humiliation.

The so-called Israeli security measures have become even tighter since the electoral success of Hamas. During the 1980s and '90s, about

---

17. Beinin and Stein, n.5: 332.
18. *Report on Israeli Settlement in the Occupied Territories*, A Bi-monthly publication of the Foundation for Middle East Peace 17(1–2) (January-February and March-April 2007): 1–8.
19. Mishal, n.15; Hamid Ansari (2000). "Continuing Myopia in West Asia", *The Hindu*, 12 March; see also Pasha, A.K. (2007). "India and West Asia: Past and Future", in N.S. Sisodia and A.K. Behuria (eds.), *West Asia in Turmoil: Implications for Global Security*. New Delhi: Academic Foundation, 2007: 441–70.
20. Erlanger, Steven (2007). "A Generation 'Lost' to Intifada Despairs", *The Hindu*, 13 March.

1.5 lakh Palestinians went to Israel daily. Now most sit idle and Hamas exploits them easily. The West Bank is cut into three parts by Israeli checkpoints.[21]

With the completion of the security wall, Israel by 2010 would have taken over 45 per cent of the West Bank which might become part of Israel. Only about 1350 square miles of territory equivalent to 12 per cent of historic Mandatory Palestine would be left for the proposed Palestinian state to accommodate more than four million Palestinians.

Mounting Global Interest

In July 2006, President Abbas called for a referendum towards the end of 2006, mainly to regain the initiative for Fatah and stave off pressure from the US, Israel, and others and to undermine the Hamas government's credibility. President Abbas' announcement brought into question his motives, because parliamentary elections are due only in 2010. The referendum idea was seen as a "recipe for civil war". Soon enough, fighting broke out between Hamas and Fatah especially in Gaza.

Meanwhile Russia took the lead in inviting the Hamas leader Khalid Mishal to Moscow for talks. President Vladimir Putin also urged a speedy end of the boycott of the Hamas-led government at the Quartet meetings. Turkey, Iran, Saudi Arabia, Egypt, and others followed the Russian example in inviting the Hamas leaders despite objections by the US and Israel. Former British Foreign Secretary Jack Straw, recognising that the Palestinian-Israeli conflict was fuelling unrest throughout West Asia, said that its resolution was even more important than a settlement of conditions in Iraq. "Its effect is so powerful, not just in West Asia but around the whole Islamic world. It is the engine of so much trouble around the world."[22]

According to the Palestinian Central Bureau of Statistics, 56 per cent of the Palestinians are under 19 and in Gaza 75 per cent of the

---

21. Pasha, A.K. (2006). "India's Policy Towards the Arab World in the 21st Century", in V.D. Chopra (ed.), *India's Foreign Policy in the 21st Century*. Delhi: Kalpaz: 215–50.
22. Pasha, A.K. (2004). "Arafat, Palestinians, and the Future", *Mainstream* (New Delhi) XLII(50) (4 December): 7–12.

population are under 30. Gazan men under 30 are virtually unable to leave their tiny poor and overcrowded territory. Few Palestinians now talk of peace, almost all talk only of "a lifetime of resistance". According to Waleed Ladadwal of the Palestinian Centre for Policy and Survey Research, young Palestinians are more supportive of armed struggle and terrorism than their parents. This generation has lost faith in political solutions. "They haven't lived one moment in a period of real hope for a real state", said Nader Said, a political scientist at Bir Zeit university in Ramallah. Some 58 per cent of those under 30, the centre's polls show, expect a more violent struggle with Israel over the next five to ten years and only 22 per cent believe that there will be a peaceful negotiated solution between Israel and the Palestinians. About 48 per cent believe that such an agreement is impossible and 20 per cent more believe it will only come "in a few generations."[23] In 2000 only 7 per cent of Palestinians were for Hamas and 46 per cent for the more secular Fatah. In 2007, even after an extremely difficult year of Hamas rule, the two Palestinian factions are roughly equal in their popular appeal.

More and more Palestinian parents see their young children turning violent. One parent said, "I was shocked but it's (all) in the news, the environment, the sound of Apaches and the F-16s and the cannons. It all affects them and they get nervous. And when you think about the violence, what future will we have here? It will be a very violent future."[24] Prime Minister Olmert recently told US Secretary of State Condoleezza Rice that he would meet regularly, but not negotiate, with President Abbas, and would not discuss borders, Jerusalem and refugees, three critical issues which must be part of any final status talks. Thus, Israeli policies promise further conflict.

India's Response

Even though India opposed the partition of Palestine by the UN in 1947 the government recognised Israel in September 1950. Ever since India's decision to establish diplomatic ties with Israel in 1992, Indo–

23. Mishal, n.15; see also Pasha, A.K. (1993). "India's West Asia Policy: Continuity and Change", *Strategic Analysis* 16(6) (September): 783–804.

24. *The Hindu*, 13 March 2007; see also *Report on Israeli Settlement in the Occupied Territories*, n.18.

Israeli ties in military, intelligence, and economic spheres have improved rapidly, especially during the NDA (National Democratic Alliance) government led by the BJP (Bharatiya Janata Party) when there was even talk of a strategic alliance with the Jewish state. The common "war on terror" and great deal of talk about Hindu–Jewish common values and ancient ties gave Indo–Israeli collaboration under the BJP a distinct ideological and communal direction. Israel has now become India's second-largest supplier of arms and its second-largest trading partner in Asia. Prime Minister Ariel Sharon visited India in 2003 (9 September) and talked about his determination to act against terror and called for greater Indian support to Israel in the UN and the Non-Aligned Movement.

Although India was keen to join the Arab–Israel peace process after the Madrid (1991) Peace Conference this did not survive for long. India more recently was also excluded from the 2003 Road Map of the Quartet. President Abbas visited India in May 2005 and India promised Rs. 65 crore in aid for infrastructure projects in West Bank and Gaza Strip, including the building of a library-cum-activity centre at the Palestinian Technical College at Deir alBalah and one at AlAzhar University in Gaza. India has been offering scholarships to Palestinian students for studies in Indian universities through the ICCR (Indian Council for Cultural Relations) as well as giving training in security to Palestinian police officers. Medicine and other humanitarian aid has also been going regularly to the Palestinians. India has reiterated its support to the Palestinian struggle for self-determination and also called for an end to violence.

Fully aware that the UPA (United Progressive Alliance) government led by the Congress Party is as keen as the NDA to consolidate its ties with Israel, cemented by a steady stream of ministerial visits and growing arms purchases, President Abbas conceded that India's ties with Israel were its own bilateral affair. Nonetheless his visit could have been used to expose Israeli policies against Palestinians and a firm call issued to end Israeli occupation in a timebound schedule. Notwithstanding the so-called "enlightened self-interest", India's acquiescence in continued Israeli occupation is perceived as not being in harmony with its widely acclaimed legacy of anti-colonial policy. Israeli policies are of a kind that the South African racist and apartheid regime pursued. The Palestine issue remains widely popular in India, with overwhelming support from all sections of Indians for an early end to the misery and sufferings of the Palestinians.

Although India is keen to join the Arab–Israel peace process it has become imperative to coordinate its efforts with Russia, China, and the regional states such as Egypt, Turkey, Saudi Arabia, and others. But with India taking a "less strident position against Israel in the UN forums much to the chagrin of the Palestinians" and having "made considerable attempts to moderate anti-Israeli resolutions" at the meetings of the Non-Aligned Movement in Durban and elsewhere, the expectations of many, especially in the Arab and Islamic world, that the Congress-led UPA government would restore the balance it had pursued in its policy towards West Asia earlier will remain largely elusive.[25] The proposition that Israel is a major arms supplier to India and hence the government should soft-pedal its stand against Israel will affect India's credibility.

As an urgent humanitarian task, India should work to lift the boycott of the Palestinian government and the unfair financial sanctions by the US and Israel on the Palestinians, who are being deprived of the basic necessities of life. India in order to regain genuine global respect must not only continue to support wholeheartedly the Palestine cause and work with other interested states to bring about an end to Israeli occupation but also ensure justice to the Palestinians. Any delay in resolving the Palestinian–Israeli issue will lead to more violence and instability in a crucial area where Indian energy interests are growing.

---

25. Abhyankar, R.M. (2007). "India's West Asia Policy: Search for a Middle Ground", in Atish Sinha and Madhup Mohta, *Indian Foreign Policy: Challenges and Opportunities*. New Delhi: Academic Foundation: 321–349; Agwani, M.S. (2005). "India and Palestine", *World Focus* 26(5) (May): 11–13; see also Pasha, A.K. (1997). "A Great Leap Forward taken by India and Israel", *India Abroad* (New York), 17 January: 2–3.

22

The Second Israel–Lebanon War

An Appraisal

V. KRISHNAPPA

> And everybody praised the Duke,
> Who this great fight did win'.
> 'But what good came of it at last?'
> Quoth little Peterkin:
> 'Why, that I cannot tell', said he,
> But 't was a famous victory'.
>
> Robert Southey, *After Blenheim*[1]

The West Asian region remained turbulent during 2006. The 34-day Israeli military campaign against Hezbollah and Lebanon in the summer added another layer to the already complex security situation in the region. The American failure to stabilise the fragile security situation in Iraq, armed hostilities between Hamas and Israel Defence Forces (IDF) in the aftermath of 25 June kidnapping of an Israeli soldier on the Gaza border, and the broader military operations of the West against terrorism provided a volatile backdrop to the Second Lebanon War. Although Israel portrayed its high-intensity military campaign as an attempt directed at Hezbollah and its military infrastructure, its aerial and artillery barrages had a debilitating impact on civilian life and property in large parts of Lebanon, including the capital city Beirut. Israel flew 15,500 sorties, attacking roughly 7000 targets. Its artillery and tank forces are reported to have fired some 100,000 rounds. Lebanon suffered 1200 civilian deaths and over two million displaced from their homes. Hezbollah is said to have fired

1. Cited in Brian Bond, *The Pursuit of Victory: From Napoleon to Saddam Hussein*. Oxford: Oxford University Press 1998: 1.

around 4000 rockets of various types, killing over 40 and displacing 300,000 civilians. In contrast to very high costs to the civilian population, the number of soldiers killed on both sides was low. Israel is reported to have lost 119 soldiers and Hezbollah about 600-700 guerrillas. The Second Lebanon War by all accounts is representative of contemporary warfare—missing battlefields, indecisive military operations, and indiscriminate violence against civilian population.

For Israel, its campaign achieved three main war objectives—(i) undermining Hezbollah's military capabilities, (ii) reassertion of Lebanese sovereignty over the South after nearly four-decades-long unfettered reign of non-state actors, and (iii) creating conditions that may eventually delegitimise Hezbollah arms. Ironically, Israel is popularly seen as a net loser while Hezbollah is riding on the crest of popularity among the Arab populations, being seen as a model of 'Resistance' against Israel, which has the support of powerful Western powers.[2]

This paper, briefly appraising the war, will address the following:

- Why did Hezbollah abduct Israeli soldiers?
- In its response what was Israel's strategy?
- What were its important war objectives?
- How far did it achieve them?
- What is the impact of the war on the Arab–Israel peace process?

---

2. "Arab World Finds Icon in Leader of Hezbollah", *New York Times*, 7 August 2006, at *http://www.nytimes.com/2006/08/07/world/middleeast/07nasrallah.html?ex=1312603200&en=b924388c96743238&ei=5090* (accessed on 7 August 2006); "A Disciplined Hezbollah Surprises Israel with its Training, Tactics and Weapons", *New York Times*, 7 August 2006, at *http://www.nytimes.com/2006/08/07/world/middleeast/07hezbollah.html? ex=1312603200&en=de52fa69d7cbb67b&ei =5088&partner=rssnyt &emc=rss* (accessed on 7 August 2006); Haseeb, Khair El-Din (2006). "The 'Israeli War on Lebanon' and its repercussions", *Daily Star* (Beirut), 14 September 2006, at *http://www.caus.org.lb/Attachments/Israeli_war_Lebanon.pdf?* PHPSESSID=3f462617a271b 3524ba1eac59 ba5dade (accessed on 14 September 2006); "The Best Guerrilla Force in the World", *Washington Post*, 14 August 2006, at *http://www.washingtonpost.com/wp-dyn/content/article/2006/08/13/AR2006081300719.html* (accessed on 14 August 2006); Abdel-Latif, Omayma (2006). "Hizbullah's Hour", *Al-Ahram Weekly* (Cairo), 7–13 September 2006, at *http://weekly.ahram.org.eg/2006/811/re81.htm* (accessed on 20 September 2006); Howeidy, Amira (2006). "Revisiting Nasarallah", *Al-Ahram Weekly*, 17–23 August 2006, at *http://weekly.ahram.org.eg/2006/808/re601.htm;* Elchoubaki, Amr (2006). "More than Resistance", *Al-Ahram Weekly,* 17–23 August 2006, at *http://weekly.ahram.org.eg/2006/808/op2.htm* (accessed on 20 August 2006).

Why Did Hezbollah Abduct Israeli Soldiers?

After Hezbollah abducted two reserve Israeli soldiers in the early hours of 12 July and informed the world that it was willing to exchange them for Arab prisoners in Israeli jails, many commentators concluded that Hezbollah's provocative act had much broader aims than what was stated. These possibly included: opening a second front to relieve pressure on Palestinian rebels; diversion of international attention from Iran; creating conditions for return of Syria into Lebanon, and dragging Israel into a region-wide conflict.[3] But these are merely assumptions: there is no evidence so far to suggest that either Syria or Iran had any hand in ordering the abductions. Hezbollah's dependence on Syria and Iran for arms and finance is almost universally acknowledged. Its ideological loyalty to Shia religious leaders in Iran is also well documented. Hezbollah depends upon Syria for the provision of material resources and transit of Iranian arms.[4] It is reasonable, therefore, to assume that Hezbollah's leadership would not ignore the interests of its close allies while deciding to undertake a major military operation. But 'Operation Sincere Promise' was not a major offensive from its perspective; in its view, "the abductions did not constitute a paradigm shift in its military strategy that necessitated an Iranian stamp of approval or

---

3. See Saad-Ghorayeb, Amal (2006). "Hizbollah's Outlook in the Current Conflict", *Policy Outlook*, Carnegie Endowment for International Peace, August 2006, at *http://www.carnegieendowment.org/files/saad_ghorayeb_final.pdf* (accessed on 15 August 2006).

4. See Saad-Ghorayeb, Amal (2002). *Hizbu'llah: Politics and Religion* (London: Pluto Press); Goldberg, Jeffrey (2002). "In the Party of God: are Terrorists in Lebanon Preparing for a Larger War?" *The New Yorker*, 14–21 October 2002; Hajjar, Sami G. (2002). "Hizballah: Terrorism, National Liberation, or Menace?" Strategic Studies Institute, U.S. Army War College, August 2002, at *http://www.intellnet.org/documents/1300/000/1300.pdf* (accessed on 17 July 2006); Norton, Augustus Richard (1999). *Hizballah of Lebanon: Extremist Ideas vs. Mundane Politics* (New York: Council of Foreign Relations, 1999); Shatz, Adam (2004). "In Search of Hezbollah Part I and II", *The New York Review of Books*, 29 April and 13 May 2004; Hersh, Seymour M. (2006). "Watching Lebanon: Washington's Interests in Israel's War", *The New Yorker*, 14–21 August 2006; Karmon, Ely (2003). "'Fight on All Fronts' Hizballah, the War on Terror, and the War in Iraq", The Washington Institute, Research Memorandum 45, December 2003; "Hizbollah: Rebel without a Cause?" *ICG Middle East Briefing* 7, 30 July 2003, at *http://www.crisisgroup.org/home/index.cfm?l=1&id=4098&m=1; http://www.crisisgroup.org/library/documents/report_archive/A401070_30072003.pdf* (accessed on 18 July 2006); "Old Games, New Rules: Conflict on the Israeli Lebanon Border", *ICG Middle East Report 7*, 18 November 2002, at *http://www.crisisgroup.org/home/index.cfm?l=1&id=4098&m=1* (accessed on 18 July 2006); "Lebanon: Managing the Gathering Storm", *ICG Middle East Report 48*, 5 December 2005, at *http://www.crisisgroup.org/library/documents/middle_east___north_africa/arab_israeli_conflict/lebanon/48_lebanon_managing_the_gathering_storm.pdf* (accessed on 18 July 2006).

warranted a massive Israeli response."[5] In the words of one of its leaders, Hezbollah "did not expect (that) the (Israeli) response would be of this magnitude."[6] It calculated that the operation would be viewed as "just another in a history of bloody tit-for-tats...more audacious and provocative, in that it occurred not in the contested Shebaa but in a non-contested area to the west, where Israeli vigilance was far lower, but not fundamentally different in its objectives."[7]

This view is corroborated by the fact that Nasarallah had called 2006 "the year of retrieving the prisoners."[8] On many occasions during 2005-6 he openly spoke of the "duty to capture Israeli soldiers and swap them for Arab prisoners in Israel." Within hours of the incident he declared that: "(F)or more than a year, I've been saying that we want to kidnap soldiers in order to exchange prisoners. Every time I said so, Israel went into high alert along the border. We decided to kidnap soldiers to end the matter of prisoners."[9] In a wide-ranging interview broadcast on the Arab news channel Al Jazeera on 20 July, Nasrallah claimed that on a number of occasions he had hinted to the Lebanese government about the seriousness of the "prisoners issue", on which his party could not afford to 'procrastinate.'[10] In the past six years Hezbollah is known to have made eleven such unsuccessful attempts.[11] Furthermore, there is a history of prisoner swap between Hezbollah and Israel mediated by Germany in 2004. Thus, it is safe to conclude that Hezbollah gravely underestimated Israel's possible

5. Amal Saad-Ghorayeb, n. 4.
6. Ibid.
7. "Israel/Palestine/Lebanon: Climbing out of the Abyss", *ICG Middle East Report 57*, 25 July 2006, at *http://www.crisisgroup.org/library/documents/middle_east___north_africa/arab_israeli_conflict/57_israel_palestine_lebanon___climbing_out_of_the_abyss.pdf* (accessed on 30 July 2006): 10.
8. Amal Saad-Ghorayeb, "Hezbollah's Apocalypse Now", *Washington Post*, 23 July 2006, at *http://www.washingtonpost.com/wp-dyn/content/article/2006/07/21/AR2006072101363.html* (accessed on 23 July 2006).
9. Nasarallah is reported to have made this comment during a press conference on 12 July 2006, cited in n. 8.
10. Transcript of the interview at *http://www.globalresearch.ca/index.php?context= viewArticle&code= AL-20060722&articleId=2790* (accessed on 5 October 2006).
11. According to Nabih Berri, the Shia Speaker of Lebanese Parliament and close ally of Hassan Nasarallah: see *as-Safir*, 17 July 2006. One Israeli military analyst believes that this was Hezbollah's fifth attempt, see Ze'ev Schiff, *Ha'aretz*, 19 September 2006.

reaction and anticipated a more customary response—"limited aggression, to be followed by a prisoners exchange."[12]

However, it would be simplistic to interpret Hezbollah's actions of 12 July narrowly. The abduction was intended to serve a broader political and ideological agenda. Ever since Israel withdrew its forces behind the internationally recognised border—Blue Line—in the summer of 2000, the retention of Hezbollah's arms was becoming increasingly untenable in the Lebanese domestic political context. The passage of the United Nations Security Council Resolution 1559 in 2004 and the subsequent withdrawal of Syrian forces in 2005 under Lebanese and international pressure dramatically changed the balance of power in Lebanon against Hezbollah.[13] The consolidation of Lebanese political forces, known as the '14 March Coalition' opposed to Syria's involvement in domestic politics, coupled with growing international interest in bolstering Prime Minister Fouad Siniora's government, was viewed with suspicion by Hezbollah.[14] The party had difficulty in convincing the larger Lebanese elite and political forces that its arms were essential for Lebanese defence against Israel. Hezbollah's claims that Israel is still in occupation of Lebanese lands, continuously violates Lebanese sovereignty, and has larger designs on Lebanese territory found favour only among certain sections of the people.[15] In these changed circumstances, Hezbollah was increasingly being seen as a 'rebel without a cause.'[16]

---

12. See Shadid, Anthony (2006). "Inside Hezbollah, Big Miscalculations", *Washington Post*, 8 October 2006, at *http://www.washingtonpost.com/wp-dyn/content/article/2006/10/07/AR2006100701054.html* (accessed on 8 October 2006); Keinon, Herb and Ryan Nadel (2006). "IDF Official: Hizbullah Jumped the Gun", *Jerusalem Post*, 12 September 2006; "Israel/Palestine/Lebanon ...", n. 7.

13. See Young, Michael 2006). "Hezbollah's Other War", *New York Times*, 4 August 2006, at *http://www.google.co.in/search?hl=en&q= Hezbollah%E2%80%99s+Other+War&btnG= Google+Search&meta=* (accessed on 4 August 2006); "Hizbollah: Rebel without a Cause?" n. 4; Amal Saad-Ghorayeb, n. 4.

14. For Hezbollah leadership views see "Israel/Hizbollah/Lebanon: avoiding renewed conflict", *ICG Middle East Report 59*, 1 November 2006, at *http://www.crisisgroup.org/home/index.cfm?id=4480&l=1* (accessed on 2 November 2006); see also Pascual, Carlos (2006). "Restoring Confidence in Lebanon's Future", Deposition before US Senate Foreign Relations Committee, 13 September 2006, at *http://www.google.co.in/search?hl=en&q=Carlos+Pascual%2C+Restoring+Confidence+in+Lebanon%E2%80%99s+Future&btnG=Google+Search&meta=* (accessed on 14 October 2006).

15. See "Lebanon: Poll shows 51 per cent want Hezbollah Disarmed", *L'Orient-Le Jour*, 28 August 2006, at *http://yalibnan.com/site/archives/2006/08/post_18.php* (accessed on 10 October 2006).

16. See "Hizbollah: Rebel without a Cause?", n. 4.

Thus, the principal motive behind Hezbollah's 'Operation Sincere Promise' was to regain some of its lost legitimacy and to undermine domestic political pressure for its disarmament. Keeping in view the historical patterns and Israel's ongoing operations in the Gaza strip, Hezbollah calculated that its opponent would respond with limited force; and the overall impact would be to bolster its own domestic situation. In the event, Israel's overwhelming response unravelled Hezbollah's careful calculations.

Israeli Strategy and Concept of Operations

In broad terms, Israel used military force not to seek a decisive victory in the battlefield but to shape the strategic choices of its adversaries, allies, and influential neutrals. The basic assumptions and core elements of Israel's Lebanon-Hezbollah engagement strategy may be summarised as follows:

(a) Force of arms alone cannot remove the Hezbollah military threat. To succeed, force should be applied in "a subtle, sophisticated and smart manner, to combine military power with the political leverage, to impose a new order" on Lebanon.[17] The application of force should be such that it creates new political realities in Lebanon unfavourable to the retention of Hezbollah's arms.

(b) Ground invasion should be considered as a last option. If it becomes necessary, it should be carried out speedily. The force should capture dominant terrain as far as the Litani River and thereafter should operate in the guerrilla mode.

(c) Ground invasion may not resolve the Hezbollah threat.

(d) Air power should be the instrument of first choice and should be employed to influence the strategic choices of the target groups.

(e) There is no foolproof military solution to a Katyusha rocket threat.

---

17. This summary of Israeli strategy is based on the statements of key figures, the strategic discourse before the war, and the observed behaviour during the war. See Keinon, Herb and David Horovitz (2006). "PM Tells Post 'I had no illusions about this job'", *Jerusalem Post*, 28 September 2006, at *http://www.jpost.com/servlet/Satellite?cid= 1159193338704&pagename= JPost%2FJPArticle%2FPrinter* (accessed on 29 September 2006).

(f) The targets of Israel's strategic influence should include the Lebanese population, especially the Shi'ite support base of Hezbollah, the Lebanese government, and the Hezbollah leadership. The use of force should seek second-order effects on regional actors, such as Syria and Iran and the 'moderate' Arab states—Saudi Arabia, Egypt, and Jordan. Military operations should aim to generate a sense of urgency to implement UN Resolution 1559 in the international community in general, and among the US and the other key players, in particular.[18]

War Objectives

What follows is an assessment of the Israeli war aims, based largely on official statements, first-person accounts of key Israeli cabinet ministers and military leaders, credible and informed commentaries published in the Israeli and Western media. The conclusions obtained through these sources are, in turn, tested against actual behaviour wherever possible and necessary. At this stage, three preliminary comments are in order. First, in some respects, there is a gap between what was stated in public by key leaders and the known accounts of deliberations and decisions within the war cabinet. Second, the Israeli strategic objectives evolved over time during the crisis. Third, what follows is a brief summary of important war aims without reference to their evolution during the war.

Bolster Israeli Deterrence

Bolstering the image of its military power was an important motive that shaped the Israeli decision to enlarge the conflict. Deterrence in essence is about shaping perceptions of one's adversaries by use or

18. See Shavit, Ari (2006). "No Way to Go to War", Interview with Moshe Ya'alon, former Chief of Staff of IDF, *Ha'aretz*, 14 September 2006, at *http://www.haaretz.com/hasen/spages/762890.html* (accessed on 15 August 2006); Schiff, Ze'ev (2006). "Let's Get Real", *Ha'aretz*, 20 October 2006, at *http://www.haaretz.com/hasen/objects/pages/printarticleEn.jhtml/itemno=777197* (accessed on 20 October 2006); Makovsky, David and Jeffrey White (2006). "Lessons and Implications of the Israel–Hizballah War: A Preliminary Assessment", *Policy Focus 60*, The Washington Institute for Near East Policy, October 2006, at *http://www.washingtoninstitute.org/pubPDFs/PolicyFocus60.pdf* (accessed on 25 October 2006); Weitz, Gidi (2006). "To Beirut if Necessary", *Ha'aretz*, 11 August 2006, at *http://www.haaretz.com/hasen/pages/ShArt.jhtml?itemNo=749190* (accessed on 13 August 2006); Benn, Aluf and Akiva Eldar (2006). "Looking for the Endgame", *Ha'aretz*, 1 October 2006, at *http://www.haaretz.com/hasen/pages/ShArt.jhtml?itemNo=769432* (accessed on 2 October 2006).

threat of force. A state seeking to deter a potential attacker should demonstrate not only its military capability but also its willingness to use it. Deterrence fails if the adversary ignores the warnings. Many view Hezbollah's attack of 12 July as a failure of Israeli deterrent power. They argue that Israel's failure to live up to its threat of exacting response in the aftermath of its withdrawal from Lebanon, coupled with its decision to swap Arab prisoners in the past, was interpreted by Hezbollah and Palestinian groups as being born out of Israeli weakness. This, they believe, led to Nasarallah's miscalculation.

Israel enjoys overwhelming conventional superiority in the region: it has monopoly over nuclear weapons and terrorism is largely contained below a tolerable threshold.[19] Ironically, a series of developments on the Lebanese and Palestinian front have led to a perception of erosion of Israeli deterrent power in the past few years.

In the immediate aftermath of Israeli withdrawal in the summer of 2000, Nasrallah claimed credit for Israel's exit from Lebanese territory after eighteen years of occupation. He exhorted the Palestinians to emulate Hezbollah, declaring, "in order to liberate your land, you don't need tanks and planes. With the example of martyrs, you can impose your demands on the Zionist aggressors...Israel may own nuclear weapons and heavy weaponry, but by God, it is weaker than a spider's web."[20] Many Israelis believe that the Second *Intifada* was inspired by Hezbollah's perceived success against Israel. History repeated itself following Israel's pullout from Gaza. The Palestinian rebels claimed credit for the exit and began to stockpile rockets.

The success of Hamas at the ballot box in early 2006 further deepened Israeli pessimism. The kidnapping of an Israeli soldier on 25 June by Palestinian rebels on the Gaza border and the violent engagement that ensued added another dimension to this never-

19. For an incisive survey of Israeli strategy see Barry Rubin, "Israel's New Strategy", *Foreign Affairs*, July/August 2006; Martin Van Creveld, *Defending Israel: A Strategic Plan for Peace and Security* (New York: Thomas Dunne Books, 2004).

20. Cited in David Makovsky, "Deterrence and the Burden of Israeli Moderates", *US News & World Report*, 3 August 2006, at *http://www.washingtoninstitute.org/templateC06.php?CID=959* (accessed on 11 August 2006).

ending conflict.[21] Predictably, at its meeting on 12 July bolstering of Israeli deterrence by overwhelming use of force was on the top of the Israeli cabinet's agenda.[22]

Shape Lebanese Domestic and International Political Context

This aim can be disaggregated into two subsets: (a) create conditions for the Lebanese government to reassert its sovereignty over South Lebanon; (b) induce a sense of urgency within the international community and the Lebanese government for implementation of UN Resolution 1559.

The most important outcome of this war was the deployment of the Lebanese Army on the border with Israel. The presence of the national army makes more credible Israel's case for holding the federal government accountable for hostile acts from its territory. The deployment of Lebanese Armed Forces along with a substantial international intervention force is expected to constrain Hezbollah's militia, both in rebuilding its military capabilities and using hidden forces against Israel, thus severely limiting its room for manoeuvre. In the words of Ehud Yaari, a leading Arab analyst,

> Nasrallah is worried about being able to continue the armed *muqawama*, or resistance, in the framework of the UN Security Council Resolution 1701. He understands that in south Lebanon, in the area below the Litani River and on the slopes of Mount Hermon, along the contours of the Hazbani, his people will no longer be able to set open military camps...in other words, Nasrallah understands that the South has ceased to be 'Hizballahstan' and he is conceding the role he had taken upon himself in the past to serve as the guardian of Lebanon's border.[23]

Although it claimed "strategic and historical victory for Lebanon",[24] Hezbollah was forced by the new circumstances to acquiesce to

---

21. See Rodenbeck, Max (2006). "War within War", *New York Review of Books* 53(14) (21 September); Robert Malley, "A New Middle East", *New York Review of Books*, 53(14); Mark A. Heller, "Israel's conflicts with Hezbollah and Hamas: are they parts of the same war?" *Strategic Assessment* 9(2) (August 2006).
22. For an account of IDF Chief Dan Halutz's recommendations to the government on 13 July see Ze'ev Schiff, n.18.
23. Yaari, "Nasarallah's Malaise." Jerusalem Post, (02 October 2006), at *http://www.washingtoninstitute.org/templateC06.php?CID=977* (accessed on 23 October 2006).
24. Nasarallah's Victory Speech, 14 August 2006, broadcast on Al-Manar TV.

Resolution 1701 and has remained faithful to its commitment to cease fire.[25] The resolution is essentially aimed at containing Hezbollah through deployment of the Lebanese army, a substantially reinforced United Nations Interim Force in Lebanon (UNIFIL), and enhanced monitoring of the borders and territorial waters to prevent Hezbollah's rearmament. The resolution itself was to a large degree dictated by Israel. Even the reference in it to Taif Accords of 1989 exclusively focuses on its disarmament provisions.[26]

It will be a mistake to suggest that Hezbollah will not resist implementation of the resolution. Ever since the cease fire its leaders are voicing their reservations about how the Lebanese government and the international community are interpreting the provisions of the resolution and the mandate of the UNIFIL. They have agreed to push their arms underground but continue to resist disarmament while projecting the Lebanese army as a counter to Hezbollah. Hezbollah leaders have so far successfully resisted international attempts to modify or reinterpret the UNIFIL mandate to station the international force on the border with Syria or at harbours and the Beirut airport.[27]

Although the Lebanese Shia population rallied behind Nasarallah during and after the conflict, many analysts believe that he is worried about losing his support base in the long run. His admission after the war that had he known "even 1 per cent (that) the capture would lead to a war at this time and of this magnitude" he would not have ordered the abduction[28] is seen by many commentators as an expression of Hezbollah's internal concerns about losing its support base. The following factors could add up to generate this backlash:

(a) The death and destruction wrought by what is seen as an unnecessary war.

25. "Nasarallah Backs Troops in South, Warns of 'Graveyard' for Enemy", *Daily Star* (Beirut), 10 August 2006 (accessed on 10 August 2006).

26. For an analysis of Resolution 1701, see *Special Research Report 06*, 25 September 2006, at *http://www.securitycouncilreport.org/site/c.glKWLeMTIsG/b.2060965/k.2EFF/Special_Research_Report_ No_6_25_September_2006.htm* (accessed on 11 November 2006).

27. See *ICG Report*, "Israel/Hizbollah/Lebanon", n. 14: 4–11.

28. Nasarallah in a widely reported interview to Lebanon's NTV on 27 August 2006, cited in Makovsky and White, n. 18: 21.

(b) Hezbollah's failure to provide the promised relief after the war; in contrast, the increased role of the Lebanese government in rehabilitation activities.

(c) War weariness among the elite and the larger population, whose two generations have suffered the consequences of Lebanon being the battlefield for others' wars.

(d) Perception among a large segment of the non-Shia population that Hezbollah is a tool of Syria and Iran, and not the national resistance force it claims to be.

(e) The increased ability of the Lebanese government after the war in terms of resources, international support, and attention to assert its sovereignty over the whole of Lebanon.

(f) Growing awareness of Lebanese identity coupled with fear of Syrian imperial intentions over Lebanon.[29] In the perception of the '14 March coalition' and the influential elite, Syria, not Israel, is the greater threat to Lebanon's national integrity.[30]

The aftermath of the war has brought these incipient factors into sharper focus. In the years to come Hezbollah will have to reckon with the increasing questioning among the Lebanese elite about the legitimacy of an armed sub-national group within their national territory. If Israel at some point in the near future removes the 'pretexts' that Hezbollah uses to justify its arms,[31] its legitimacy will be further eroded. The recent pronouncements and political manoeuvres by Hezbollah's leadership show their increasing discomfort about the evolving political and security situation in Lebanon. They are increasingly suspicious that the present constellation of political forces is conspiring with international actors, such as the UK, the US and Israel, to strangulate resistance. Some Hezbollah leaders have asked for a change of government "to ensure (that) the government would not take hostile decisions."[32] Ideologically, however, Hezbollah loathes civil war and especially a

29. Summary of Lebanese views expressed in the media.

30. Ibid

31. See David Horovitz, "Removing the Pretext", *Jerusalem Post*, 25 August 2006.

32. See "Israel/Hizbollah/Lebanon ...", n. 14: 11.

Sunni–Shia confrontation. It has aspirations for national leadership and believes in converting Lebanese society to its point of view through patience and persuasion. The spectre of civil war would be detrimental to its long-term ideological interests.[33]

Reduction of Hezbollah Arms, Especially its Rocket Forces

Reduction of Hezbollah arms involved a two-pronged approach. First, direct attrition of fielded forces. Second, denial by interdiction of logistical and resupply routes. Ever since the war, this aim has been the most controversial. Though in the early days of the war Israeli leaders publicly claimed that the war would not end without the destruction of Hezbollah it is now apparent that this was not among its war aims. Moshe Ya'alon, former Chief of Staff of the IDF, notes:

> I understood there was no military action which could smash or pulverise Hezbollah. I understood that there is no way to uproot Hezbollah from the hearts of the Shi'ites in Lebanon. I also understood that there is no gimmick that will remove the Katyusha threat instantly. Accordingly, I proposed that we take combined political-military action to contain Hezbollah, to constrict its maneuvering space and in the end to bring about a situation in which the organisation would be perceived as illegitimate in Lebanon itself.[34]

The conduct of war itself suggests that Israel had very limited aims and did not seek a decisive battlefield victory. Its aim was not to destroy but to cause significant damage to the guerrilla force, especially its rocket forces. Israel claims that it destroyed most of the medium-and long-range rockets and missile launchers of Iranian origin in the first two days of the war. However, its campaign against short-range Katyusha rockets was demonstratively unsuccessful. Hezbollah retained an undiminished capacity to fire these at will till the very end of the war. Around 4000 rockets landed in various parts of northern Israel during the war, killing 42 and injuring over 4000 civilians. Many in Israel and elsewhere see Hezbollah's uninterrupted

33. Saad-Ghorayeb, *Hizbu'llah* ..., n. 4.

34. Ari Shavit, "No Way to Go to War", n. 18.

launching of the short-range rockets as a singular failure of Israeli leadership.[35]

Israel's claims to have significantly degraded Hezbollah arms are currently difficult to verify. Israeli counter-rocket and guerrilla operations appear to have had little impact on Hezbollah's counter-strategies until the very end of the war. This gave an impression of an Israeli strategic failure and fuelled adverse public perception against Prime Minister Ehud Olmert's government. In contrast, Hezbollah's show of strength and resilience in confronting a powerful adversary created an image of its invincibility. However, it is apparent that the operational and tactical performance of either party had a small role, if any, in shaping the strategic choices. Neither sought a decisive battle. Both resorted to punitive strategies to affect the will of their adversary. In the end, Israel prevailed.[36]

Reducing Iranian Influence and Involvement

For many years, the Israeli leadership has viewed Hezbollah "as a frontal commando unit of the Iranian Revolutionary Guards."[37] Some even term it as the Western Command of Iran. During the war, Israel saw an opportunity to expose Iranian complicity in arming the disruptive groups in the region. Some analysts believe that Hezbollah's provocation provided an opportunity to undermine Iran's strategic arm before it acquired nuclear capability, which would have rendered military operations extremely risky. A large section of the Israeli public and elite believe that Iran "has been heading steadily towards a confrontation with Israel for some time now, and its aid to Hezbollah was meant to ensure that it would have a ready strategic response if Israel took action against it."[38] Undermining Iran's influence and involvement in the region was a key objective of the war.

This war having fettered and weakened Hezbollah, its utility for Iran has declined in any future conflict with Israel or the United

---

35. Makovsky and White, n. 18; See also, Cordesman, Anthony H. (2006). "Preliminary 'Lessons' of the Israeli-Hezbollah War" CSIS 11 September, at *http://www.csis.org/media/csis/pubs/060817_isr_hez_ lessons.pdf* (accessed on 01 October 2006).

36. Makovsky and White, n. 18

37. Schiff, Ze'ev (2006). "Israel's War with Iran", *Foreign Affairs*, November-December 2006.

38. Ibid.

States. Nasarallah conceded during the war that this conflict was not in the interest of Iran. He denied any Iranian role in ordering the 12 July abduction but admitted that a premature exposure of Hezbollah rocket forces was not in Iranian interests, if they were engaged at all.

Create Conditions for Return of Soldiers without a Prisoner Swap

Within minutes of the abduction, Israel launched an unsuccessful rescue operation in which eight of its soldiers were killed. Israel justified its bombing of Beirut airport on 13 July as part of its strategy to disrupt the removal of soldiers outside of Lebanon. However, it is now becoming evident that within hours of the abduction the IDF placed the return of the soldiers on low priority. The military leadership calculated that there was no military solution and the international community would interpret massive military operations for the recovery of two soldiers as disproportionate use of force. Instead of direct military operations, Israel hoped to create conditions for the return of its soldiers without a prisoner swap.[39]

Return of the abducted soldiers is a key component of UN Resolution 1701. The war did not create conditions for their return without a prisoner swap, contrary to the claims of the Israeli leadership. As on date, there is no sign of any possible resolution. It does not appear that the Israeli leadership is unduly concerned about the matter. The current political environment is not conducive to a negotiated settlement. This issue is likely to remain unresolved for some more time.

Conclusion

A close examination of Israeli war aims and the impact of the second Lebanon war suggests that Israel attained most of its important war objectives, namely, altering perceptions about Israeli deterrent power; shaping of Lebanese domestic political and strategic context; and reduction of Hezbollah arms. In the aftermath of the war, Hezbollah appears to be on the defensive, manoeuvring to protect its political and military flanks in an increasingly hostile political environment. The Hezbollah leadership is viewing with concern the

39. Ibid.

growing international interest and commitment that has emboldened the Lebanese government.

Though the war has significantly weakened Hezbollah, it still enjoys support among large sections of the Lebanese Shi'ite population. Its popularity in the Arab lands can act as a useful source for funds and arms. In other words, Hezbollah is down but not out. Realism and a sense of proportion is essential in assessing the possibilities of sustainable peace. Even though Israel is far better placed to secure its interests, public perceptions within and the larger political context in the region do not give much cause for hope. A comprehensive settlement of the Arab–Israel conflict through negotiations looks seems remote. A large number of stakeholders and interested international actors are now pushing for progress on multiple tracks—Syria–Israel, Israel–Palestine, and Israel–Lebanon.

On the Syria–Israel track there is little hope for. A weak, and to large degree discredited, government in Jerusalem is unlikely to make any bold move in the near future. On the Palestinian front, hope and despair alternate like the crest and the trough on a sinusoidal curve on a daily basis. The principal political plank of the Olmert government—convergence plan—is increasingly becoming unpopular, a casualty of public loss of faith in the government. As regards the Israel–Lebanon track, if Israel were to remove the pretexts that Hezbollah uses to justify its arms, such as Sheeba farm, minor territorial disputes along the Blue Line, and visible violation of Lebanese airspace and territorial waters, possibilities do exist for sustaining momentum on this track. But even this task is not going to be easy unless Syria is part of the solution.

In general, the West Asian peace process faced a bleak future before the war. There is little to show that the war has altered that outlook in any fundamental sense, except in the limited context of Lebanon. The war has created conditions for reordering of Lebanese politics. It still remains an incomplete task. Wars do not on their own settle fundamental differences between the combatants. That is the task for statecraft in the coming months and years. The true measure of success will be whether or not Hezbollah is persuaded to become one among the many political parties in Lebanon.

23

Major Powers in Central Asia

Imperatives for India

MEENA SINGH ROY

Over the last three years the Central Asian Republics (CARs) have witnessed significant geopolitical shifts: the resurgence of Russia; rise in China's profile; 'Colour Revolution' in Kyrgyzstan; unrest in Andijan leading to a significant change in Uzbekistan's foreign policy; closing of American military base in Uzbekistan; and the growing prominence of the Shanghai Cooperation Organization (SCO). The death of Turkmen President Saparmurat Niyazov on 21 December 2006 added yet another angle to the Central Asian dynamics, although the new President, Gurbanguly Berdymukhammedov, elected on 11 February 2007, is expected to continue his predecessor's policy. Berdymukhammedov clearly stated, "Everything positive that was created and fixed in the national state system will not undergo a change."[1]

Is Central Asia on the verge of witnessing a paradigm shift? Will competition among the major powers intensify? Will the 'Great Energy Game' in the region continue? Can India, Iran, and Pakistan play a greater role? Will Japan become a player in the region? Will NATO and US forces be able to control a resurgent Taliban? And how would the CARs respond to these pushes and pulls? These issues will determine the future course of geopolitical development in the region.

The region witnessed intense competition among the major players to bring CARs under their strategic fold and to control the energy resources. However, while the US, Russia, and China continue to be

1. Interview of the President of Turkmenistan for the Turkmenistan Magazine, at *www.turkmenistan.ru/?page_id=12&lang_id=en&elem_id=9363&type=event&layo...*

the major players, the balance of power in the region has shifted in favour of Russia and China. Recently, Japan, Iran, and Pakistan are also seen as increasing their profiles in the region. This review evaluates the major-power engagement in Central Asia during 2006 and assesses the imperatives for India. India's evolving strategic interests in CARs surely demand a new forward policy.

Russia's Increasing Profile

Geographical proximity, past linkages, and politico-economic realities stamp Russia as an influential player in the region. The CARs see Russia as a guarantor of security, and Moscow is exploiting its identity as an energy superpower by signing major energy deals,[2] thereby reinforcing its political and economic clout in the Eurasian region.

Uzbekistan has emerged as a major ally and strategic partner of Russia. In March 2006 the two states signed a new commitment, which stipulates that they would help each other in case of a military threat.[3] The treaty has raised Russia's status, particularly its role in strengthening security in the region. Uzbekistan also joined the Eurasian Economic Community (EEC) in March 2006[4] and then rejoined the Collective Security Treaty Organization (CSTO) in August 2006, which it had quit in 1999.[5] After Uzbekistan ratifies all CSTO agreements, it will join the CSTO's rapid deployment forces in Central Asia.[6] On 10 March 2006 Uzbekistan also signed a law enabling its exit from GUUAM, the regional organisation that was made up of Georgia, Ukraine, Uzbekistan, Armenia, and Moldova.[7]

---

2. During the year the highest profile move by Russia was the signing of an energy deal with Kazakhstan in April, where Kazakhstan pledged to significantly increase the amount of oil it exports *via* Russia.
3. "Uzbek Leader Signs Ratified Treaty on Allied Relations with Russia", ITAR-TASS News Agency, Moscow, 7 March 2007, at *http://www.eurasianet.org/resource/uzbekistan/hypermail/200603/0006.shtml*
4. "Uzbek President Signs law on Eurasian Economic Community", *Uzbekistan Daily Digest*, at *http://www.eurasianet.org/resource/uzbekistan/hypermail/200603/0007.shtml*
5. This regional security group, comprising Russia, Armenia, Belarus, Kazakhstan, Kyrgyzstan, and Tajikistan, seeks to promote military and political cooperation aimed at ensuring the collective security of its member states. "Uzbekistan Rejoins CSTO", *Uzbekistan Daily Digest*, at *http://www.eurasianet.org/resource/uzbekistan/hypermail/200608/0012.shtml*
6. *Interfax*, 14 March 2007, at *http://www.silkroadstudies.org*
7. *http://www.eurasianet.org/resource/uzbekistan/hypermail/200603/0012.shtml*

All these developments point towards Uzbekistan's increasing attempt to distance itself from the US and the other western powers and position itself closer to Russia.[8] Moscow's latest strategic inroads came in late December 2006 when it gained access to the Navoi airfield. In return, Moscow has agreed to provide Uzbekistan with modern navigation systems and air defence weapons.[9]

Apart from its upswing in relations with Uzbekistan, Moscow also cemented its political, military, and economic ties with Kazakhstan, Kyrgyzstan, and Turkmenistan. The visit of Kazakh President Nursultan Nazarbayev to Moscow in April 2006 is a potential turning point in the struggle for control of the Caspian Basin's oil and gas reserves. During the visit, President Nazarbayev announced that the volume of Kazakhstan's oil transported *via* the Caspian Pipeline Consortium (CPC) route would rise to 67 million metric tonnes (m.t.) from the current 28 m.t., and that Kazakhstan and Russia would work jointly to develop three offshore oil fields of Kurmangazy, Khvalynsky, and Tsentralnoye. The Russian energy conglomerate LUKoil has recently invested roughly $3 billion in Kazakhstan for new joint projects, including an expansion of the CPC pipeline. The two countries also signed an agreement to process natural gas from Kazakhstan's Karachaganak gas field.

Russia–Kazakhstan trade in 2005 reached nearly $10 billion, a 35 per cent increase over 2004. During the first two months of 2006, bilateral trade hit a rough patch, totalling $1.13 billion, down 4.5 per cent from the corresponding period in 2005. Notable defence and security agreements were also signed between the two countries. They agreed to reduce the lease payments for test site and firing ranges by $3 million per year. In addition, the two countries signed an agreement granting an orbital position to Kazakhstan's communications and broadcasting satellite, Kazsat.[10] While

8. In 2005 Russia was Uzbekistan's main trading partner accounting for 21.7 per cent of its trade. There are 411 Uzbek-Russian joint ventures and enterprises with 100 per cent Russian capital in Uzbekistan. There are 267 enterprises with Uzbek capital in Russia. At *http://www.eurasianet.org/resource/uzbekistan/hypermail/200603/0009.shtml*
9. Blank, Stephen, "An Uzbek air base: Russia's newest achievement in Central Asia", at *http://www.eurasia.org/departments/insight/articles/eav011107a_pr.shtml*
10. Blagov, Sergei, "Russia Registers Significant Victory in Caspian Basin energy contest", at *http://www.eurasianet.org/departments/business/articles/eav040506_pr.shtml*

maintaining its strong strategic ties with Russia and China, Asthana was also able to conclude an Individual Partnership Action Plan with NATO, the first Central Asian State to do so, thereby displaying its ability to balance the major powers through its 'multi vector' foreign policy.[11]

Russia's economic and strategic influence in Kyrgyzstan also expanded significantly after the visit of President Kurmanbek Bakiyev to Moscow in April 2006. There was an expansion of the Russian airbase at Kant and a joint Russian–Kyrgyz anti-terrorism exercise was held. In addition, Bakiyev agreed to enhance Bishkek's participation in regional economic and security groupings, including the CSTO and the SCO. Russia announced that it would assist Bishkek in completing two power plants. In addition, Bakiyev agreed, in principle, during a 25 April 2006 meeting with the Gazprom chief executive officer, Alexei Miller, on a joint venture involving the Kyrgyz national energy company, Kyrgyzneftigaz.[12]

Moscow also increased its influence in Tajikistan. The Tajik Ministry of Defence has promoted its close ties with Russia at every turn. More than 100 Tajik nationals graduated from Russian military institutions and academies in 2006. Russia also trains officers in air defence, engineering, and communications. The Norak opto-electronic reconnaissance centre, a part of Russia's space-tracking system in Tajikistan, is among the best military units of the Russian Space Troops. Tajikistan now supplies the reconnaissance centre with electric power, communication channels, fuel, water, and other services. Russia introduced artificial intelligence into the "Okno" system, including precision optics and high-tech computer systems, making the facility among the best in the world. Such technological innovations provide Moscow immense political leverage.[13] The two countries also agreed

11. "Russia and Eurasia", *Strategic Survey* (London: International Institute of Strategic Studies/ Routledge, 2006): 194–6.

12. Open joint stock company (OAO) Gazprom is the world's largest gas company engaged in natural gas, gas condensate and oil prospecting, production, transmission, processing and marketing both inside and outside Russia. Russia controls 50.002 per cent of the company's shares. Gazprom possesses the richest natural gas reserves in the world, with its share in the global and Russian total making up 16.9 per cent and 60 per cent, respectively. Gazprom owns the gas trunklines integrated in the Unified Gas Supply System of Russia (UGSS).

13. McDermott, Roger, "Tajikistan Cautious on Ties with Western Militaries", at *http:// jamestown.org/edm/article.php?article_id=2371262*

on the terms for financing the jointly built Sangtudin hydroelectric plant.[14]

Besides bilateral relations, Russia has continued its engagement with regional groupings like CIS (Commonwealth of Independent States), EEC, Central Asian Cooperation Organization (CACO), and SCO. These groupings provide Russia with ample opportunities to further its interest in the region. SCO helps to bolster its ties with CARs and offers space for engaging China economically while simultaneously balancing US influence in the region. CIS border guards held joint operations on the Tajik–Afghan border and in the Caspian and Black seas in 2006. With an aim of integrating the region, the Eurasian Development Bank was recently established. Russia's estimated trade with CARs is more than $6 billion. These developments indicate that Russia stands to retain its economic and strategic gains, regardless of how the situation unfolds in Central Asia.

China's Accelerating Engagement

In 2006, China enhanced its role and influence in Central Asia, both through the SCO and at the bilateral level. An assessment of China's Central Asia policy in 2006 reflects a continuation of its overall approach of cooperation, multilateralism, and integration, particularly with neighbouring states.[15] The SCO mirrors China's carefully calibrated approach towards Central Asia. These are mainly to integrate the Xinjiang region, address the problems of separatism, extremism, and terrorism within China's Xinjiang province,[16] and gain access to the region's energy resources.[17]

14. *Interfax*, 5 March 2007; *The China and Eurasia Forum: Weekly Newsletter* No. 50, 6–13 March 2007, at *http://www.chinaeurasia.org*
15. Clarke, Michael (2005). "China's Strategies in Xinjiang and Central Asia: Towards Chinese Hegemony in the 'Geographical Pivot of History'"? *Issues and Studies* 41(21) (June): 86–87; Ong, Russell (2005). "China's Security Interests in Central Asia", *Central Asian Survey* 24(4) (December): 425–39.
16. China faces a host of Uygur insurgent groups—United Revolutionary Front of Eastern Turkestan, Xinjiang Liberation Organization, Uygur Liberation Organization, Wolves of Lop Nor, Free Turkistan Movement, Home of East Turkistan Youth, and Organization for the Liberation of Uyguristan. See McNeal, Dewardic (2001). "China's Relations with Central Asian States and Problems with Terrorism", in US Department of State, Congressional Research Service Report for Congress, 17 December 2001, at *http://fpc.state.gov/documents/organisation/7945.pdf; Russell Ong, n. 15.*
17. Lifan, Li and Ding Shiwu (2004). "Geopolitical Interests of Russia, the U.S. and China in Central Asia", *Central Asia and Caucasus* (Sweden) 3(27): 144.

The SCO plans to set up a Free Trade Zone in the region. During the June 2006 Summit, several documents were signed. A resolution of the SCO Business Council and an action plan of the SCO Interbank Association on supporting regional cooperation were finalised. On the sidelines, business contracts and loan agreements worth some $2 billion were signed.[18] An important feature of this summit was the Russian proposal for creating an energy club within SCO. Prospects for development of a model and a concept for an SCO energy club were discussed in Tashkent at an energy round table of SCO on 27 February 2007.[19]

Under the SCO umbrella Beijing has already set aside $900 million for Kazakhstan, Kyrgyzstan, Tajikistan and Uzbekistan. By 2004, China invested $4 billion in CARs. China Development Bank has issued a $15.567 million loan to Uzbekistan's Aloqabank. The Export-Import Bank of China (Eximbank) has expressed readiness to invest $360 million in the construction of a 150 MW hydropower plant in Zerafshan, northern Tajikistan.[20] Beijing has agreed to implement projects to build and reconstruct the Dushanbe–Chanak Road in northern Tajikistan and to provide capital and technology for the construction of the highway linking Kyrgyzstan and Uzbekistan, two high-tension power transmission lines in Tajikistan, a cement plant in Kyrgyzstan and a hydropower station in Kazakhstan.[21] China's estimated trade with CARs is around $95 billion (Statistics from the Chinese General Administration of Customs and the Ministry of Commerce of PRC).

China has been able to access Central Asia's energy resources. The Xinjiang Uygur Autonomous Region received its first flow of crude oil through a cross-border pipeline from Kazakhstan.[22] In addition, China's CITIC (China International Trust and Investment Company) Group

---

18. Wenzhao, Tao, "SCO Offers Model of Effective Co-operation", at ***http://www.chinadaily.com.cn/opinion/2006-06/26/content_625569.htm***
19. Intexfax, 27 February 2007.
20. "China Development Bank issues $15.6 million loan to Uzbekistan's Aloqabank", *Interfax*, 6 March 2006; "China's Bank to Finance Hydropower Plant in Tajikistan", *Itar-tass*, 6 March 2006.
21. Tao Wenzhao, "SCO offers model of effective co-operation", at ***http://www.chinadaily.com.cn/opinion/2006-06/26/content_625569.htm***
22. "China-Kazakhstan pipeline carries crude oil to NW China", at ***http://news.xinhuanet.com/english/2006-07/29/content_4891739.htm; http://news.monstersandcritics.com/energywatch/news/article_1180693.php/Energy_Watch_-_July_13***

acquired Kazakh oil assets of Canada's Nations Energy Company Ltd for $1.91 billion—the third largest overseas oil acquisition made by Chinese companies[23]—which allows CITIC to develop the Karazhanbas oil and gas field in Mangistau Oblast, Kazakhstan, until 2020. Karazhanbas has proven reserves in excess of 340 million barrels of oil and currently produces over 50,000 barrels of oil a day.

China has successfully established partnerships with Turkmenistan. Turkmen and Chinese officials signed a series of economic and technical cooperation agreements on 21 August 2006. Both countries are continuing work on a pipeline scheduled for completion in 2009, thus enabling Ashgabat to supply 30 billion cubic metres of gas annually to China. Plans to build the pipeline were first discussed during President Niyazov's visit to Beijing in April 2006.[24]

The volume of railway cargo traffic between Kazakhstan and China is expected to reach 18–20 million tonnes by 2015.[25] China's transportation role is growing in Eurasia. The building of rail and road networks to link China's west to the oceans not only demonstrates its economic rise but also its influence in Central, South-West, and South Asia.[26] Though China has not been able to acquire any military base in these Republics, it has been able to establish strategic partnership. Its current level of involvement is directed towards engaging these states economically.

United States' Weakening Strategic Position

The United States' strategic interests, seen to be growing stronger in Central Asia during the past few years, weakened considerably in 2006.[27] Washington came out with new plans and worked towards

23. "CITCIC buys Kazakg oil assets for $1.9b", at *http://www.chinadaily.com.cn/china/2006-12/31/content_772608.htm*
24. Torbakov, Igor, "Russia watches warily as Turkmen-Chinese economic cooperation expands", at *http://www.eurasianet.org/departments/insight/articles/eav082906_pr.shtml*
25. *http://eng.gazeta.kz/art.asp?aid=78672*
26. For details, see Garver, John W. (2006). "Development of China's Overland Transportation Links and with Central, South-West and South Asia", *China Quarterly* No. 185 (March): 1–22.
27. Maher, Heather, "Central Asia: U.S. Helsinki Commission concerned about SCO's influence", at *http://www.edi.org/russia/johnson/2006-217-40.efm, and www.rferl.org;* The Overseas Basing Commission in its May 2005 Report acknowledged that US national security might be enhanced by future Cooperative Security Locations (CSLS) in Central Asia. For details see Nichol, Jim (2006). "Central Asia: Regional Developments and Implications for U.S. Interests", *CRS Brief for Congress*, Foreign Affairs, Defense, and Trade Division, Update 12 May 2006 at *http://digital.library.unt.edu/govdocs/crs/data/2006/upl-meta-crs-8922/1B93108-2006may12.pdf*

creating stronger Central–South Asian energy and trade links to balance the Russian influence. Richard A. Boucher, Assistant Secretary of State for South and Central Asian Affairs, stated:

> Our goal is to revive ancient ties between South and Central Asia and to help create new links in the area of trade, transport, democracy, energy and communications. At the same time, we seek to preserve and enhance the ties of Central Asian countries to Europe, especially through organisations like NATO and its Partnership for Peace (PfP) and the Organization for Security and Cooperation in Europe (OSCE) as well as the important interests Japan has in Central Asia.[28]

These plans were premised on the fears that China and Russia were pulling the region into their strategic fold and marginalising the US. The dramatic events in Kyrgyzstan and Uzbekistan[29] alarmed the ruling elite in the region that their position was threatened not only by international terrorist and extremist Islamist groups but also by the US, which was supporting the 'coloured revolutions.' The changed perception of the CARs not only provided a new geopolitical role for the SCO but also eroded United States' strategic space.

The US has pursued three sets of interests in Central Asia: security cooperation, commercial and energy interests, and political and economic reforms. In 2006, Washington adhered to the policy of providing more options to the CARs and keeping them under its influence. A manifestation of this policy was Washington's decision to transfer responsibility from the Department of State for the Central Asian States to a new Bureau of South and Central Asian Affairs.[30]

Since the disbanding of its military base in Uzbekistan,[31] the US has been trying to improve its relations with Kazakhstan, Kyrgyzstan,

---

28. "U.S. Policy in Central Asia: Balancing Priorities (Part II)", Richard A. Boucher, Assistant Secretary of State for South and Central Asian Affairs, Statement to the House International Relations Committee, Subcommittee on the Middle East and Central Asia, 26 April 2006, at *http://www.state.gov/p/sca/rls/rm/2006/65292.htm*
29. In Kyrgyzstan the 'coloured revolution' resulted in a violent overthrow of the ruling regime and in Uzbekistan (in Andijan) an armed uprising was crushed by the use of military power of the state.
30. n. 28.
31. The changed attitude of the Central Asian regimes towards the US following events in Kyrgyzstan and Andijan resulted in the SCO member states (in July 2005, during the Asthana Summit) calling on the US to set a deadline for its military presence in the region; the US closed down its airbase in Uzbekistan in November 2005.

and Tajikistan. During 2006 Washington tried to expand its military bases in the region. After the 'tulip revolution' Kyrgyzstan allowed the US to continue its key Manas airbase but only after it agreed to increase the rent.

While the US administration has rejected the idea of permanent military bases in these states, there is little doubt that its military presence would continue for a long time.[32] Acquiring bases in Central Asia seems to be a short-term need to achieve long-term interests in the region. More than 50,000 US military personnel are stationed on ships and military bases stretching from Turkey to Oman and eastward to Manas airport, 30 km outside of Bishkek and 480 km from the Chinese border.[33] Uzbekistan provided a base for US operation at Karshi-Khanabad until it pulled out in November 2005. Tajikistan permitted the use of its international airport in Dushanbe for refuelling and hosted French forces, which pulled out in November 2005. Kazakhstan and Turkmenistan provided over-flight and other support.[34] On 24 January 2007 the US Ambassador to Kyrgyzstan, Marie Yovanovitch, specified that US military personnel would remain in Kyrgyzstan as long as counter-terrorist operations continued in Afghanistan. A joint Tajik–US military training was scheduled at Fakhrobod military training complex (35 km south west of Dushanbe) from 28 January to 9 March 2006. Future plans include a team of US infantrymen giving tactical training to the special task forces of the Tajik State Committee on National Security (SCNS) and the Tajik border troops on counter-terrorism. This training will be the first of its kind in Tajikistan and may stimulate greater interest in specialist anti-terrorist training.[35] Throughout the region, the US has funded the construction of new border crossing checkpoints, including most

32. For example, no sooner had Gen. Tommy Franks, head of the US Armed Forces Command said that the US had no plans to create permanent military bases than he was contradicted by US Assistant Secretary of State Elizabeth Jones that American presence in Kyrgyzstan would be significant and long-term. See *The Current Digest of the Post-Soviet Press* 54(5) (27 February 2002): 5. Also see Jim Nichol, n. 27.

33. Loeb, Vernon (2002). "Footprints in Steppes of Central Asia", *Washington Post*, 9 February: AO1

34. Jim Nichol, n. 27.

35. McDermott, Roger, "U.S. Military Needs Long-term Stay in Manas", at *http.//Jamestown.org/edm/article.php?artic;id=2371855*

recently, in Turkmenistan on the Iranian and Afghan borders.[36] It has also been providing aid to the CARs.

In 2006, Kazakhstan emerged as the critical US ally in the region. Vice President Dick Cheney visited Kazakhstan in May 2006 and President Nazarbayev visited the US in September 2006, his first to Washington in five years. The US stance towards Kazakhstan is part of Washington's endeavour to reposition its role in Central Asia following the expulsion of US and NATO forces from Uzbekistan in 2005. The US needs continued air access to Afghanistan, where terrorist groups are increasing their operations.[37]

Similarly, Washington tried to mend fences with Tashkent. When Boucher met Uzbek President Islam Karimov in Tashkent on 9 August 2006, the latter told him, "Your visit after a long interruption will provide a chance to develop our relations." Boucher replied, "Our views on observing human rights in Uzbekistan and about assessing the Andijan events differ. However, we are ready to cooperate with Tashkent in the fight against drug trafficking, threats of terrorism, and illegal distribution of arms." Boucher made it clear, however, that a further deterioration in US-Uzbek ties could lead the US to "take retaliatory measures."[38]

There are indications that the Uzbek government is exploring the possibility of restoring relations with the US and the European Union. *Pravda Vostoka*, the official mouthpiece of President Islam Karimov's administration, recently published a commentary declaring, "the existing stalemate in relations does not serve the interests of Uzbekistan, the US or the EU" and even states that a rapprochement is possible: "It is necessary to jointly think over ways for new, promising opportunities for cooperation and modernising traditional relations." It is not clear, however, if Washington would be ready to

36. Ibid.; Davis, Jacquelyn K. and Michael J. Sweeney (2004). *Central Asia in U.S. Strategy and Operational Planning: Where do we go from here?* Washington: The Institute for Foreign Policy Analysis, February; "Taieban 'Convenient Reason' for USA to Enter Central Asia", *Delovaya Nedelya*, 8 March 2002, Almaty, in BBC Monitoring Global Newsline Central Asia Political File, 11 March 2002, at fromtopic@mon.bbc.co.uk

37. Economic Intelligence Unit (EIU), (UK), Country Report on Kazakhstan, July 2006: 16.

38. "U.S. Official Meeting with Uzbek President", *Uzbekistan Daily Digest*, at *http://www.eurasianet.org/resource/uzbekistan/hypermail/200608/0007.shtml*

accept the Uzbek government's terms for rapprochement.[39] The current US engagement with the region indicates that American attempts to develop closer ties with the CARs are still complicated.[40]

India's Evolving Interests and Stakes in Central Asia

The major powers' engagement and the resultant power game in Central Asia has enormous significance for India. First, how does it impact India? Second, what is at stake for India in Central Asia and how is it engaging this strategically important region in the changing security situation?

India's engagement and role in Central Asia cannot be delinked from its larger role in Asia. While Central Asia continues to be of great strategic significance to India, its engagement with the region has been more reactive than proactive. While Tajikistan, Uzbekistan, and Turkmenistan stand out to be of security interest for India's Afghanistan-Pakistan policy, Kazakhstan and Kyrgyzstan are important for India's relations with China. Tajikistan's importance for India lies in its geostrategic location as it shares a border with Afghanistan and China and is located in proximity to Pakistan Occupied Kashmir (POK).

Tajikistan is part of an established drug route for Afghan opium to the West. In the past, it was important for India's support to the Northern Alliance; in the future, it can play an important role in maintaining peace along Afghanistan's northern border, as well as to fight jihadis and drug traffickers and to stop the flow of illegal weapons.[41] India needs to carefully monitor the activities of jihadi forces from Pakistan operating in Tajikistan, given its proximity to POK and the likely proliferation of this problem into the state of Jammu and Kashmir.

Uzbekistan is the only republic which has a common border with all the Central Asian states and Afghanistan. It has been a reliable

39. "Uzbekistan sends up trial balloon for rapprochement with western countries", at *http://www.eurasianet.org/departments/insight/articles/eav022607b_pr.shtml*
40. Sands, David R. (2006). "'Strategic' Accord Planned for Nazarbayev's U.S. Visit", *Washington Times*, 8 July 2006, at *http://washingtontimes.com/world/20060707-094335-4336r.htm*
41. Views expressed by former Director Jasjit Singh, IDSA, in Rahul Bedi, "India Dabbles in the New 'Great Game'", *Jane's Intelligence Review* 13(6) (June 2002): 19.

partner of India. While Kazakhstan cannot be ignored because of its economic potential, especially energy resources, Kyrgyzstan is significant because of its proximity to the Xinjiang province of China and the Wakhan corridor, which is on the trijunction of China, Tajikistan, and POK. This is underscored by mounting evidence that the Central Asian militant group, the Islamic Movement of Uzbekistan, remains active in tribal areas near the Pakistan–Afghanistan border. Activities of this groups and Chechen rebels have been reported in POK which provides them sanctuaries. Further radicalisation and militarisation of Islamist movements within CARs would only deepen the strategic conundrum India already confronts in Jammu and Kashmir.

Turkmenistan's importance, as stated, lies in its energy reserves, especially gas, and its importance as a transit route for the rest of CARs. Moreover, its proximity to Iran and Afghanistan—which India views as strategically important—cannot be overlooked. Though India's frontiers are not contiguous with Central Asia, the close proximity, long cultural, historical ties, and economic potential of the region have earmarked it as an area of priority.

Throughout 2006, India continued to develop and establish dynamic and multifaceted ties with each Republic. From India's point of view two important developments need to be highlighted. First, the visit of Prime Minister Manmohan Singh to Uzbekistan, and second, the visit of Tajik President Emomali S. Rakhmonov to India. During President Rakhmonov's visit, five documents on energy, trade, security, science and technology, and culture were signed.[42] The other significant development was the meeting of the Joint Working Group on Counter Terrorism between India and Tajikistan, held in January 2006 in Dushanbe and a second in August 2006 in Delhi. During the January meeting, a protocol was signed on mutual assistance to combat criminal activities.[43]

---

42. Joint Declaration by Republic of India and the Republic of Tajikistan on Further Development of Relations, Friendship and Cooperation, at *http://meaindia.nic.in/declarestatement/2006/08/07jd01.htm*

43. *http://mediandia.nic.in/speech/2006/08/04js01.htm*; Kumar, B.R. Mutu (2006). "India–Tajikistan Relations: An Appraisal and Agenda for Future", Paper presented in the International Seminar on "India and Tajikistan in International Affairs", at Indian Council of World Affairs, New Delhi, 8 August 2006.

Prime Minister Manmohan Singh's visit to Uzbekistan in April 2006—the first by an Indian prime minister in more than a decade—reaffirmed India's interest by stating that "Central Asia is strategically an important region and has historically been at the crossroads of the Eastern and Western worlds. We wish for continued stability and economic prosperity..."[44] In July 2006, during his meeting with President Nazarbayev, Prime Minister Singh acknowledged the importance of Kazakhstan for India and stressed that "Kazakhstan is an important economic and political partner of India and the country is interested in extension of bilateral collaboration."[45]

The results for India in the energy sector are somewhat mixed. Although there have been no major breakthroughs in Central Asia's energy sector,[46] on 26 April 2006 India's Ministry of Petroleum and Natural Gas and GAIL (Gas Authority of India Limited), signed memorandums of understanding with Uzbekistan to conduct oil and gas exploration there. Under this agreement, Tashkent will allow exploration on the condition that future profits are split on a parity basis. Uzbekistan is also ready to allocate geological territory to Indian companies to explore for hydrocarbons.[47] It was agreed in June 2006 that GAIL and Uzbekneftegaz would work together to build facilities in Uzbekistan to produce liquefied petroleum gas (LPG) at a cost of $50–60 million each, and have a production capacity of 100,000 tonnes per year. It is not clear how many plants the two companies plan to construct.[48]

Though Tajikistan wants India to invest in its hydroelectric power projects, no plans have been concretised. India's state-owned National Hydro Power Corporation (NHPC) has completed pre-feasibility study of the project. The government, however, approved rehabilitation of 12 MW Varzob-I hydropower plant outside Dushanbe through a $13 million grant. Iran and Russia are already constructing the hydropower

44. Opening remarks by Prime Minister Dr. Manmohan Singh at the joint press conference with Uzbekistan President, Tashkent, 26 April 2006, at http://www.mea.gov.in

45. *http://www.trend.az/?mod=shownews&news=23574&lang=en*

46. Some Kazakh experts are of the opinion that India being a late entry into the Kazakh energy sector it would be difficult for India to make any major breakthrough soon.

47. *http://www.eurasianet.org/resource/uzbekistan/hypermail/200604/0020.shtml*

48. *http://www.eurasianet.org/resource/uzbekistan/hypermail/200605/0006.shtml*

station and China, Pakistan, and Kazakhstan are negotiating with Tajikistan on realization of the projects in this field.[49]

In addition, ONGC Videsh concluded a deal with Denmark's Maersk Oil and German oil and gas firm Wintershall for taking up to 33 per cent stake in Blocks 11 and 12 in offshore Turkmenistan. Maersk Oil with an 80 per cent holding is the operator of the blocks, which cover about 5663 sq km, while Wintershall, a unit of the BASF chemicals group, owns the remaining 20 per cent stake.[50]

India is viewed in the Central Asian region as a reliable partner and a benign power. While terrorism remains the major issue of cooperation, the CARs are looking for Indian involvement in the IT (information technology) sector and using India's experience in setting up various industrial units related to agriculture and defence, providing training in financial and banking sectors, and helping build their national economy through scientific and technological cooperation. India could be a principal driver in establishing cooperation among these states.[51] Central Asians view India as a route to progress in what they perceive as their "southern arc of instability" involving Afghanistan and Pakistan.[52]

Existing power politics in South and Central Asia and lack of direct land route to the region limit India's ability to play a major role. Both Moscow and Washington regard India as a reliable partner. The possibilities of cooperation in economic, transport, and energy sectors between Russia-India-China-Iran-Afghanistan and CARs are promising. In fact, India could play a central role in strategising cooperation with Afghanistan-Turkey-Japan and CARs.

Other than Pakistan, which always has tried to gain 'strategic depth' in Afghanistan and Central Asia, India enjoys good relationship

---

49. "Tajikistan President Seeks Increased Economic Cooperation with India", *The Hindu*, 8 August 2006; "Tajikistan Seeks Investment in Hydel Power, Mining", at *http://www.dailyindia.com/show/49167.php/tajikistan_seeks_investment_in_hydel_power....*
50. IRIS News Digest, 6 January 2007, at *http://www.myiris.com/newsCentre*
51. Views based on discussion during "III India Central Asia Regional Conference", 6–8 November 2003, Tashkent. Also in interaction with scholars, officials, and other experts in Tashkent.
52. Stobdan, P. and K. Santhanam (2003). "Central Asia is Central to India", *Indian Express* (Delhi), 28 November.

with other regional players like Iran and Turkey. Today the major concern for India is the security situation in Afghanistan. So far, the US and NATO forces have not been able to provide stability in Afghanistan. Moreover, Pakistan's ethnic linkages provide ample opportunity for Pakistan's Directorate of Inter Services Intelligence (ISI) to counter any Indian plans in Afghanistan. While Pakistan is in no position to neutralise India's influence in Afghanistan and Central Asia, it can impede India's infrastructure projects in Afghanistan.

The Russian factor is also important. Given India's close strategic partnership with Russia, and given the latter's growing influence in Central Asia, India can leverage its relations with CARs. The US engagement in Central Asia is unlikely to affect India in the short term. So far, India has been cooperating with both the US and Russia in the global war against terrorism. The fall of the Taliban regime has been a positive development for India, facilitating its effort to build roads within Afghanistan, which could be extended to Central Asia in future. However, Pakistan's attempt to contain India's presence might delay these infrastructure projects.

Assessment

Central Asia is witnessing a paradigm shift in terms of emerging alignments and realignments. Russia, as a major player, is seen to be sharing the strategic space with China in the region and this trend will continue. The cooperation between Moscow and Beijing both bilaterally and within the SCO may serve as a counterbalance to the United States' Central Asia policy. The United States' strategic position would depend upon how it is able to balance its policy of promoting democracy and human rights on one hand, and seeking closer economic, political, and security relations with the CARs, on the other. The Central Asian regimes suspect the United States' intentions in the region but it is unlikely that Washington's interest there will wane in the near future.

China's influence in Central Asia is expected to expand in the long term. While China has used economic diplomacy to build strategic ties with the region, Russia has pursued both economic and military diplomacy to strengthen its strategic position. Despite China's entry in the Central Asian energy sector, Russia will remain the major player. It seems that the Central Asian regimes are using the Chinese offers in the energy sector as a bargaining chip with Russia to get a better price for their energy resources. Moreover, unlike the US, China and Russia do not pressurise the CARs to democratise, liberalise their markets, nor do they raise human rights issues.

Confrontation among the major players is unlikely, but competition for greater influence in the region is likely to intensify for two reasons. First, the energy demand of China and India will increase and competition between the US and Russia would intensify to gain control over the energy transit routes. Second, the rise in Chinese and Russian influence and US attempts to create a support base for its long-term strategy in South Asia and Persian Gulf region are likely to bring about realignment of regional and extra-regional powers in the region.

The other important trend is Japan's renewed interest in Central Asia. Japan's accelerating dialogue with CARs reflects Tokyo's desire to play a proactive role in the region and Eurasia as well as countering the influence of Russia and China.[53] The US may encourage NATO and Japan for greater engagement to counterbalance Chinese and Russian domination in the region. Consequently, regional players like India, Pakistan, Iran, and Turkey are likely to reorient their policies either independently or with their strategic partners.

During 2006 both Pakistan and Iran, in an effort to find a foothold in the region tried to acquire full membership of SCO. The recent initiatives taken by Pakistan in Central Asia indicate a marked improvement in its overall relations with the CARs.[54] Likewise, visits by Central Asian heads of state point to the fact that these regimes are trying to develop new equations with Pakistan. Countries like

53. Masaki, Hisane, "Japan Joins the Energy Race", at *http://www.atimes.com/atimes/Japan/HG28Dh01.html*

54. For details see Roy, Meena Singh (2006). "Pakistan's Strategies in Central Asia", *Strategic Analysis* 30(4) (October-December).

Uzbekistan are looking for new allies in the light of their deteriorating relations with the US.[55]

India may not as yet be a key player in Central Asia but it is an important one. Its foothold in the region is limited to Afghanistan and Tajikistan. Russia could remain an important partner of India in Central Asia. However, India's increasing strategic partnership with Washington may work as a handicap as it pursues bilateral and multilateral initiatives in the region. Nonetheless, the United States' interests cannot be excluded. Therefore, a big challenge before India is to see that the US becomes a stabilising force rather than a destabiliser.

India will have to carefully manage its relations in this high-stakes region. At one end, it will have to engage Pakistan, Iran, and Turkey; and at the other, it will have to envisage cooperation within the ongoing trilateral framework of India-Russia-China. To achieve any meaningful relation with Central Asian states, India needs to promulgate a unified political-economic and strategic planning and implement them both at bilateral and multilateral level. Whatever steps India may take to reclaim its strategic space in Central Asia, it is important that it remains integral to Eurasian energy politics.

---

55. During his visit in May 2006 President Islam Karimov acknowledged the importance of Pakistan. He stated that Pakistan "possesses great power in terms of its economy, population and, if you like, in terms of military and technical potential." The official Uzbek news agency noted in its report on the visit that "following the Andijan events [in May 2005], at the UN General Assembly, Pakistan supported the position of Uzbekistan." Karimov last visited Pakistan in 1992. "Uzbek president visits Pakistan..." at *http://www.eurasianet.org/resource/uzbekistan/hypermail/200605/0000.shtml* 3 May 2006.

V

Statistical Appendix

Table A-1

GDP, Defence Expenditure, and Armed Forces Personnel: Top 25 Defence Spending Nations in Asia, including Australia and New Zealand

(In US Dollars)

Country	*Rank*	*GDP (in $ bn)*	*Defence Budget (in $ bn)*	*Armed Forces Personnel (Active/Reserves)*
Japan	1	4560	41.1	2,255,000/800,000
People's Republic of China (PRC)	2	2620	35.3	240,400/41,800
Republic of Korea (RoK)	3	885	23.7	687,000/4,500,000
India	4	839	22.3	1,316,000/1,155,000
Australia	5	749	15.1	51,610/18,973
Taiwan	6	351	7.73	290,000/1,657,000
Singapore	7	132	6.4	72,500/312,500
Myanmar	8	83.84[1]	[a] 6.23 (2005)	375,000
Pakistan	9	119	4.14	619,000
Vietnam	10	61.1	3.43	455,000/5,000,000
Malaysia	11	143	3.08	109,000/51,600
Indonesia	12	346	2.59	302,000/400,000
Democratic People's Republic of Korea (DPRK)	13	40[2]	[a] 2.3	1,106,000/4,700,000
Thailand	14	207	2.13	306,600/200,000
New Zealand	15	105	1.31	8951/2228
Philippines	16	118	0.909	106,000/131,000
Bangladesh	17	58.8	0.843	126,500
Sri Lanka	18	27.8	0.686	150,900/5500
Kazakhstan	19	149	0.648	65,800
Brunei	20	12.6[3]	0.343	7000/700
Turkmenistan	21	45.1[4]	0.181	26,000
Nepal	22	7.7	0.139	69,000
Cambodia	23	6.6	0.123	124,300
Uzbekistan	24	58.5	[a] 0.084	55,000
Tajikistan	25	9.4	0.0707	7,600

Note: GDP: Gross Domestic Product; [a]: estimated.

1. *http://www.cia.gov/library/publications/the-world-factbook/geos/bm.html*
2. *http://www.cia.gov/library/publications/the-world-factbook/print/kn.html*
3. *http://www.oxfordbusinessgroup.com/country.asp?country=58*
4. *http://www.cia.gov/library/publications/the-world-factbook/print/tx.html*

Source: IISS, "East Asia and Australasia", *The Military Balance*, 107(1) (March 2007): 331–81; IISS, "Central and South Asia", *The Military Balance*, 107(1) (March 2007): 301–30.

Table A-2

Major Platforms and Equipment Inventories: Top 20 Defence Spending Nations in Asia, including Australia and New Zealand

Country	*Army*			*Navy*			*Air Force*		
	MBT	*AIFV/APC*	*Arty*	*Sub's*	*PSC*	*PCC*	*FTR*	*FGA*	*Tpt*
People's Republic of China (PRC)	7580+	1000/3500	17,700+	58	76	242	1179	1242	296+
Japan	980	70/730	1980	16	53	9	260		30
Republic of Korea (RoK)	2330	2040/2480	10,774+	20	43	75	210	295	34
India	3978	1700+/817+	10,360+	16	58	19	137	674	288
Australia	119	/740	566	6	13	13	29 (BBR)	104	54
Taiwan	926+	225/950	1815+	4	33	71	282	150	39
Singapore	100	294/1280	326+	4	7	17	0	97	9
Myanmar	150	/325	388+	0	3	59	58	22	15
Pakistan	2461	/1266	4291+	8	6	6	209	104	27
Vietnam	1315	300/1380	3040	2	11	39	140	64	28
Malaysia	26 (Lt Tk)	111/1020	414	0	10	17	28	16	31
Indonesia	350 (Lt Tk)	11/356	1060	2	28	37	24	48	62
Democratic People's Republic of Korea (DPRK)	3500+	/2500+	17,900+	63	8	335+	299	211	318
Thailand	333	/950	2473	0	20	89	87		54
New Zealand	0	/105	74	0	2	6	0	0	7
Philippines	65(Lt Tk)	85/370	282+	0	1	59	0	0	17
Bangladesh	180	/180+	190+	0	5	44	24	18	7
Sri Lanka	62	62/217	963	0	0	123	3	13	14
Kazakhstan	930	573/770	986	0	0	0	99	65	3
Brunei	20(Lt Tk)	/39	24	0	0	6+	O	0	1

Note : MBT: main battle tank; Lt Tk: light tank; AIFV: armoured infantry fighting vehicle; APC: armoured personnel carrier; Arty: artillery; Subs: submarines; PSC: principal surface combatants (includes aircraft carriers, destroyers, frigates, and corvettes); PCC: patrol and coastal combatants; FTR: fighter aircraft; BBR: bomber aircraft; FGA: fighter ground attack; Tpt: transport aircraft.

Source : IISS, "East Asia and Australasia", *The Military Balance* 107(1) (March 2007): 331–81; IISS, "Central and South Asia", *The Military Balance* 107(1) (March 2007): 301–30.

Table A-3

World Nuclear Forces: Warheads, Delivery Systems, and Ranges (in km)

Country	Total Warheads (Deployed)	Delivery Systems (Range in km): Bombers (Range)	ICBMs (Range)	SLBMs (Range)	IRBMs/MRBMs/ SRBMs (Range)
United States	5521	B-52 H (16,000); B-2 (11,000)	Minuteman III (Mk-12, Mk-12A) (13,000)	Trident II (Mk-4, Mk-5) (7400)	
Russia	5682	Tu-95MS6, Tu-95MS16 (6,500-10,500); Tu-160 (10,500-13,200)	SS-18 (11,000-15,000); SS-19 (10,000); SS-25/27 (10,500);	SS-N-18 M1 (6500); SS-N-23 (9000)	
United Kingdom	185			Trident II (D-5) (7400)	
France	348	Mirage 2000N (2750); Super Etendard (650)		M45 (6000)	
Peoples Republic of China (PRC)	130	Hong-6 (3100); Qian-5	DF-4 (5500); DF-5A (13,000); DF-31 (8000); DF-31A (12,000)	Julang-1 (1000); Julang-2 (8000)	DF-3A (3100); DF-21A (2100)
India	50	Mirage 2000H (1850); Jaguar IS (1400)			Agni I (800); Agni II (2000-2500); Prithvi I (150)
Pakistan	60	F-16 A/B (1600)			Ghauri I (Hatf-5) (1200); Shaheen I (Hatf-4) (600-800); Ghaznavi (Hatf-3) (290)
Israel	100-200	F-16 A/B/C/D/I (1600)			Jericho II (1500-1800)

Notes: 1. The Democratic People's Republic of Korea (DPRK), which tested a plutonium device on 9 October 2006, is believed to have enough separated plutonium currently for 4-13 nuclear weapons. See David Albright and Paul Brennan (2006). "The North Korean plutonium stock mid-2006", Institute for Science and International Security (ISIS), 26 June. Available at *www.isis-online.org/publications/dprk/dprkplutonium.pdf.*

2. SLBM: sea-launched ballistic missile; ICBM: intercontinental ballistic missile, >5500 km in range; IRBM: intermediate-range ballistic missile, 2400–5499 km; MRBM: medium-range ballistic missile, 800-2399 km; SRBM: short-range ballistic missile, 150-799 km. See Andrew Feickert and Alan K. Kronstadt (2003). "Missile Proliferation and Strategic Balance in South Asia", CRS Report for Congress, 17 October, at *http://www.fas.org/spp/starwars/crs/RL32115.pdf.*

Source: SIPRI (2006). *SIPRI Yearbook, 2006: Armaments, Disarmament, and International Security*. Oxford: Oxford University Press, pp.639-68.

Table A-4

Major Conflicts in Asia, Insurgent/Terrorist Groups, Fatalities, Current Status

Country	*Insurgent/Terrorist/ Extremist/Radical Groups*	*Fatalities*	*Current Status/ Remarks*
Afghanistan	Al-Qaeda, Taliban	578 coalition forces (From 2001-May 2007)[1]; >4000 civilians (2006)[2]	Increasing Talibanisation; record drug output; growing cross-border support.
India	Left-wing extremists; North East insurgent groups; Jammu and Kashmir insurgents	Left-wing extremism (949); North East (1012); Jammu and Kashmir (1352)[3]	76 out of 299 districts in 9 states 'badly affected' by Maoist violence; 9 year old cease fire with NSCN (IM) extended; bomb blasts by ULFA in November; peace process encouraging in J&K.
Indonesia	Free Aceh Movement (GAM); Free Papua Movement (OPM)	37 GAM members, 44 civilians, 17 soldiers killed in 2005; sharp decrease in killing by security forces[4]	August 2005 peace agreement with GAM holding; OPM's unilateral cease fire in July 2006.
Iraq	Islamic State of Iraq (Sunni), Mehdi Army (Shia), Islamic Army of Iraq (different elements), Army of Ansar Al-Sunna (Kurds and Sunnis)	3467 US deaths since 2003; >30,000 Iraqi security forces and civilian deaths since January 2006[5]	US 'troop surge' to control the Sunni-Shia carnage, domestic political and regional diplomatic efforts in progress, no let-up in casualties.
Israel	Fatah, Hamas, Palestinian Islamic Jihad, Popular Front for the Liberation of Palestine	Nearly 700 in 2006 (>650 of them Palestinians)[6]	Intra-Palestinian faction fighting on the rise; Israel-Palestinian peace initiatives continuing.
Lebanon	Hezbollah	160 Israelis, >1000 Lebanese killed	UN Security Council Resolution 1701 ended the conflict, multinational force in place.
Myanmar	Karen National Union (KNU), Shan State Army-South (SSA-South)	>20,000 killed till date	Military operations against KNU increased, major offensive, led to >16,000 ethnic Rohingyas being displaced[7].

Contd...

.contd...

Nepal	Communist Party of Nepal-Maoist (CPN-M)	>12,000 people killed, in a decade of violence (from 1996-2006)	Interim coalition government formed, following November 2006 peace agreement, elections due in November 2007.
Pakistan	Al-Qaeda, Taliban, Baluch Liberation Army (BLA), Religious extremists, Sectarian strife	Nearly 1000 killed in 2006 in more than 650 terror attacks[8]	80,000 Pakistan Army troops in FATA; killing of Nawab Bugti on 27 August intensified the Baluch crisis; prominent Shia cleric killed in Karachi in July.
Philippines	Maoist New People's Army (NPA); Moro Islamic Liberation Front (MILF); Abu Sayyaf Group (ASG)	>50,000 deaths till 2005 (against NPA and MILF)	Peace talks with NPA collapsed; ASG coordinating with pan-South East Asian Jemaah Islamiyah (JI).
Sri Lanka	Liberation Tigers of Tamil Eelam (LTTE)	>3500 killed in fresh eruption of fighting in 2006	Escalation in conflict, Deputy Army Chief killed in June; 61 school girls killed in Sri Lankan air bombardment on 14 August.
Thailand	National Revolutionary Front Coordinate (BRN-K), Islamic insurgency in provinces of Narathiwat, Patani, and Yala	>1000 deaths since escalation of violence in January 2004	Large-scale attacks launched by the insurgents, efforts on to train the 20,000 strong village defence organisations more effectively.

Notes:

1. "Enduring Freedom Casualties", at http://www.cnn.com/SPECIALS/2004/oef.casualties
2. "Suicide bomber near Afghan Parliament kills 6", *Reuters*, 6 April 2007, at http://in.news.yahoo.com/070406/137/6e8f6.html
3. "India fatalities", at http://www.satp.org/satporgtp/countries/india/database/indiafatalities.htm. Data are from January 2006–8 May 2007.
4. "Country Reports on Human Rights Practices 2006: Indonesia", at http://www.state.gov/g/drl/rls/hrrpt/2006/78774.htm
5. "Iraq coalition casualty count", at http://icasualties.org/oif
6. "B'Tselem: Israeli Security Forces killed 660 Palestinians during 2006", *Haaretz*, 28 December 2006, at http://www.haaretz.com/hasen/spages/807007.html
7. Amnesty International, *Myanmar*, Country Report 2007, at http://thereport.amnesty.org/eng/Regions/Asia-Pacific/Myanmar
8. "South and Central Asia Overview", *Country Reports on Terrorism 2006*, at http://www.state.gov/s/ct/rls/crt/2006/82734.htm

Sources: SIPRI (2006). *SIPRI Yearbook, 2006: Armaments, Disarmament, and International Security.* Oxford: Oxford University Press: 116-19; IISS (2007). "Central and South Asia", *The Military Balance* 107(1) (March): 301-30; IISS (2007). "East Asia and Australasia", *The Military Balance* 107(1) (March): 331-81.

Table A-5

Top 15 Energy Consumers in Asia

Country	*Energy Consumed in Quadrillion (10^{15}) Btu (British Thermal Units)*	*Rank*
China	59.57	1
Japan	22.62	2
India	15.41	3
South Korea	8.98	4
Ukraine	6.48	5
Iran	6.44	6
Saudi Arabia	6.10	7
Indonesia	4.68	8
Taiwan	4.39	9
Thailand	3.42	10
Malaysia	2.51	11
UAE	2.33	12
Kazakhstan	2.33	13
Uzbekistan	2.22	14
Pakistan	1.98	15

Source: US Department of Energy, Energy Information Administration, 2006, at http://www.eia.doe.gov/pub/international/iealf/tablee1.xls

Table A-6

Top 15 Energy Producers in Asia

Country	*Energy Produced in Quadrillion (10^{15}) Btu (British Thermal Units)*	*Rank*
China	55.94	1
Saudi Arabia	24.15	2
Iran	12.05	3
India	11.05	4
Indonesia	8.84	5
UAE	7.42	6
Kuwait	5.70	7
Iraq	4.37	8
Malaysia	4.09	9
Japan	4.03	10
Libya	3.60	11
Qatar	3.45	12
Ukraine	3.24	13
Turkmenistan	2.61	14
Uzbekistan	2.51	15

Note: 1. The total energy consumption of Russia is 30.062 10^{15} BTU and its total energy production is 51.689 10^{15} BTU. Russia therefore is in second position in the Eurasian region both as a consumer and producer of energy.

Source: US Department of Energy, Energy Information Administration, 2006, at http://www.eia.doe.gov/pub/international/iealf/tablef1.xls